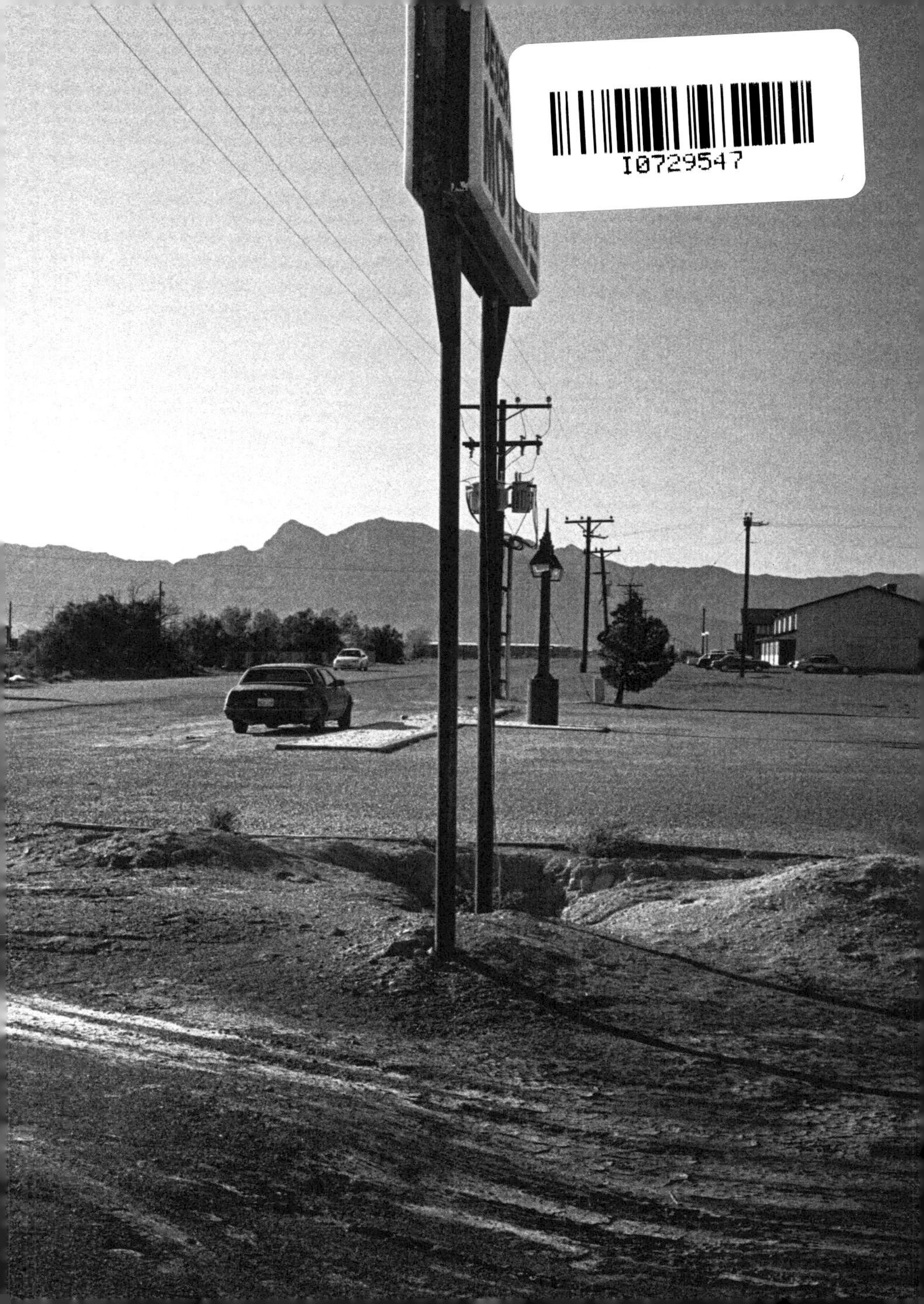

I0729547

PETER LINDBERGH
Untold Stories

TASCHEN

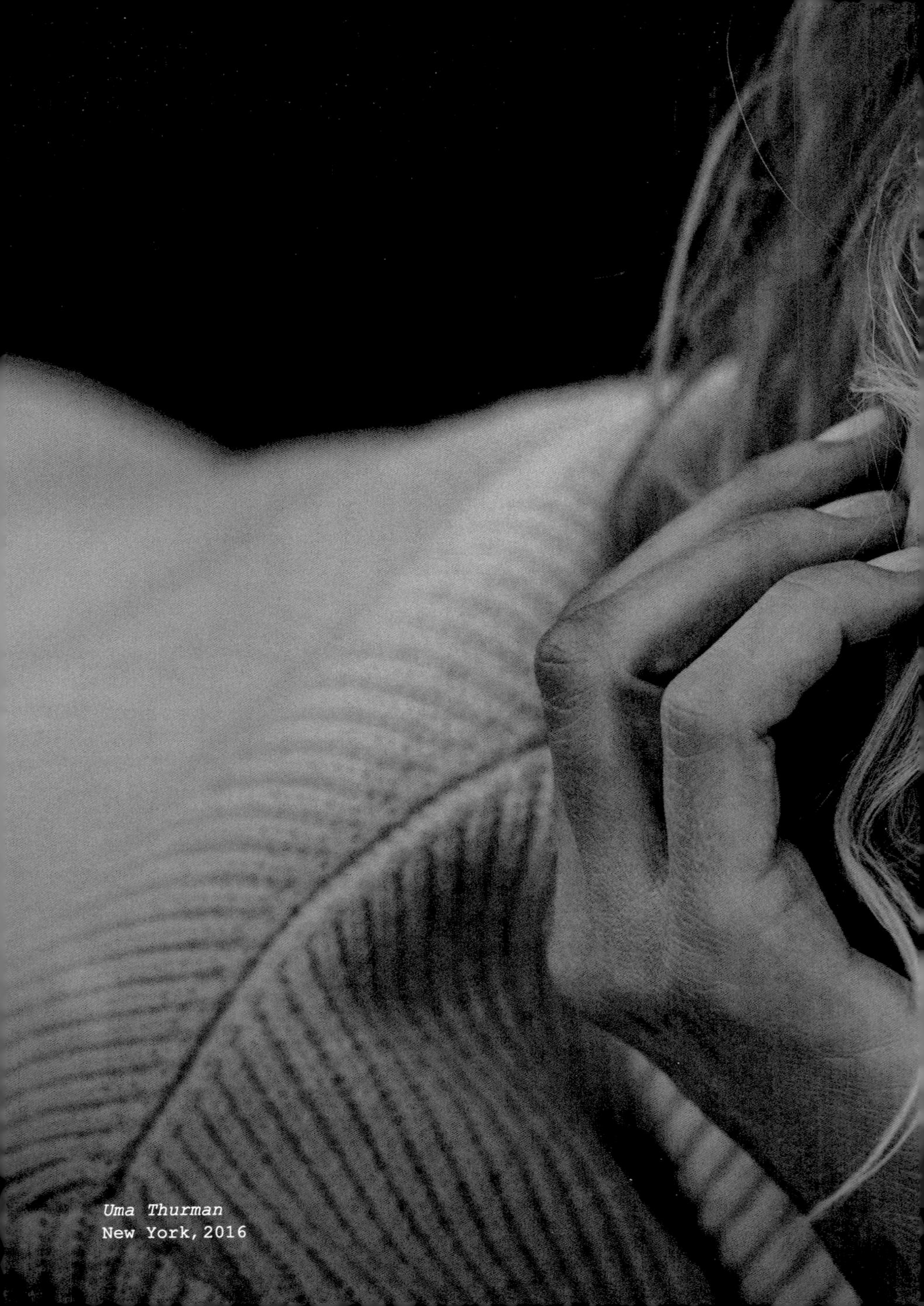
Uma Thurman
New York, 2016

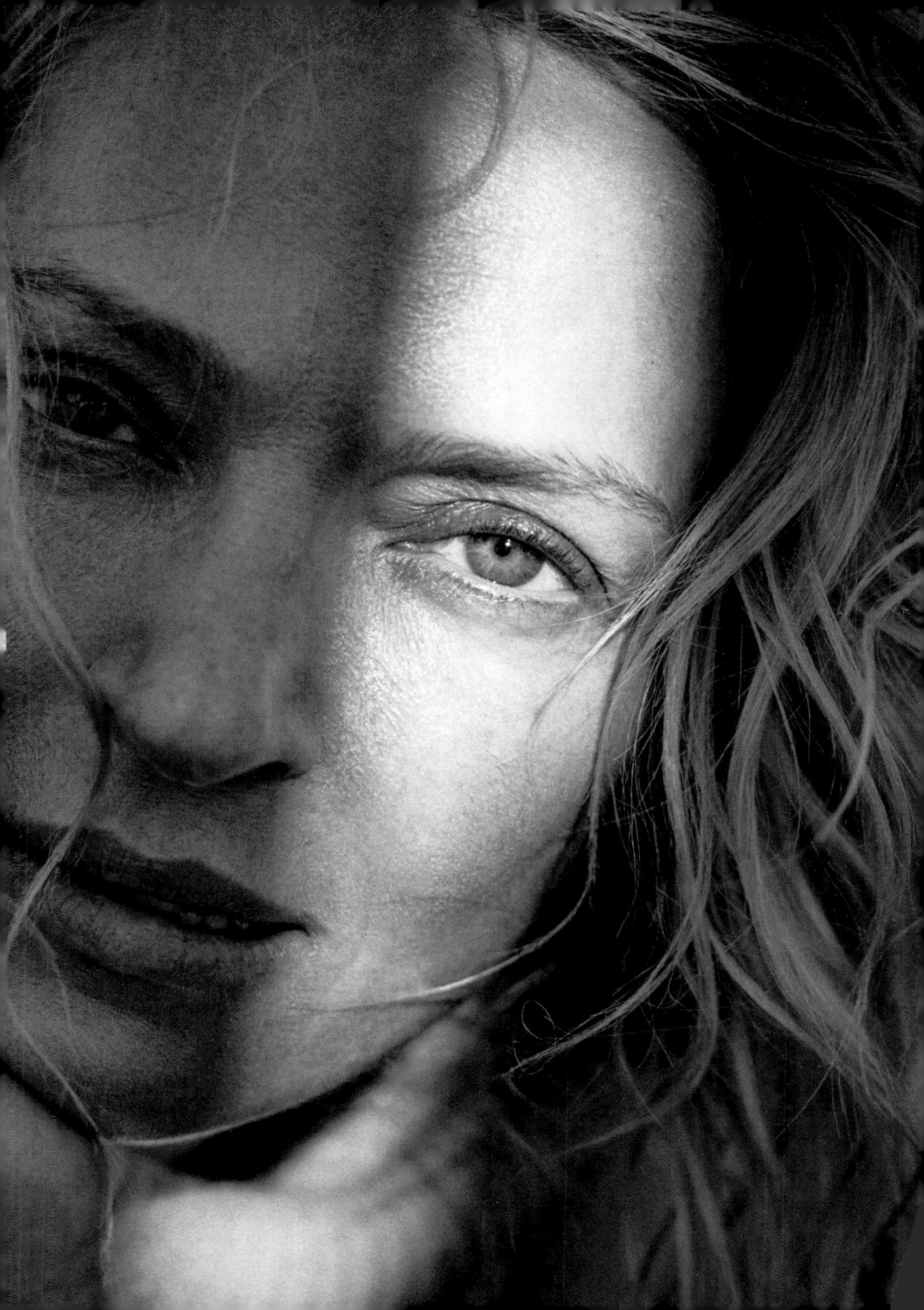

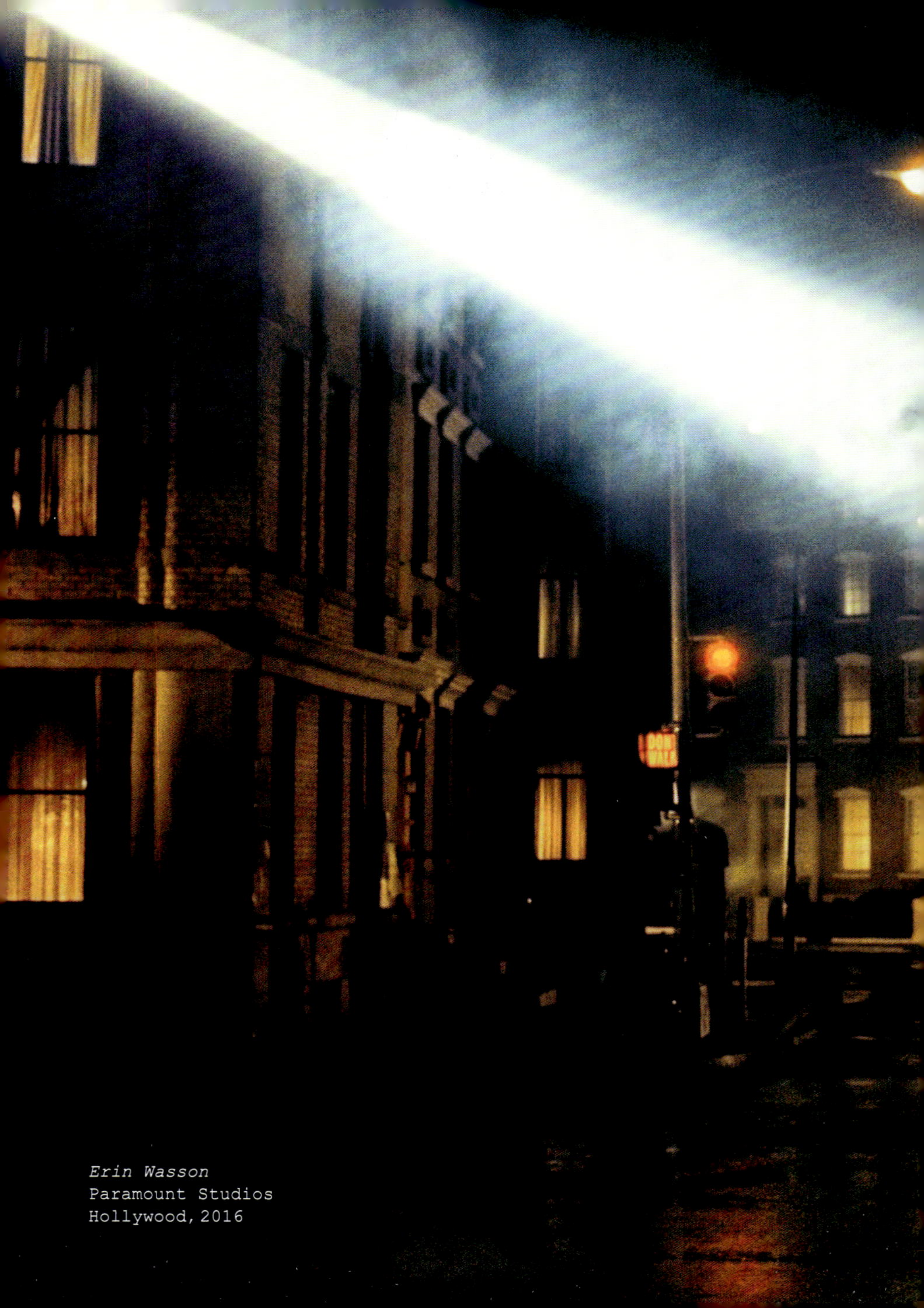

Erin Wasson
Paramount Studios
Hollywood, 2016

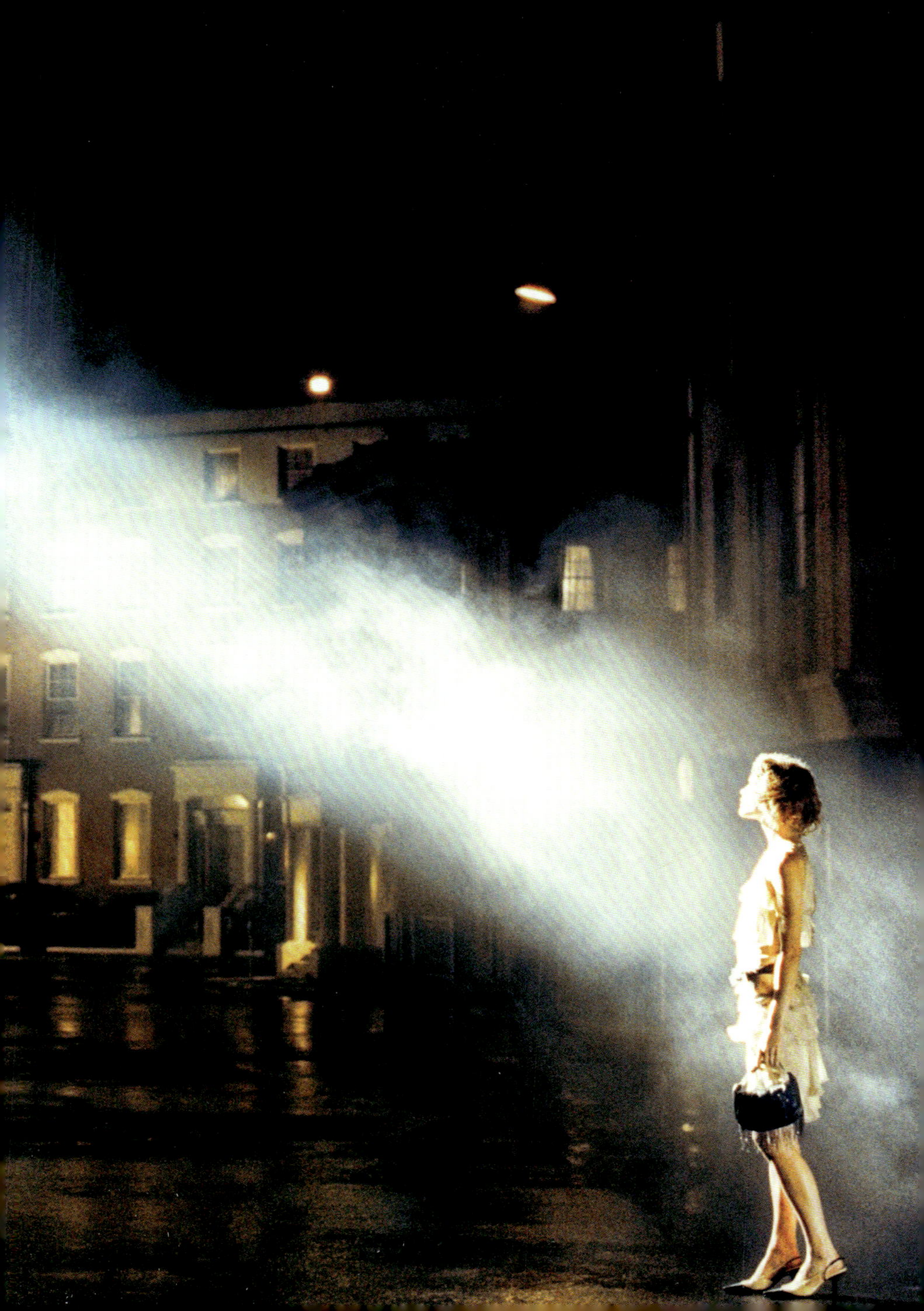

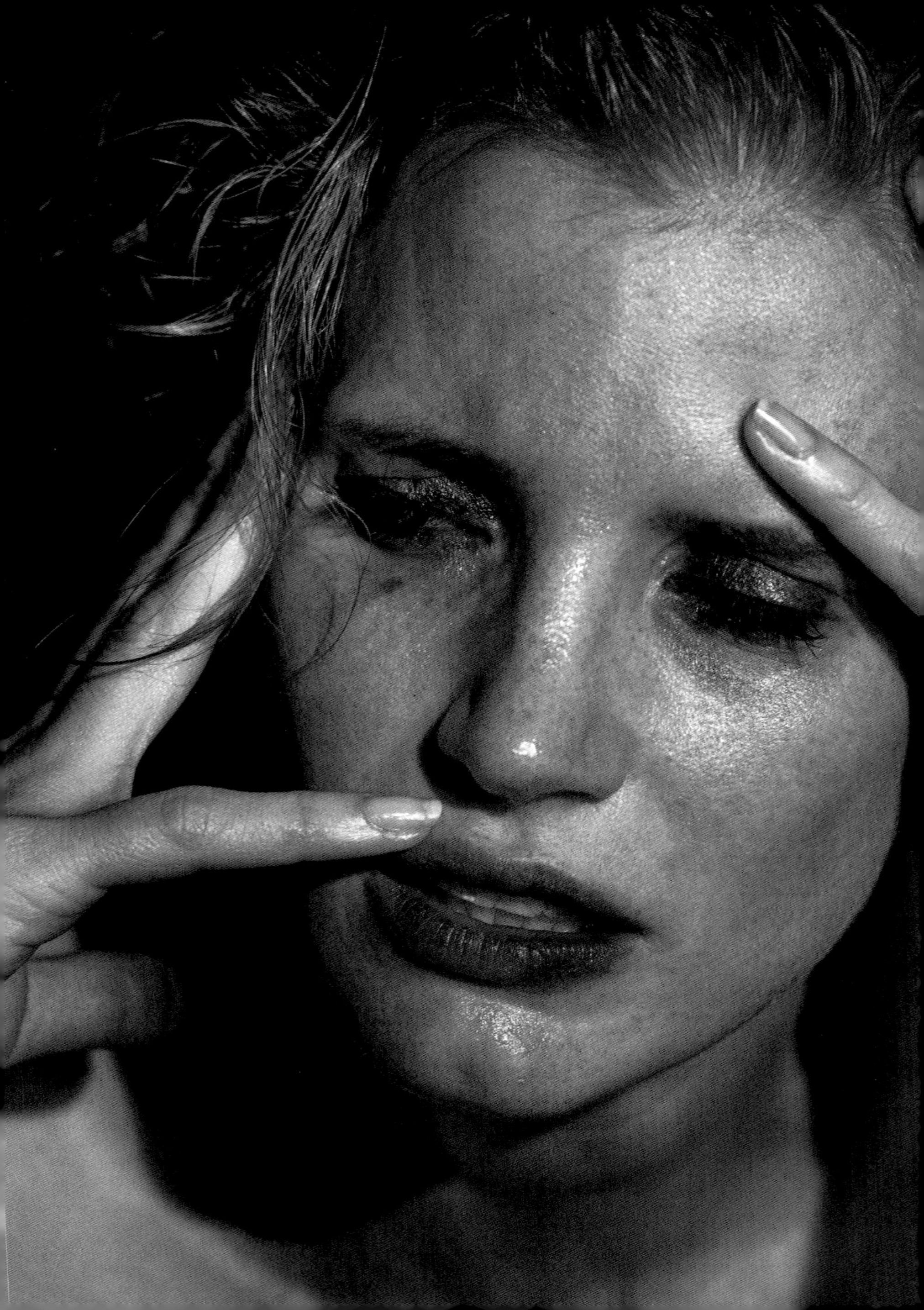

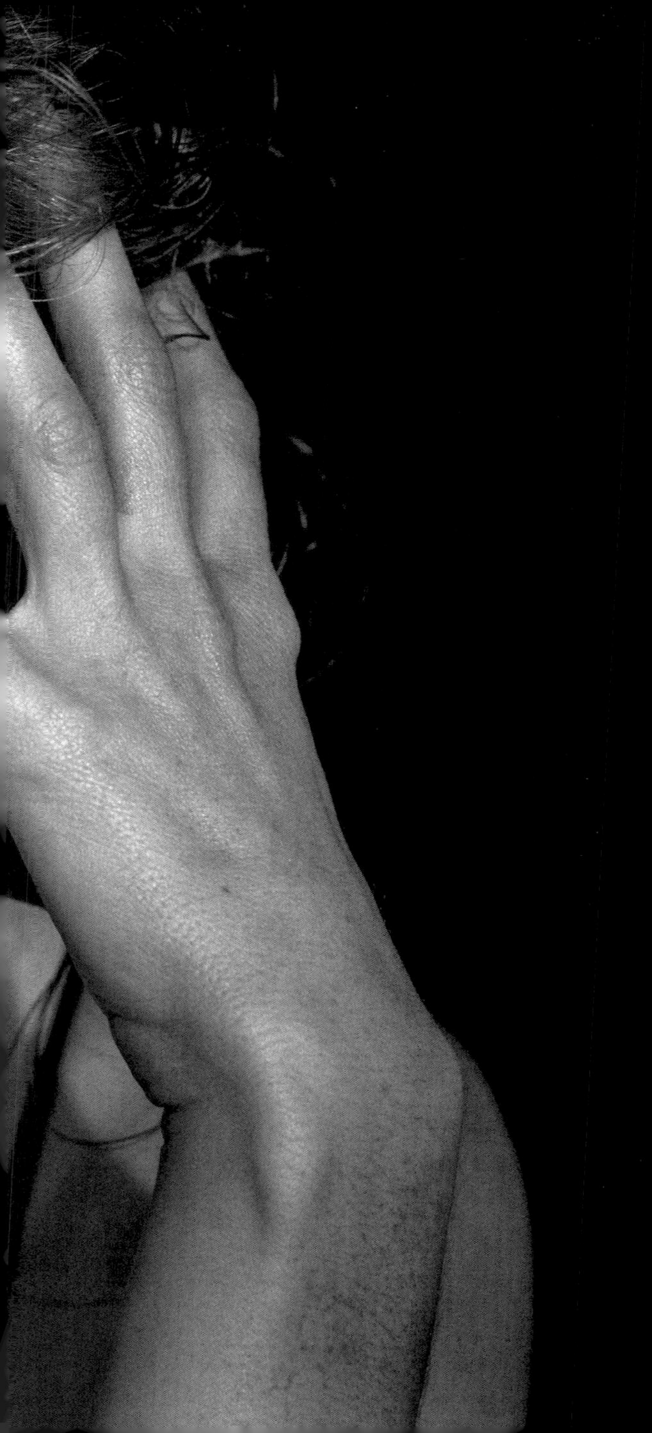

Jessica Chastain
New York, 2011

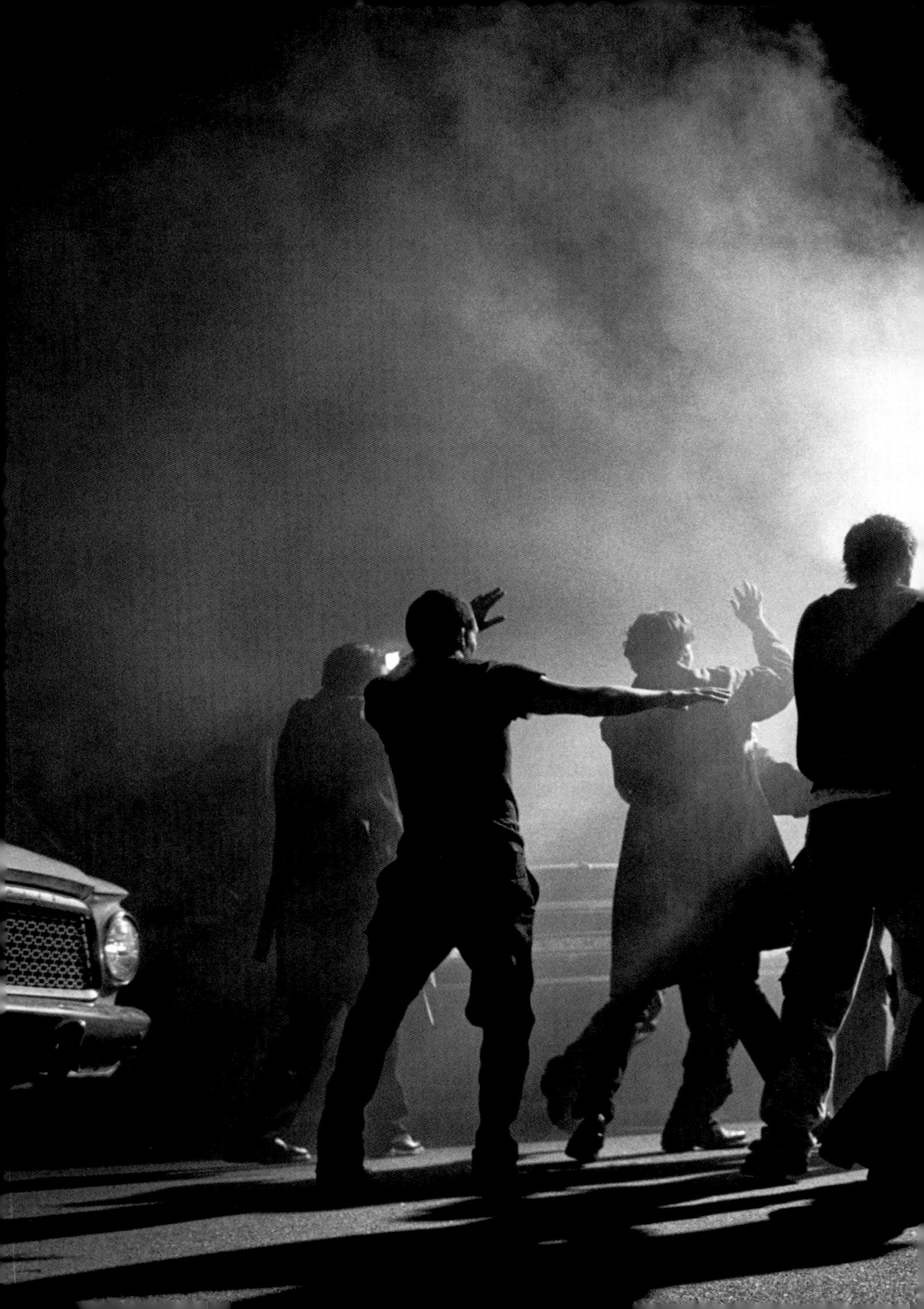

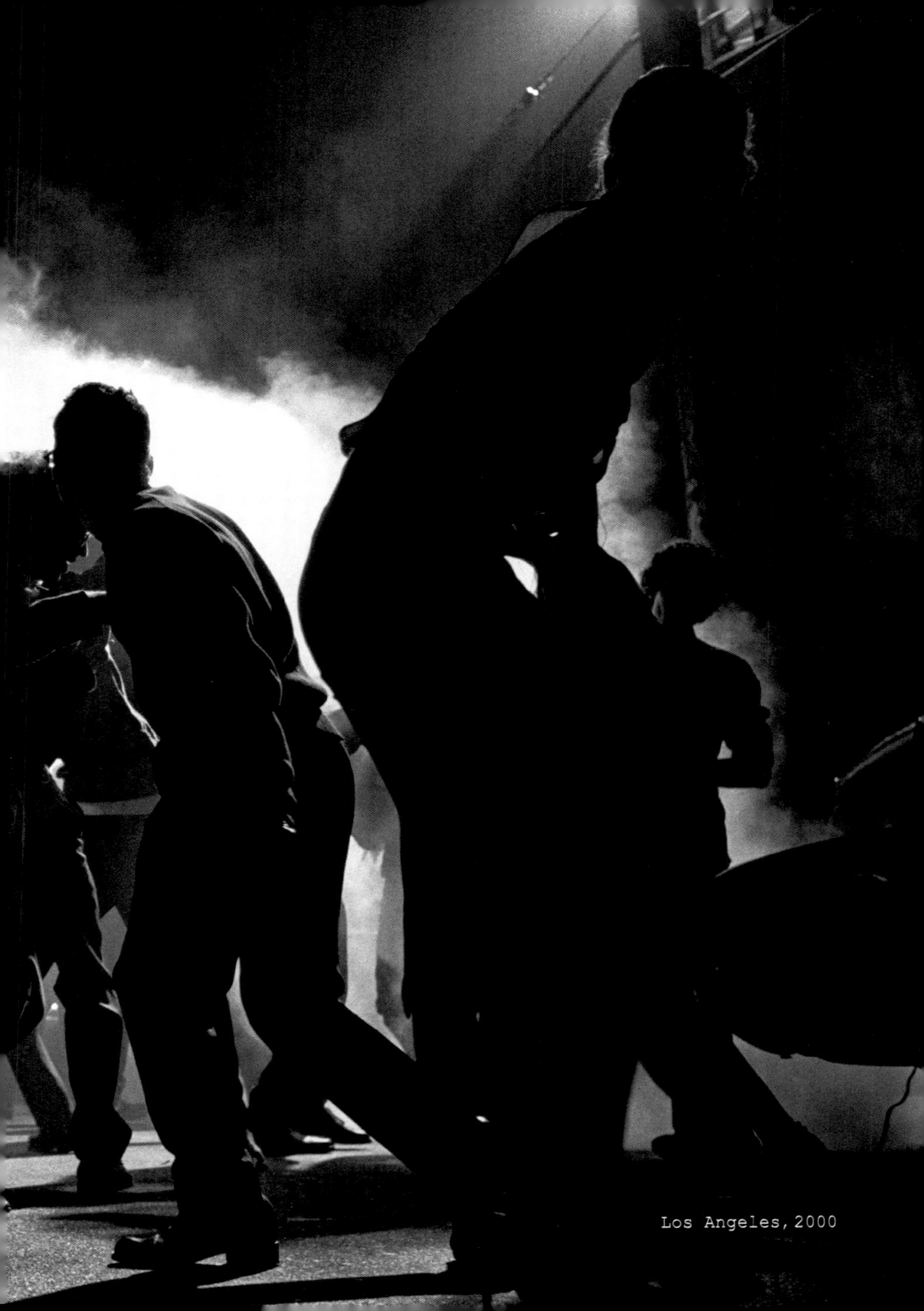

Los Angeles, 2000

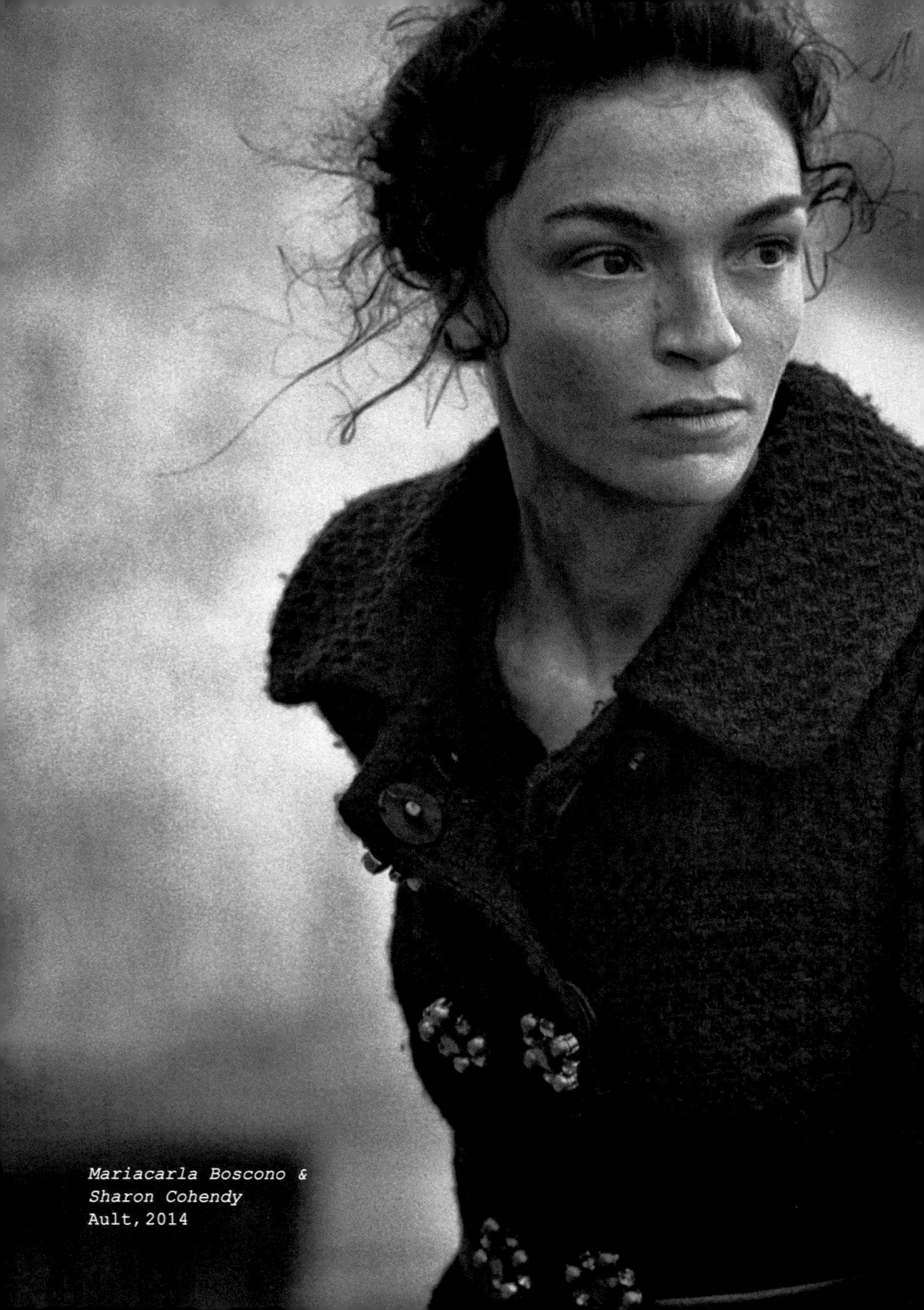
Mariacarla Boscono &
Sharon Cohendy
Ault, 2014

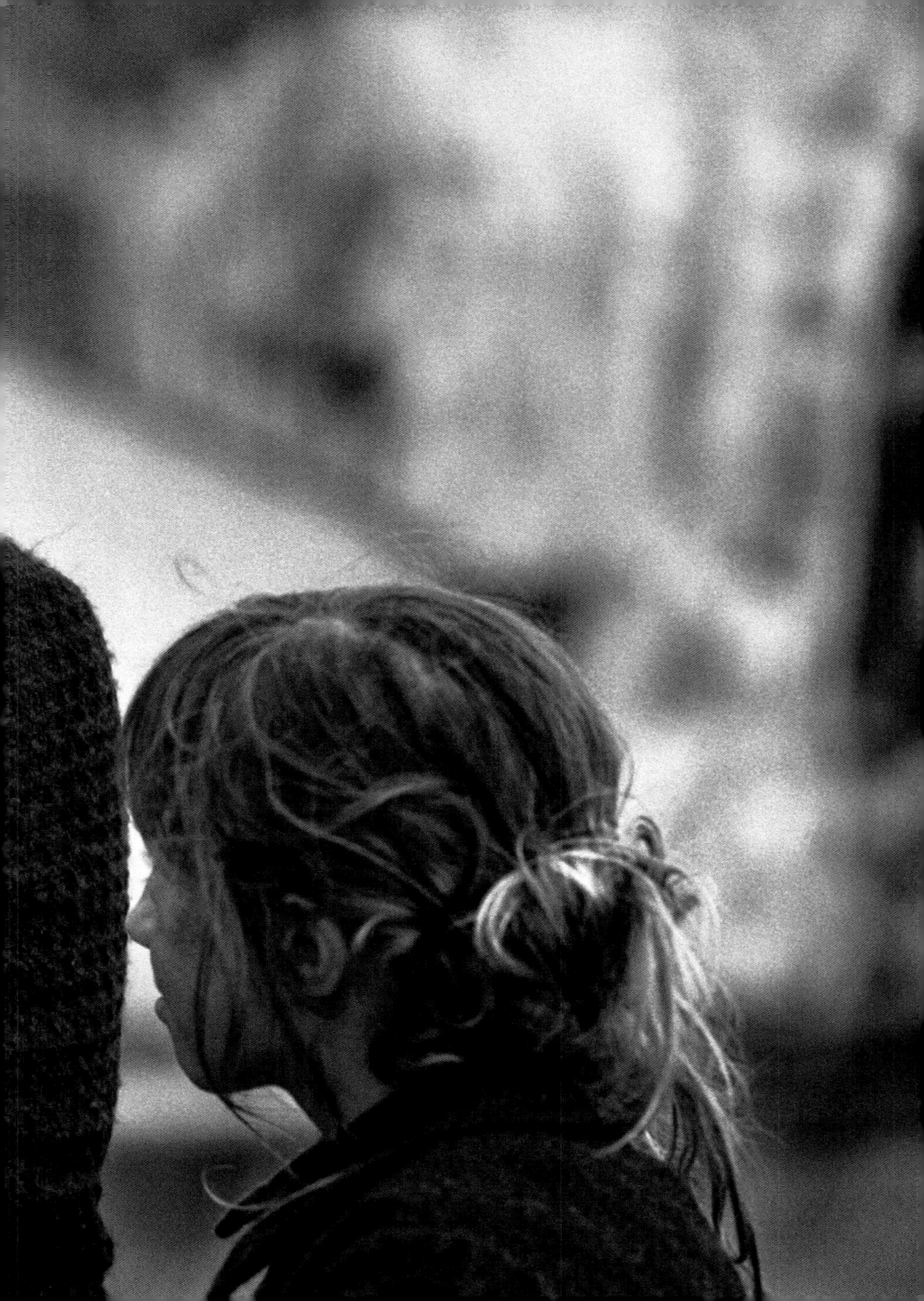

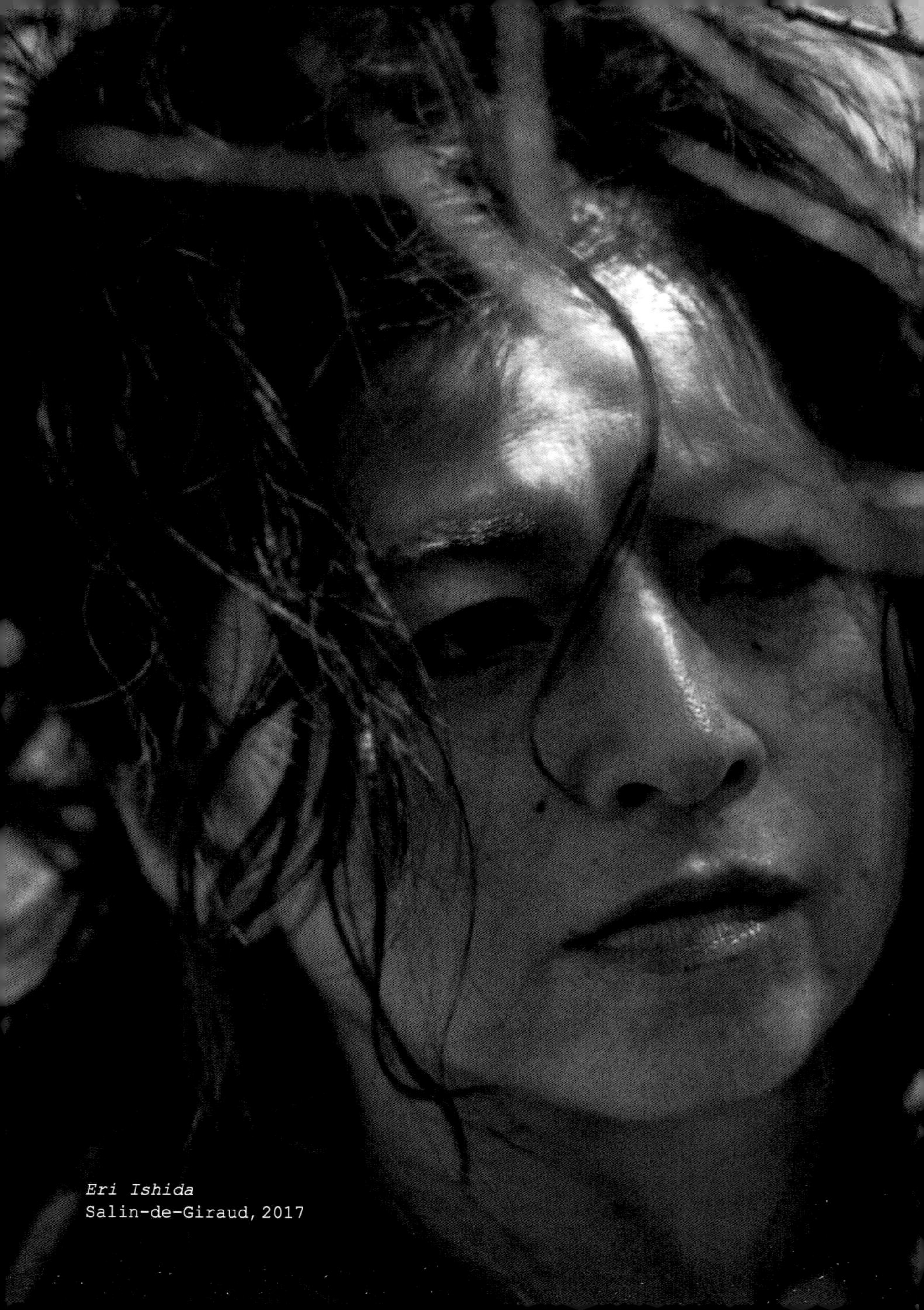

Eri Ishida
Salin-de-Giraud, 2017

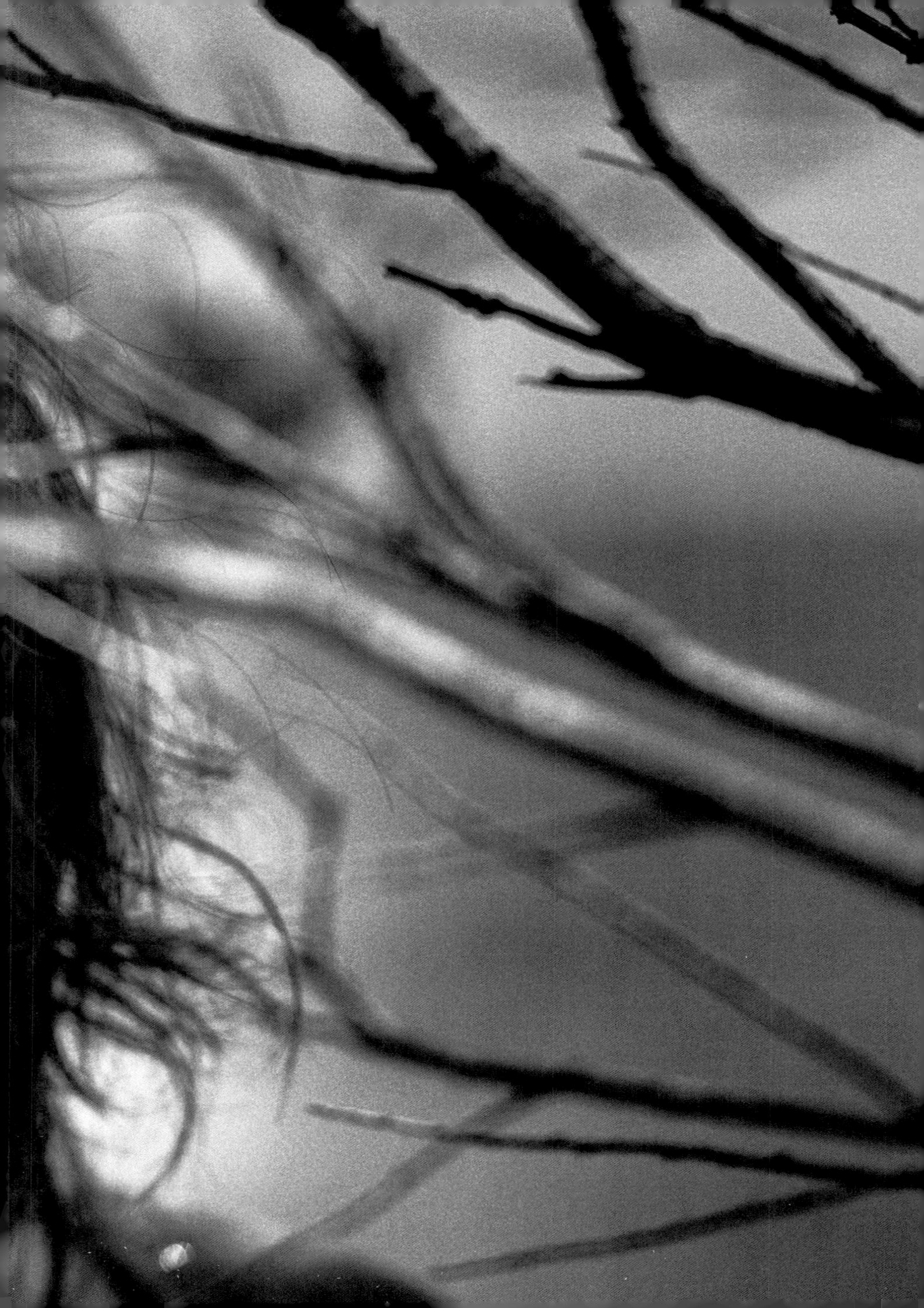

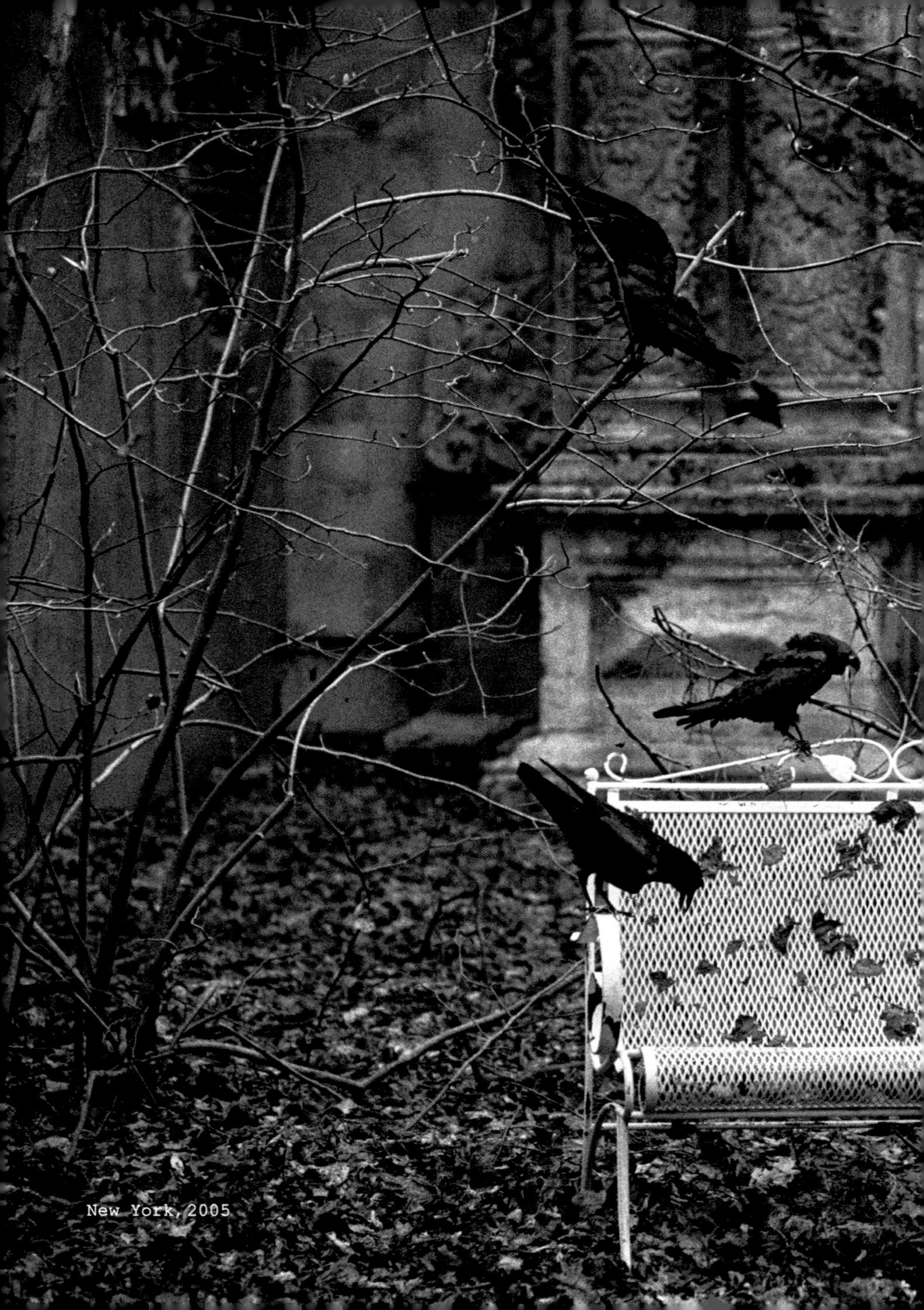
New York, 2005

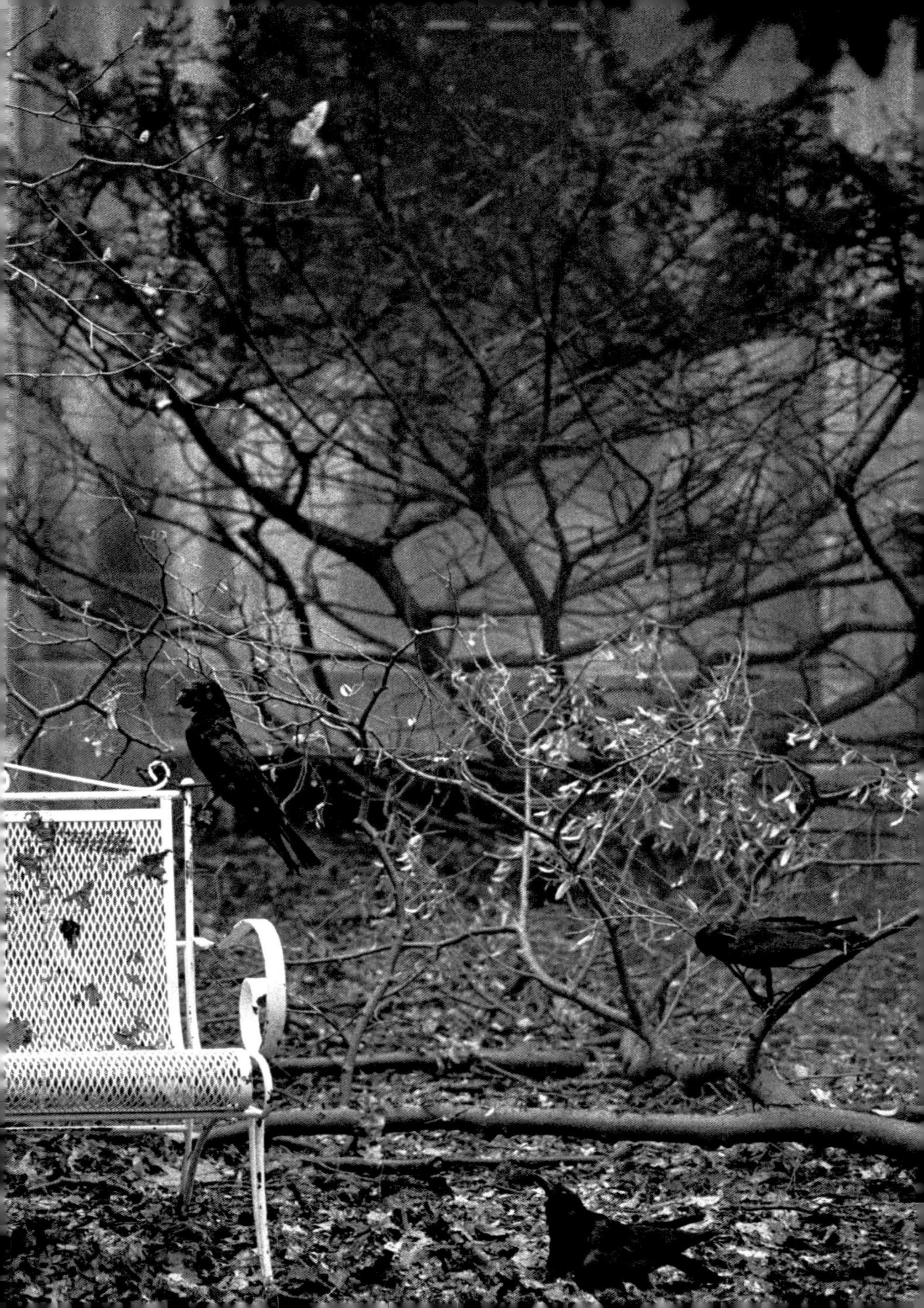

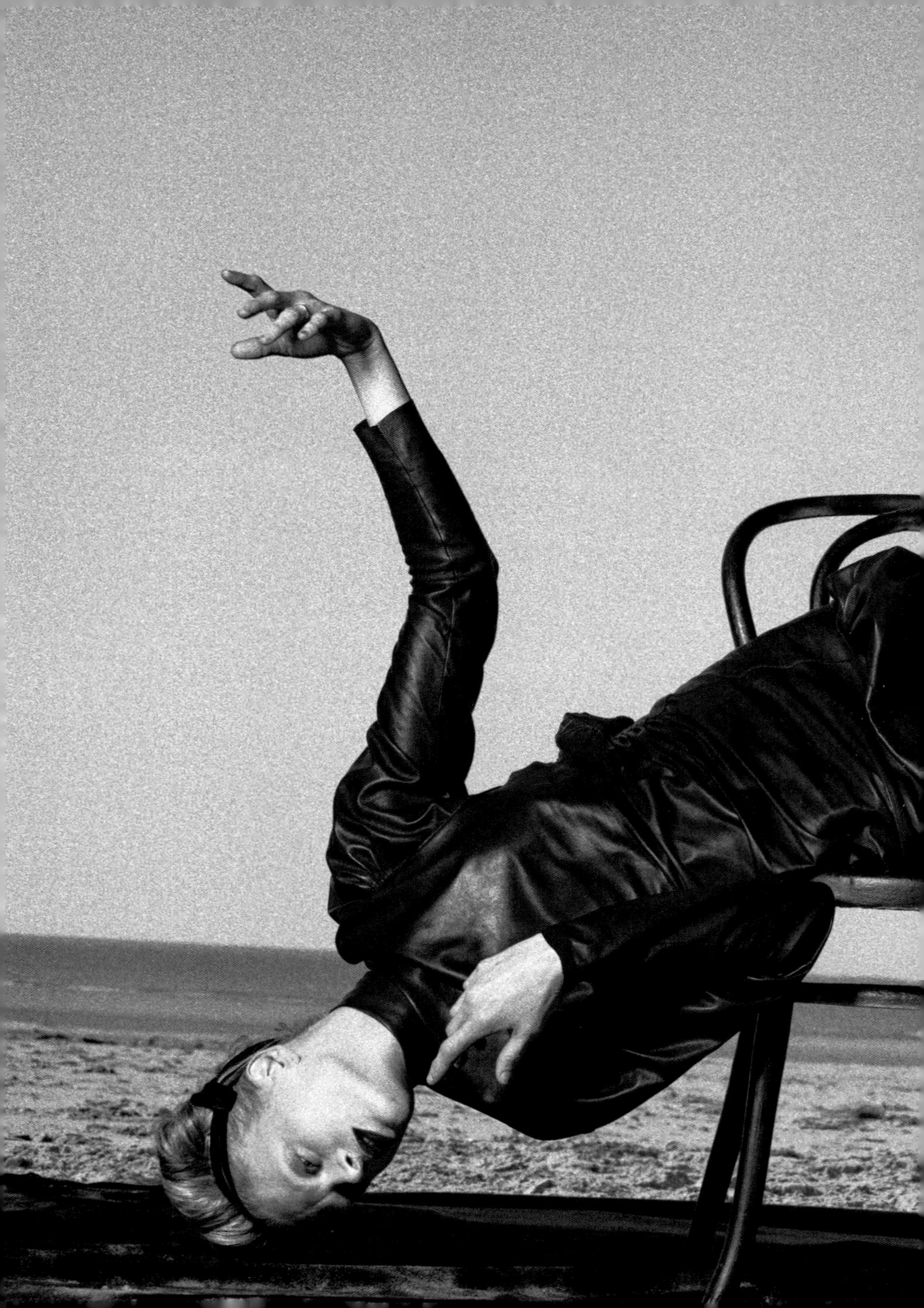

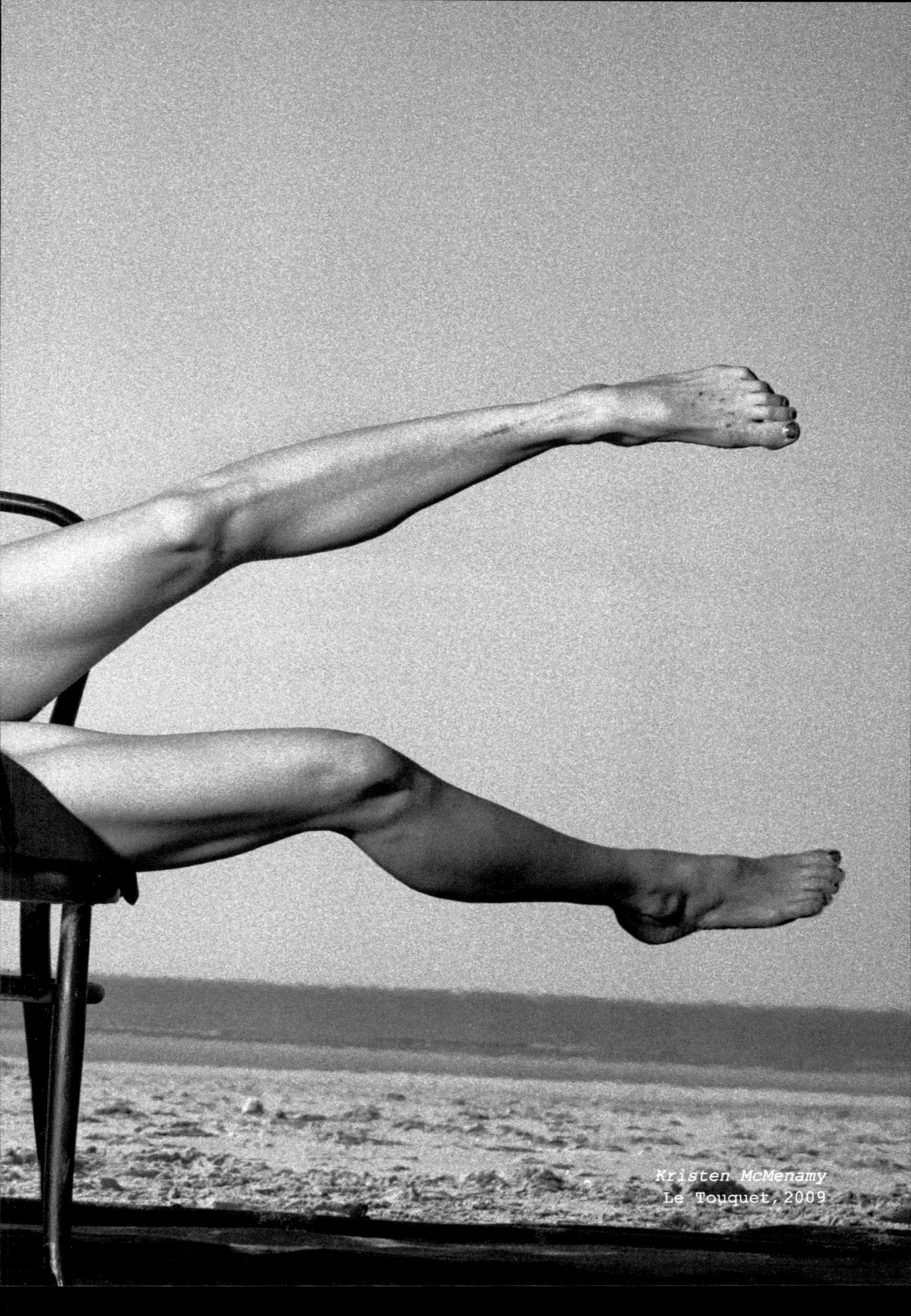

Kristen McMenamy
Le Touquet, 2009

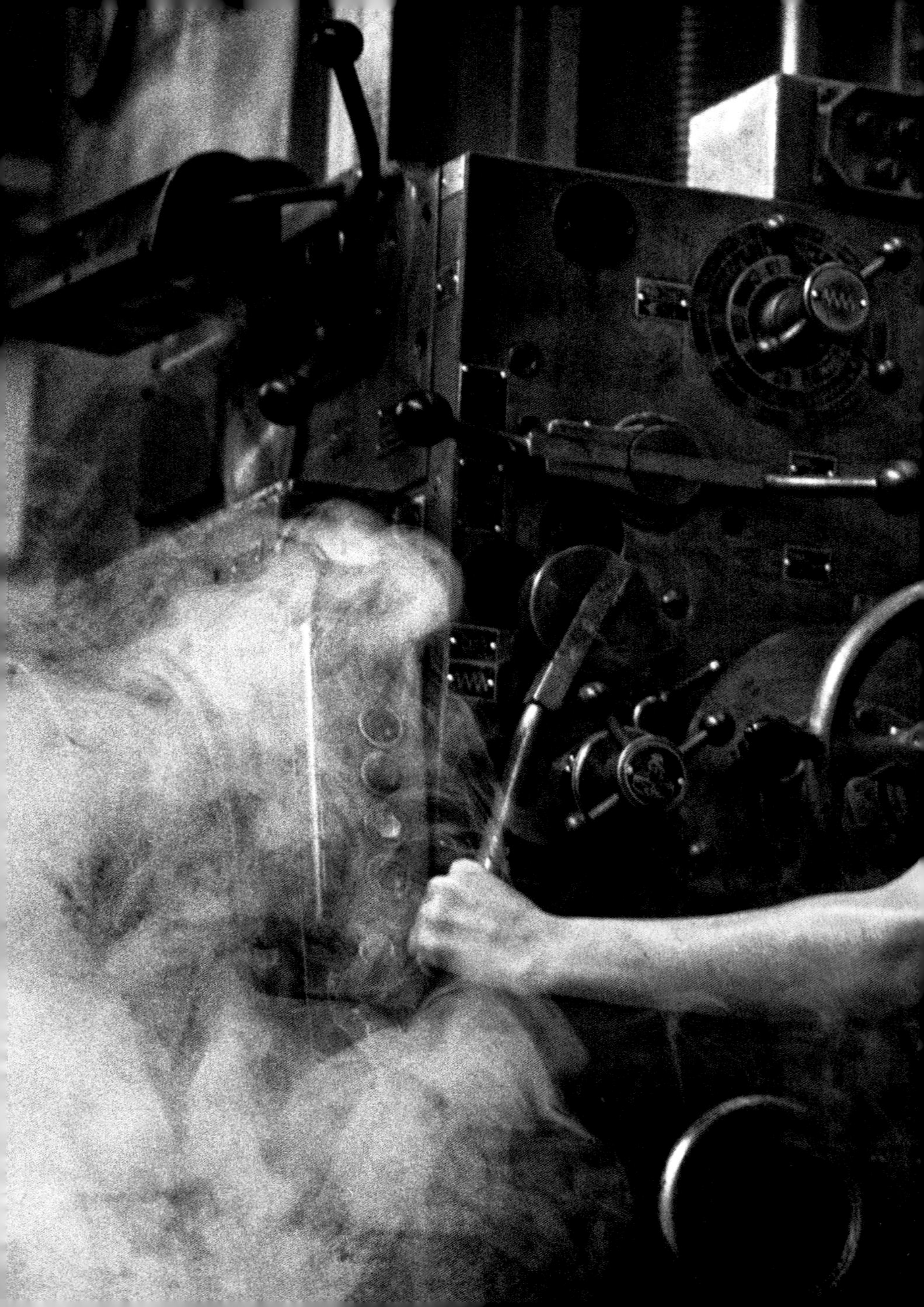

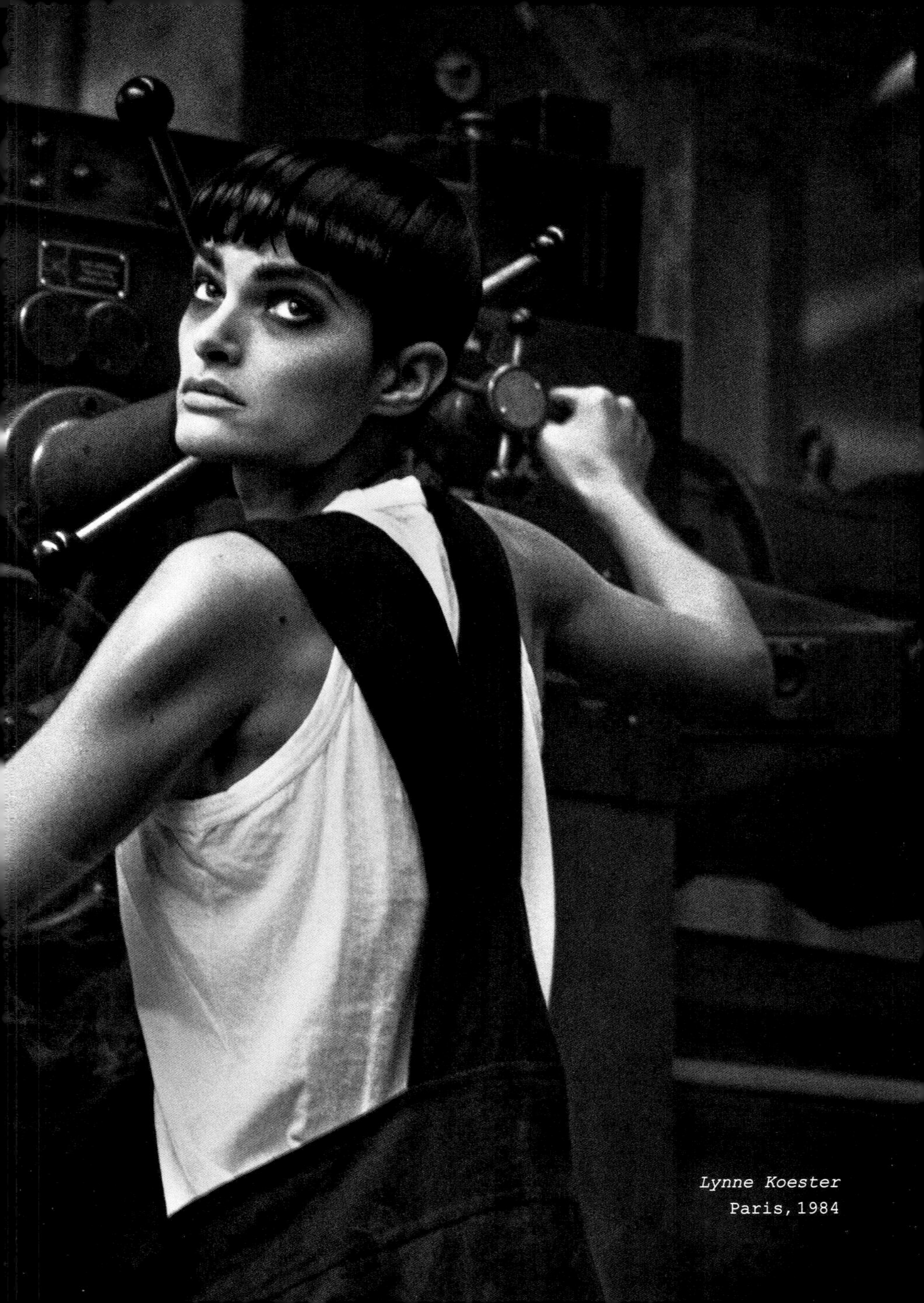

Lynne Koester
Paris, 1984

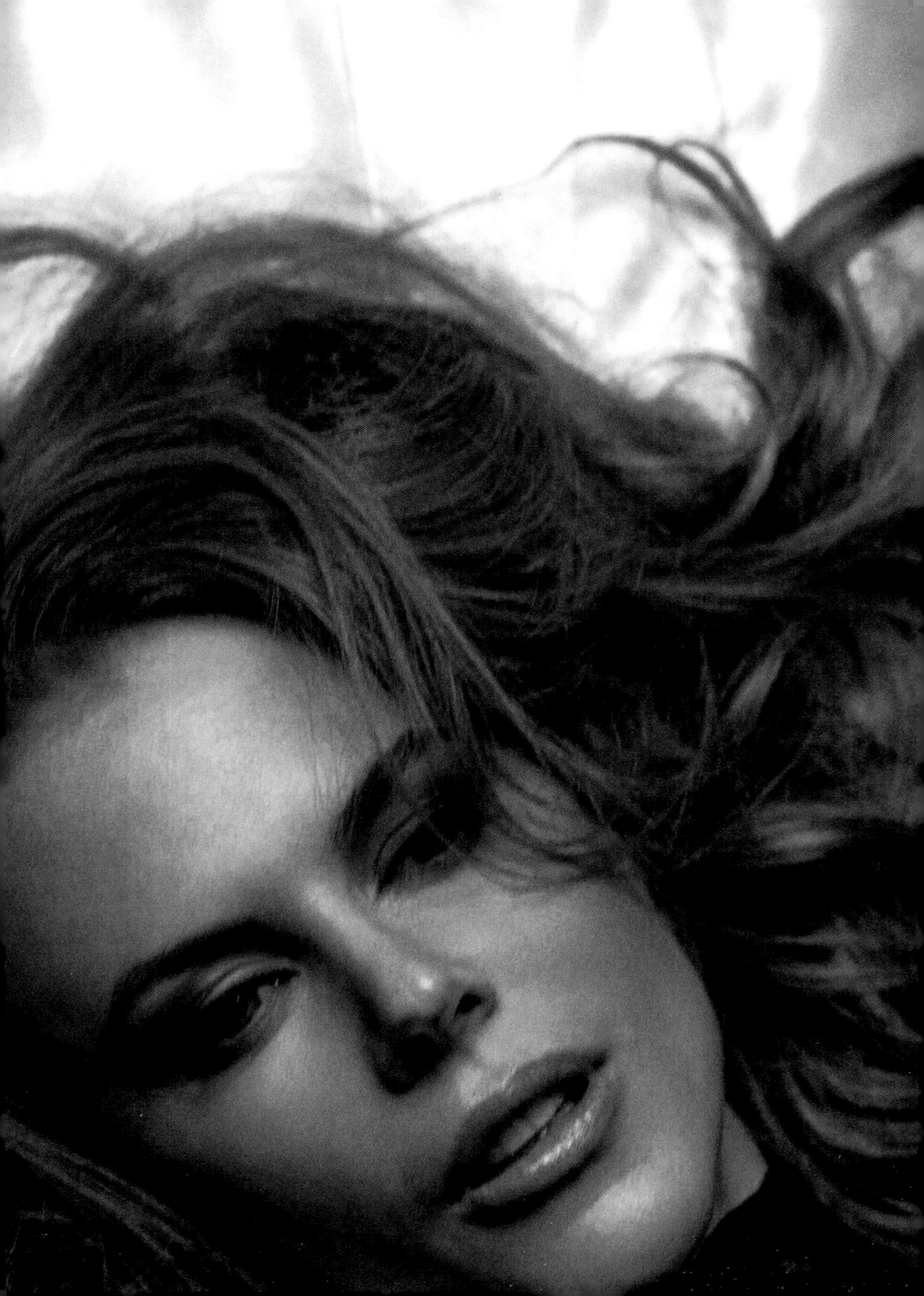

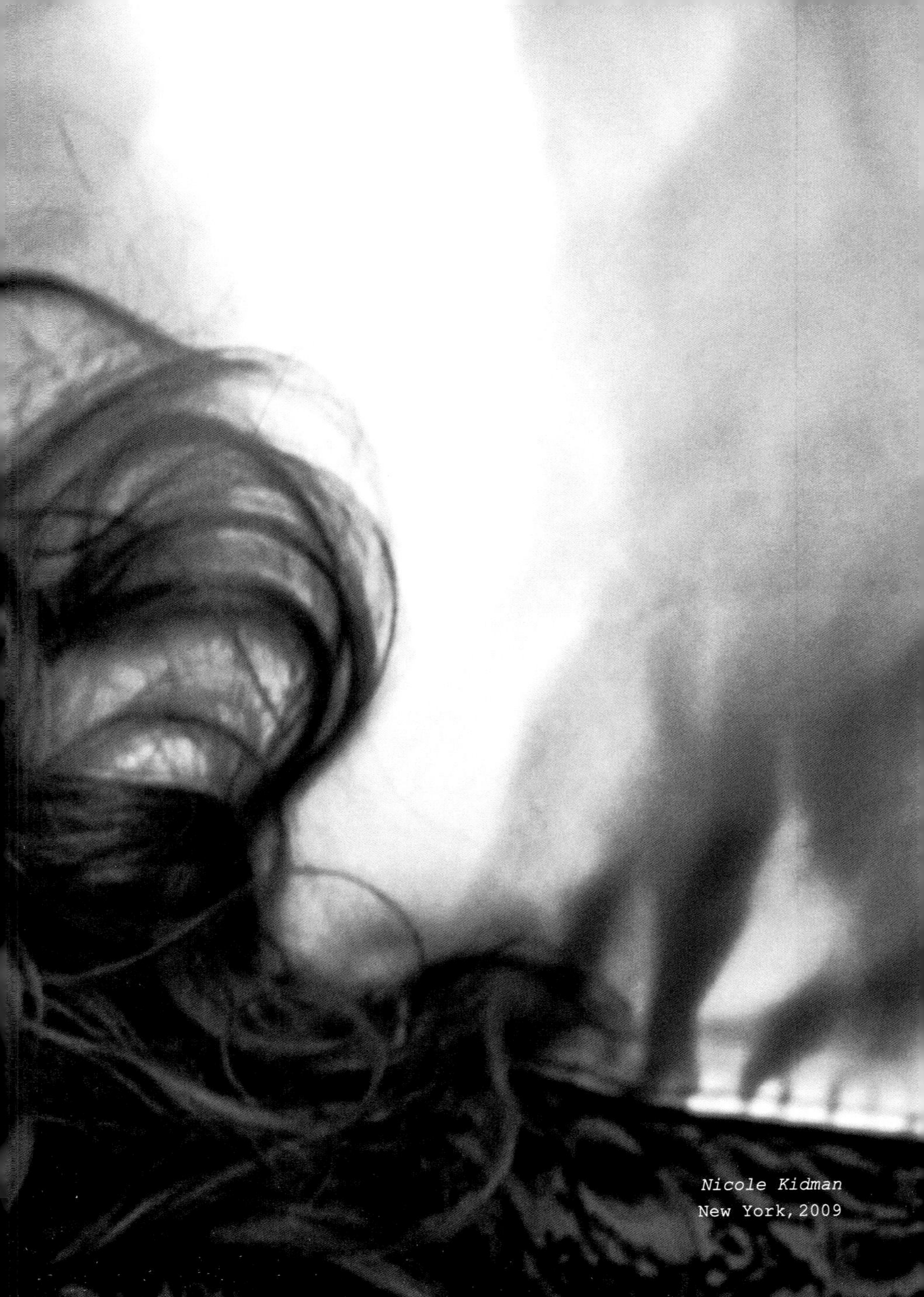

Nicole Kidman
New York, 2009

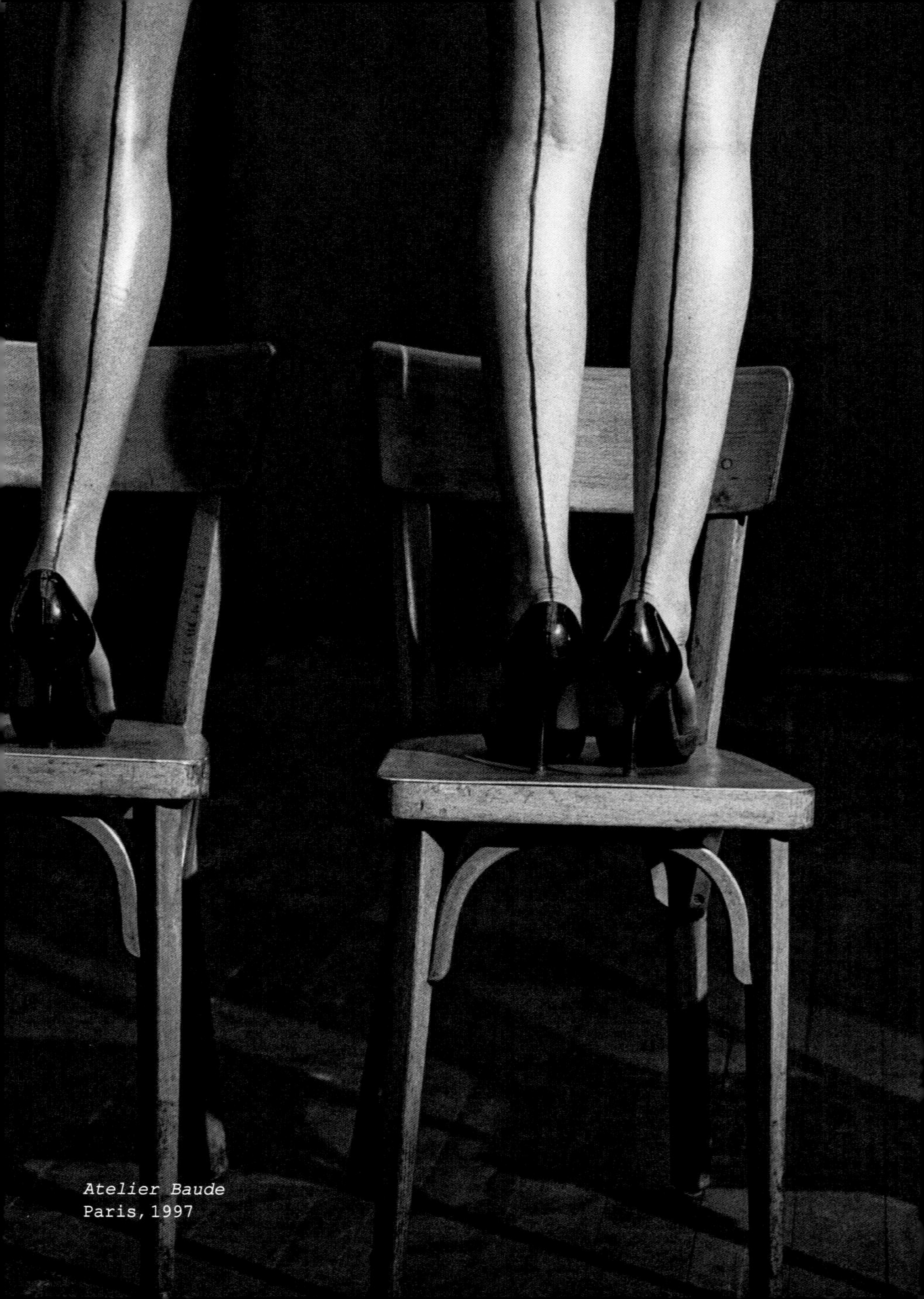

Atelier Baude
Paris, 1997

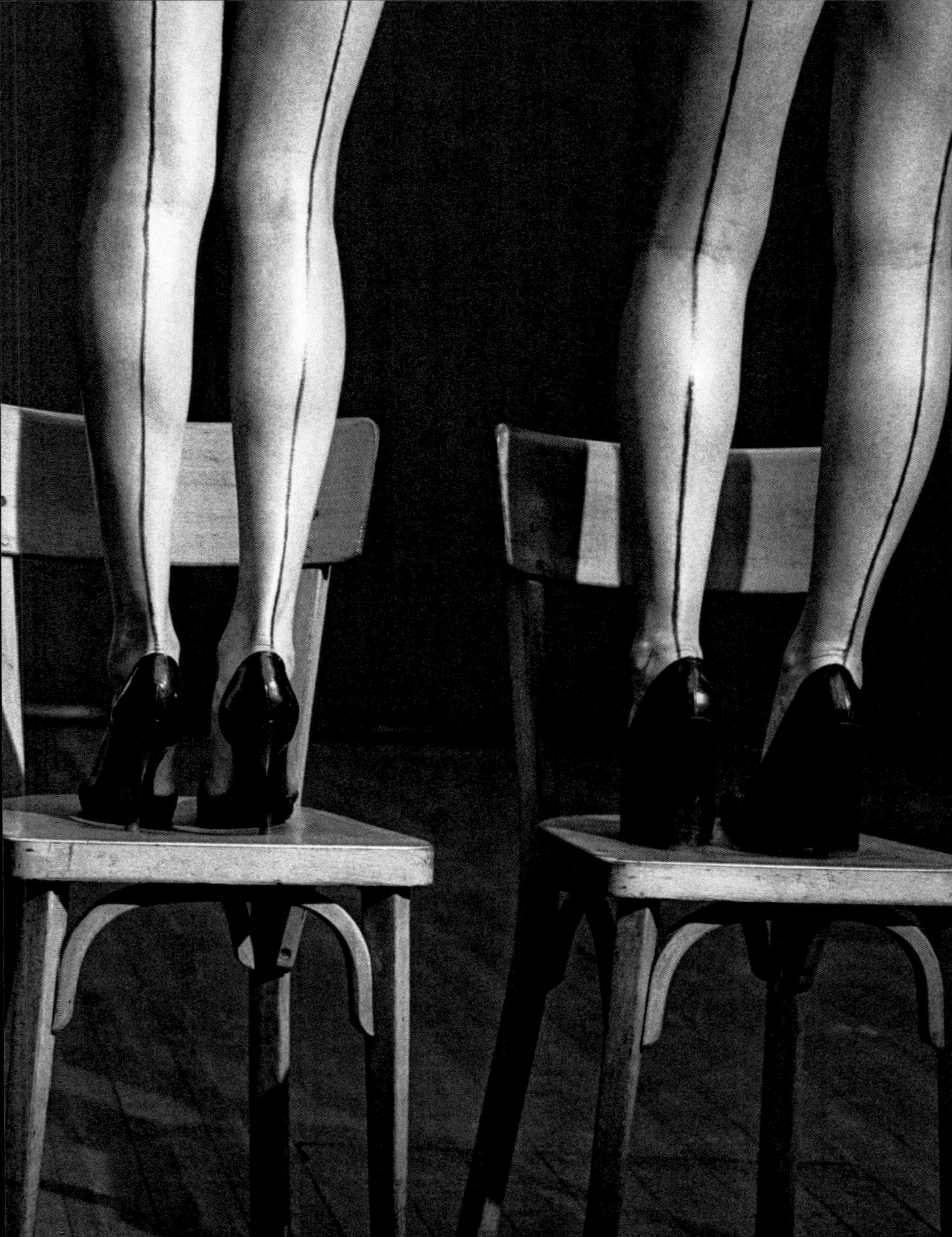

Jessica Chastain
New York, 2016

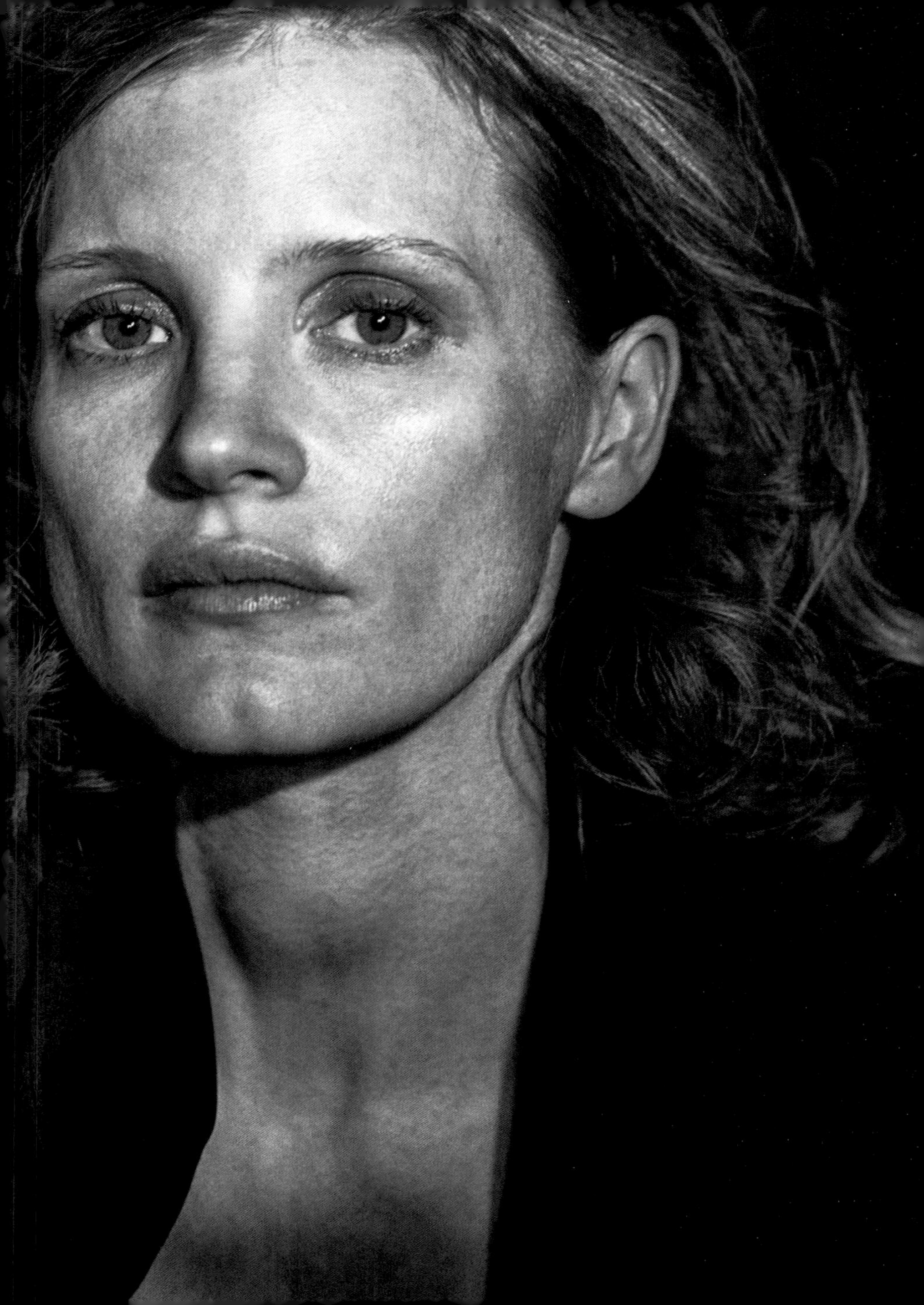

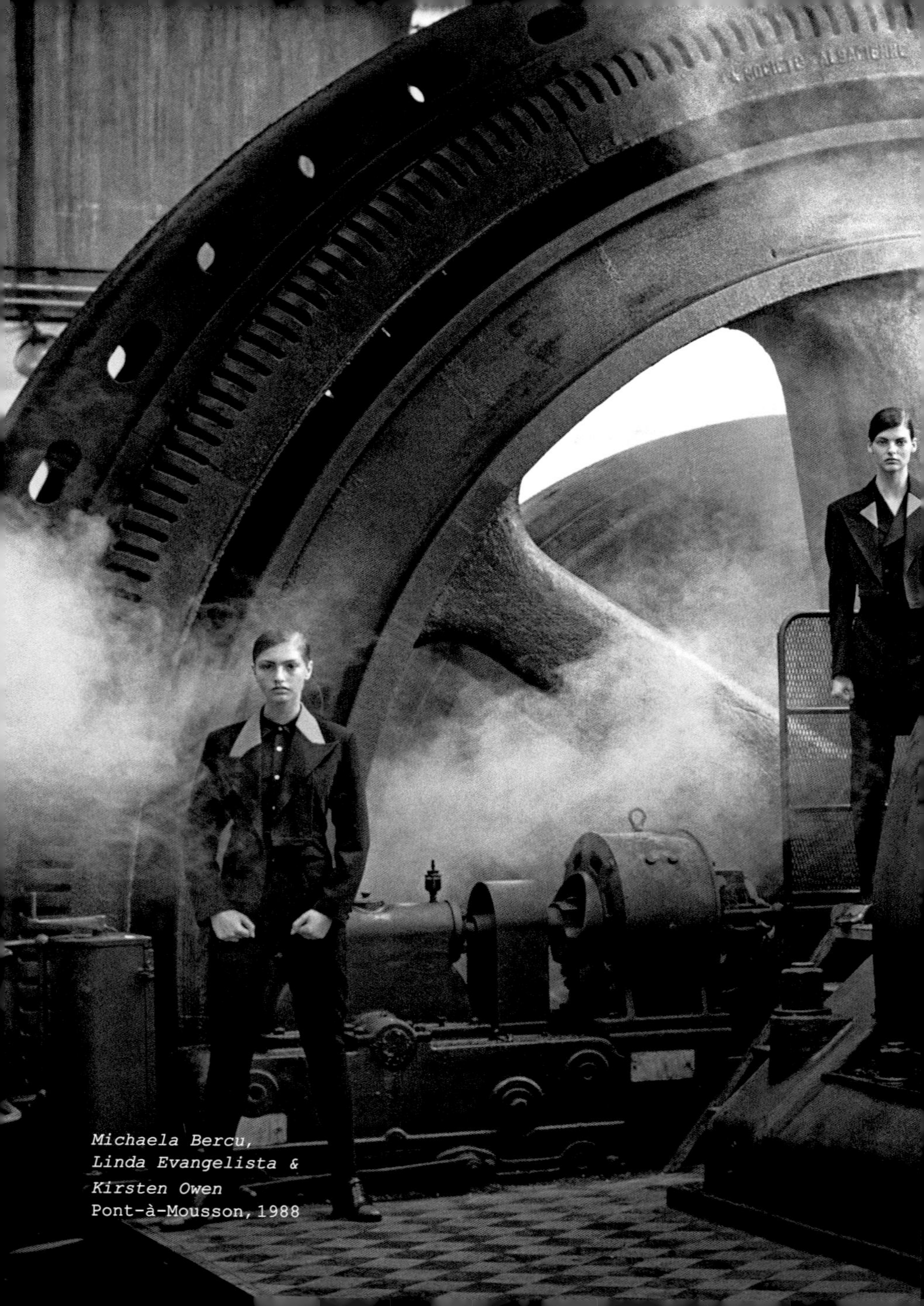

Michaela Bercu,
Linda Evangelista &
Kirsten Owen
Pont-à-Mousson, 1988

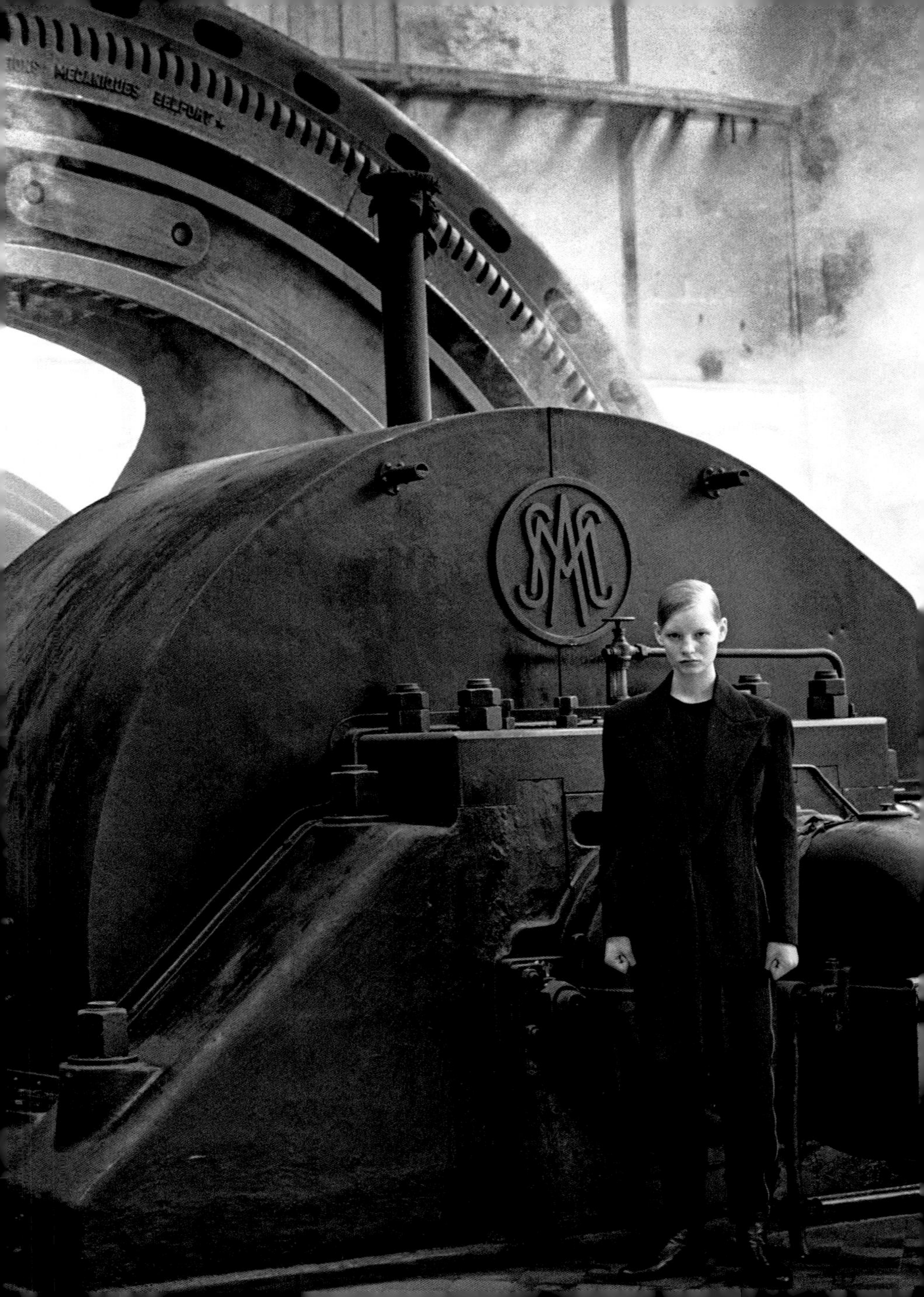

MÉCANIQUES BELFORT

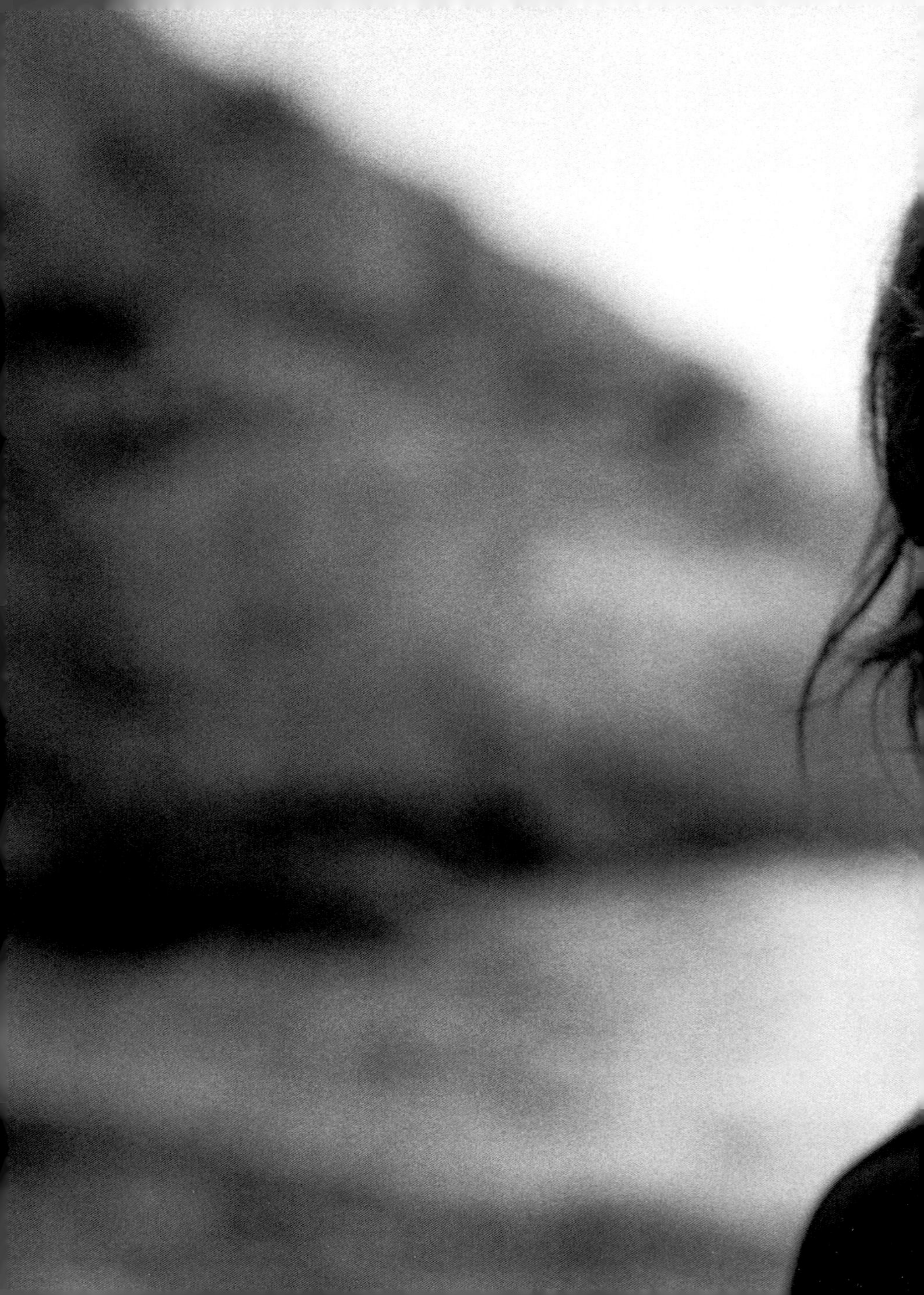

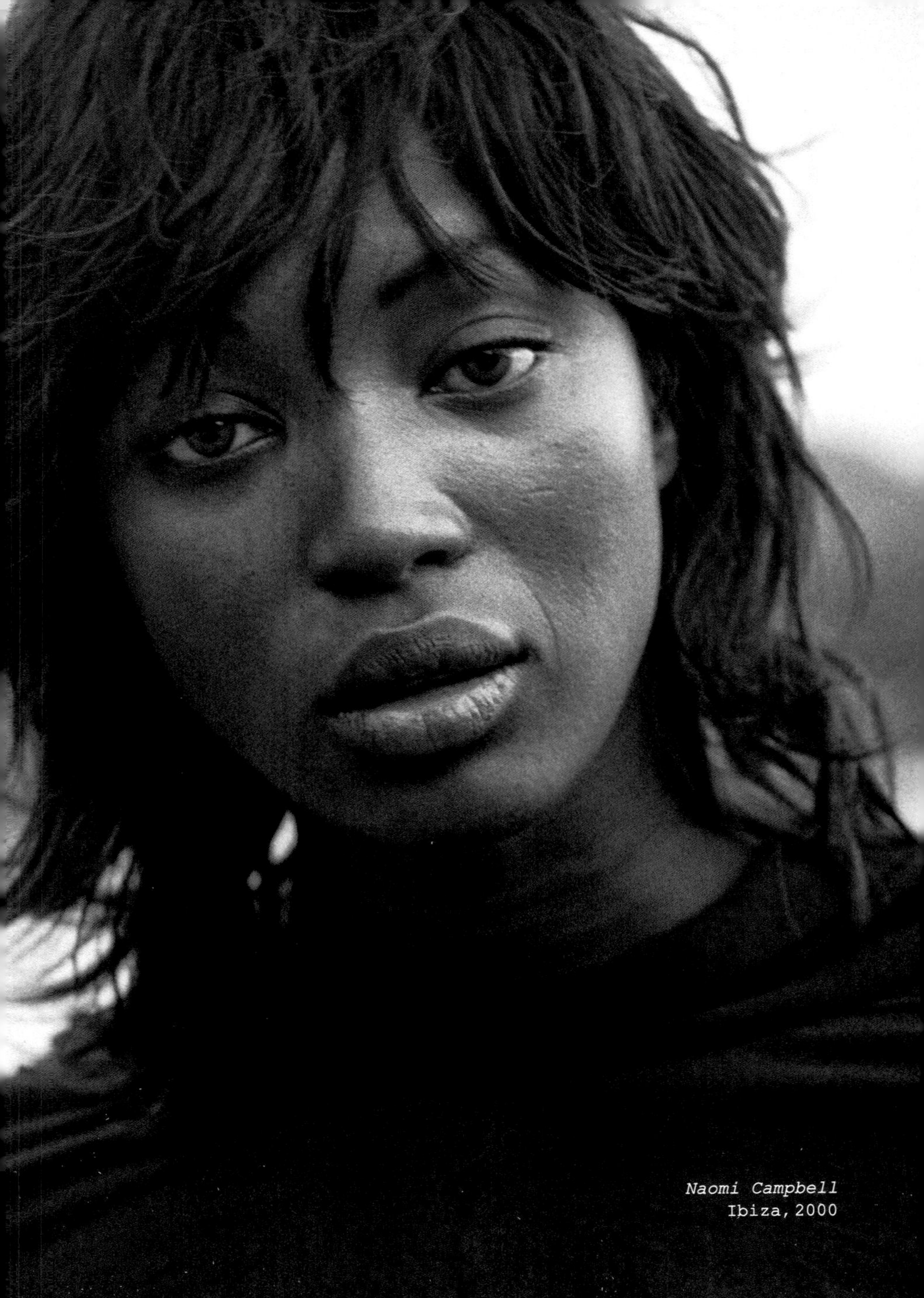

Naomi Campbell
Ibiza, 2000

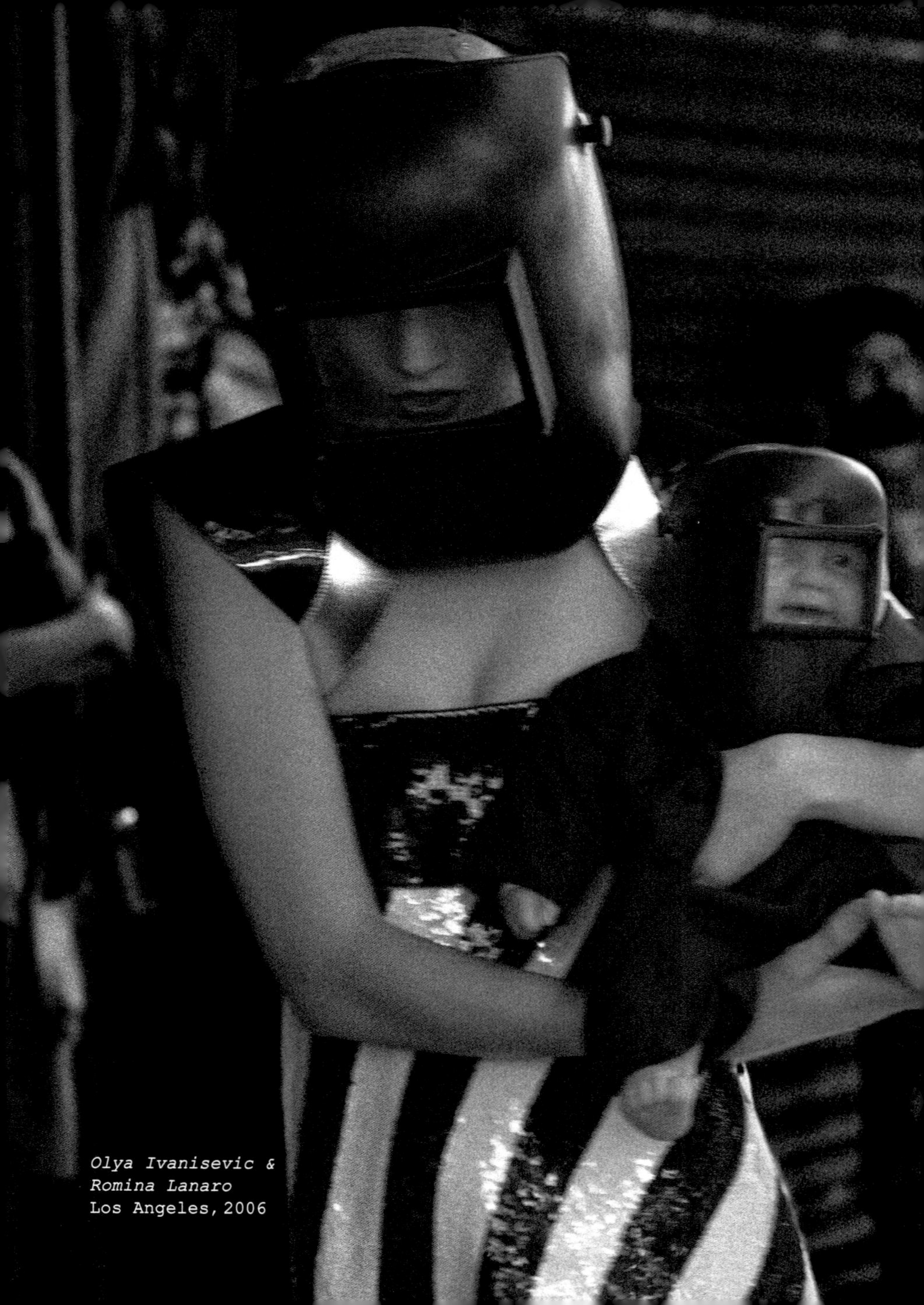

Olya Ivanisevic &
Romina Lanaro
Los Angeles, 2006

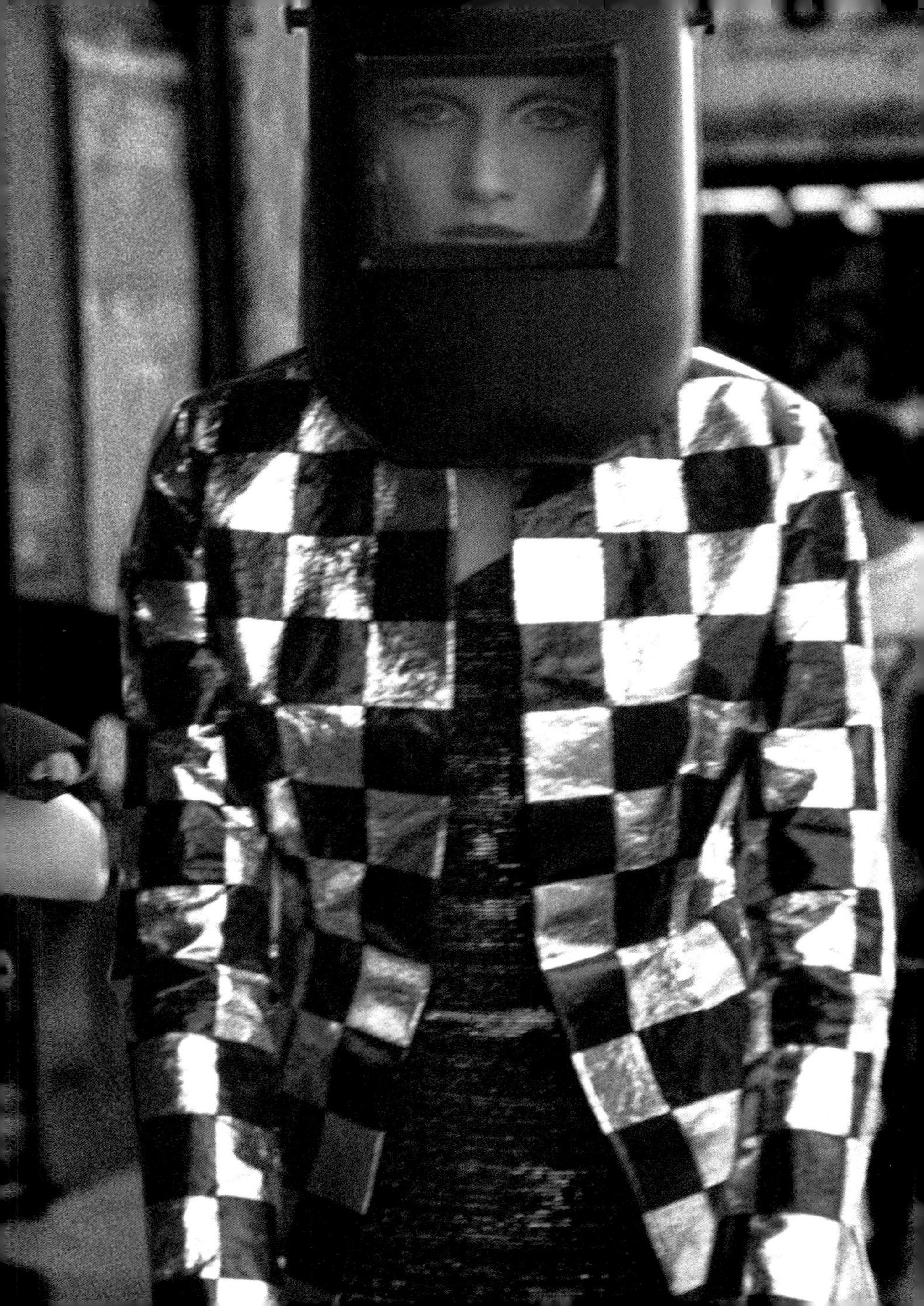

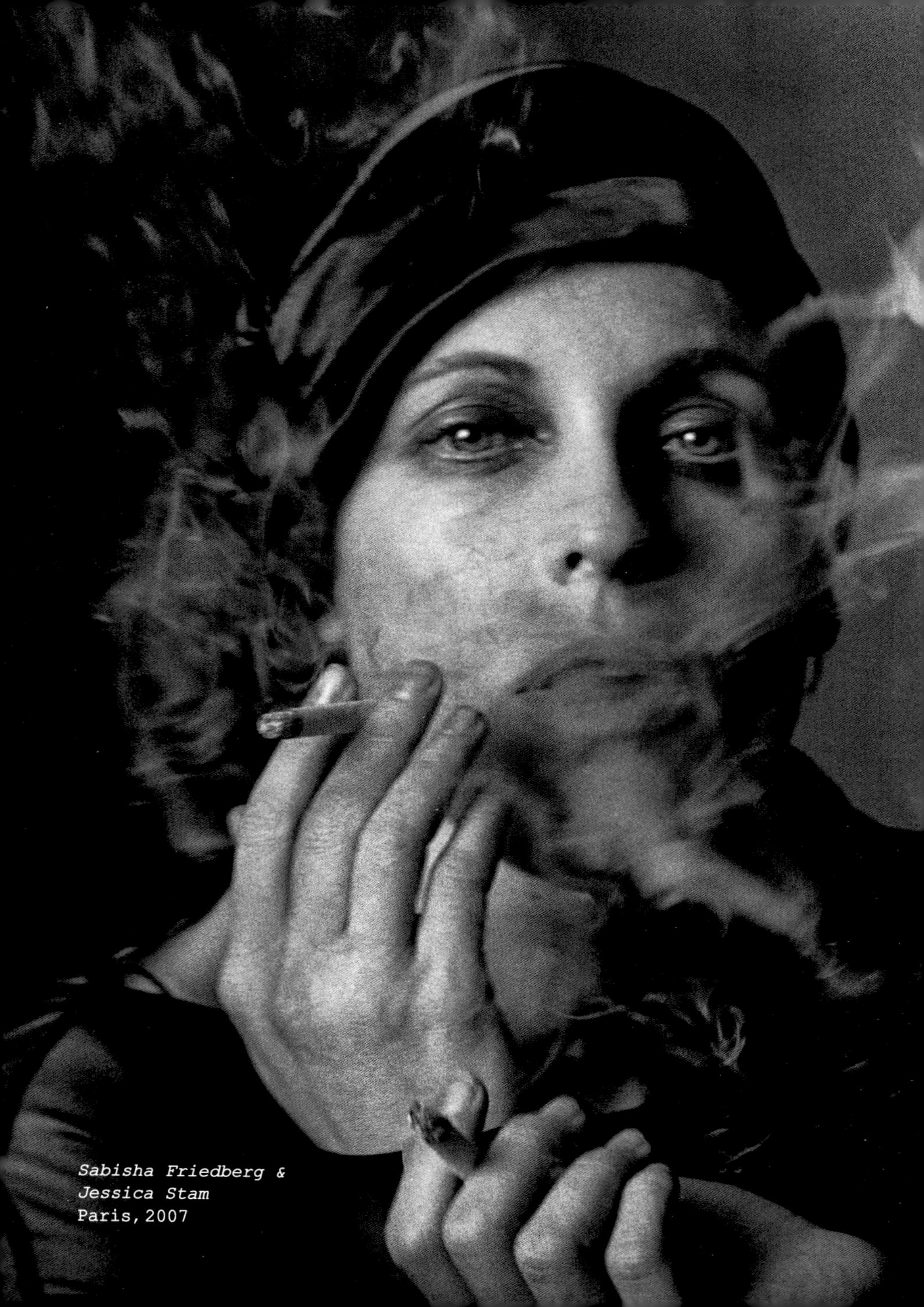
Sabisha Friedberg &
Jessica Stam
Paris, 2007

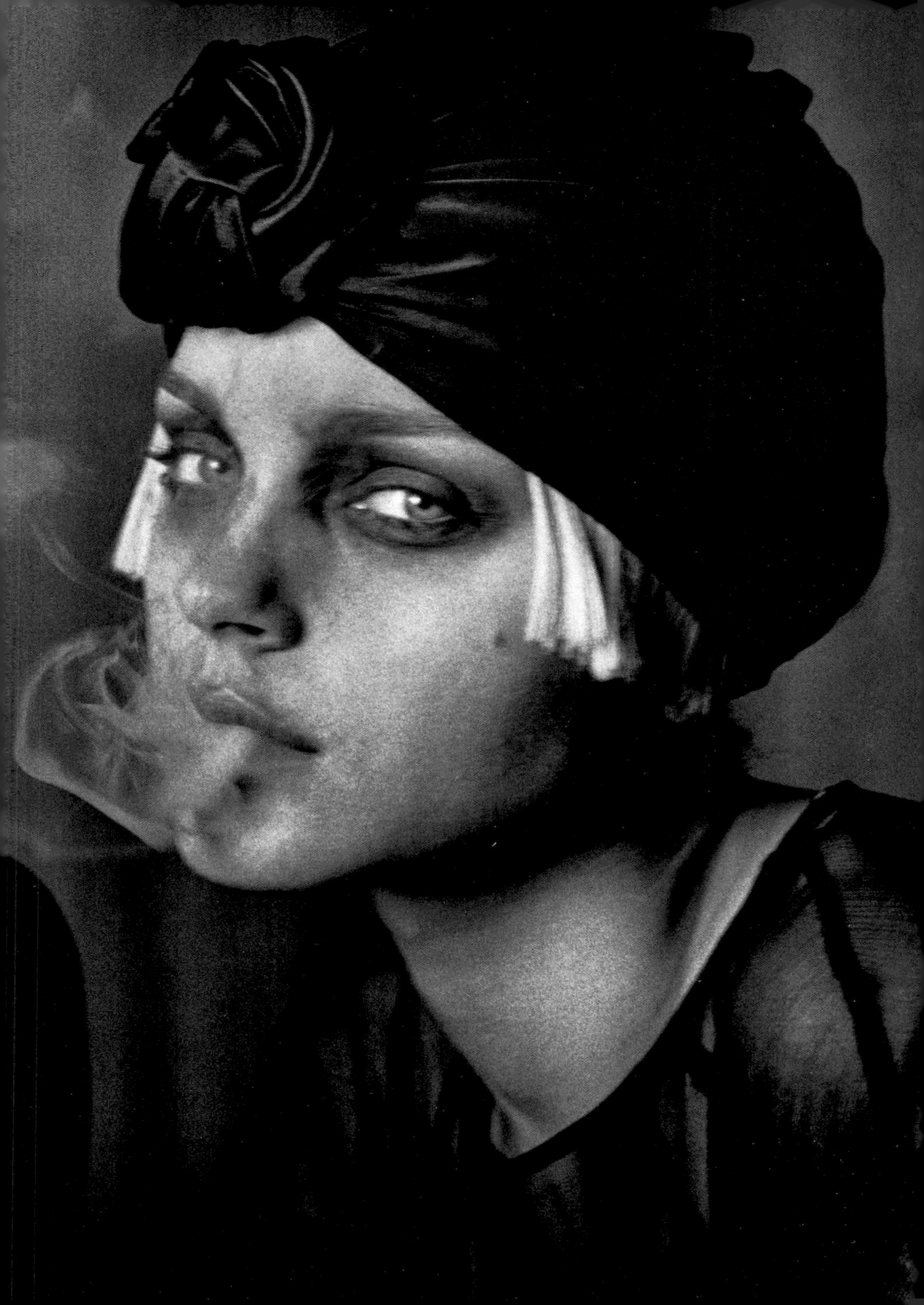

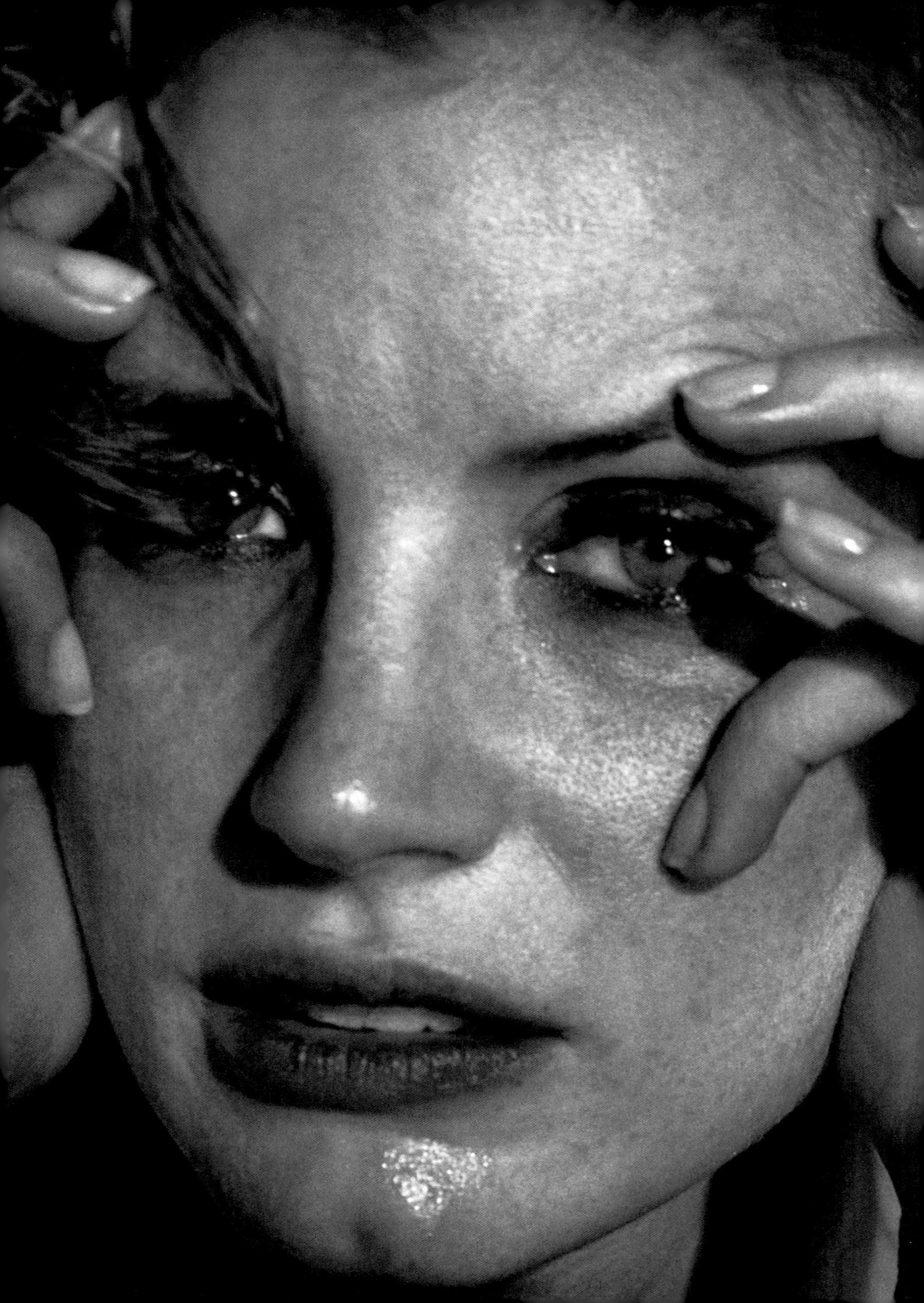

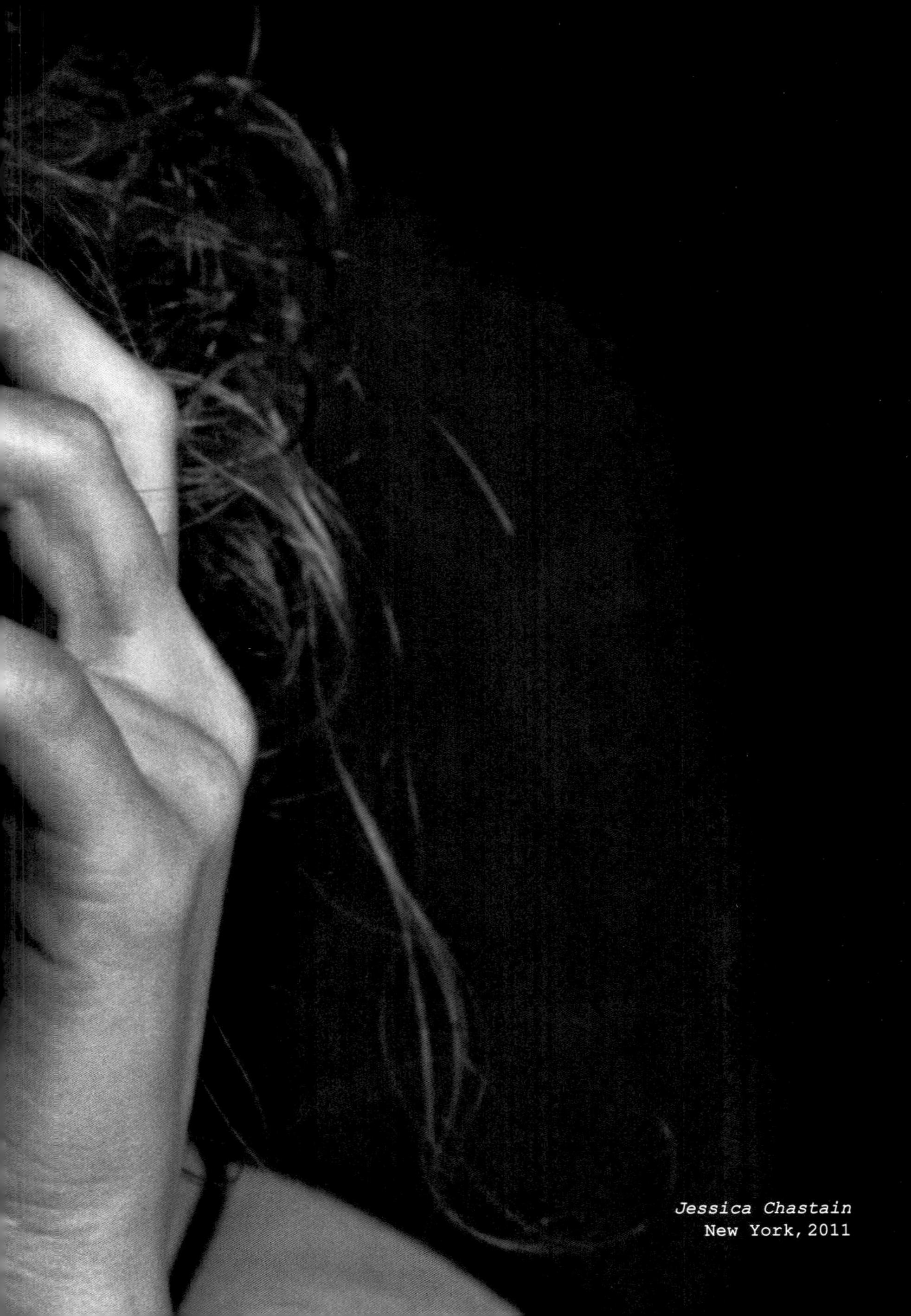

Jessica Chastain
New York, 2011

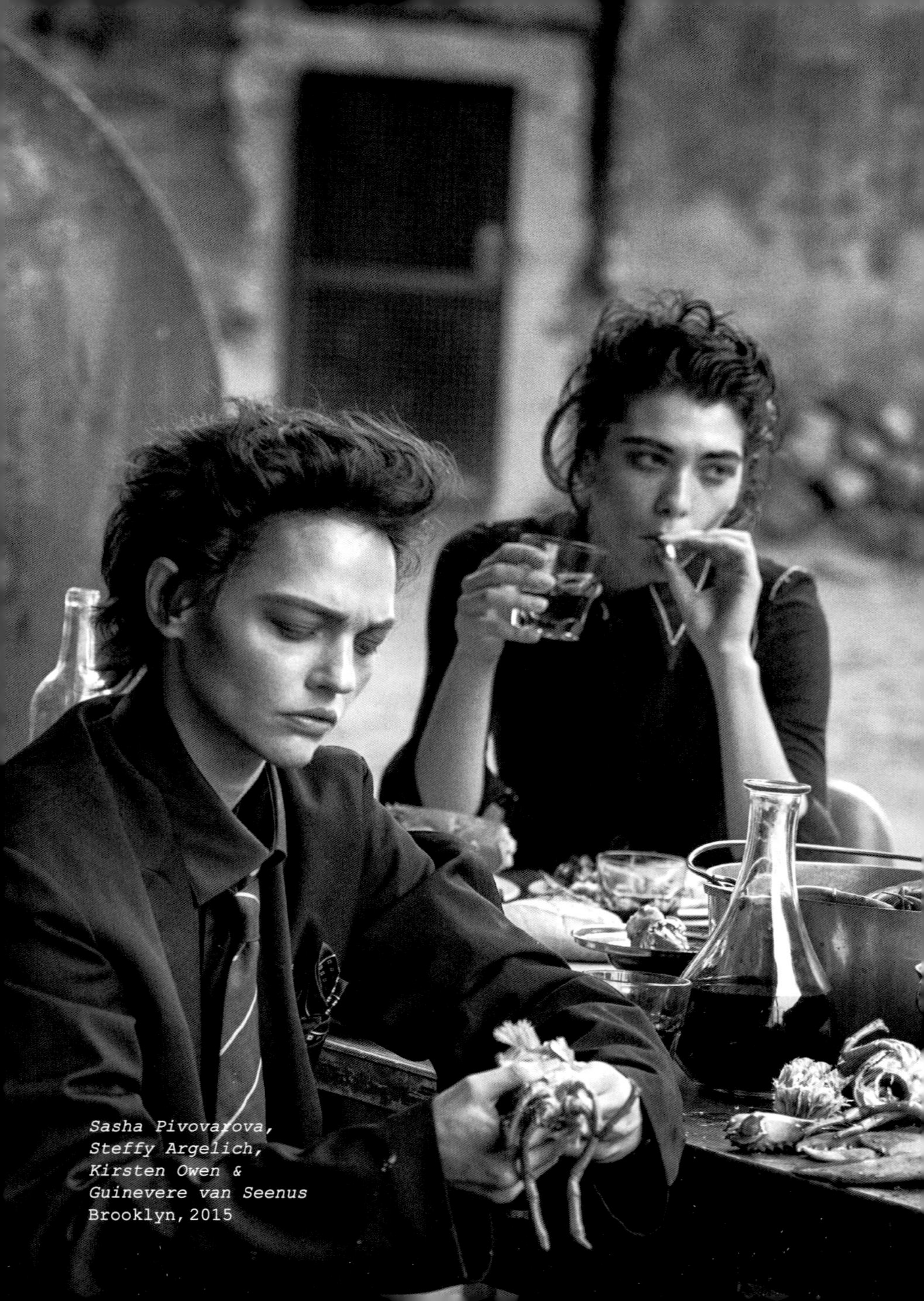

Sasha Pivovarova,
Steffy Argelich,
Kirsten Owen &
Guinevere van Seenus
Brooklyn, 2015

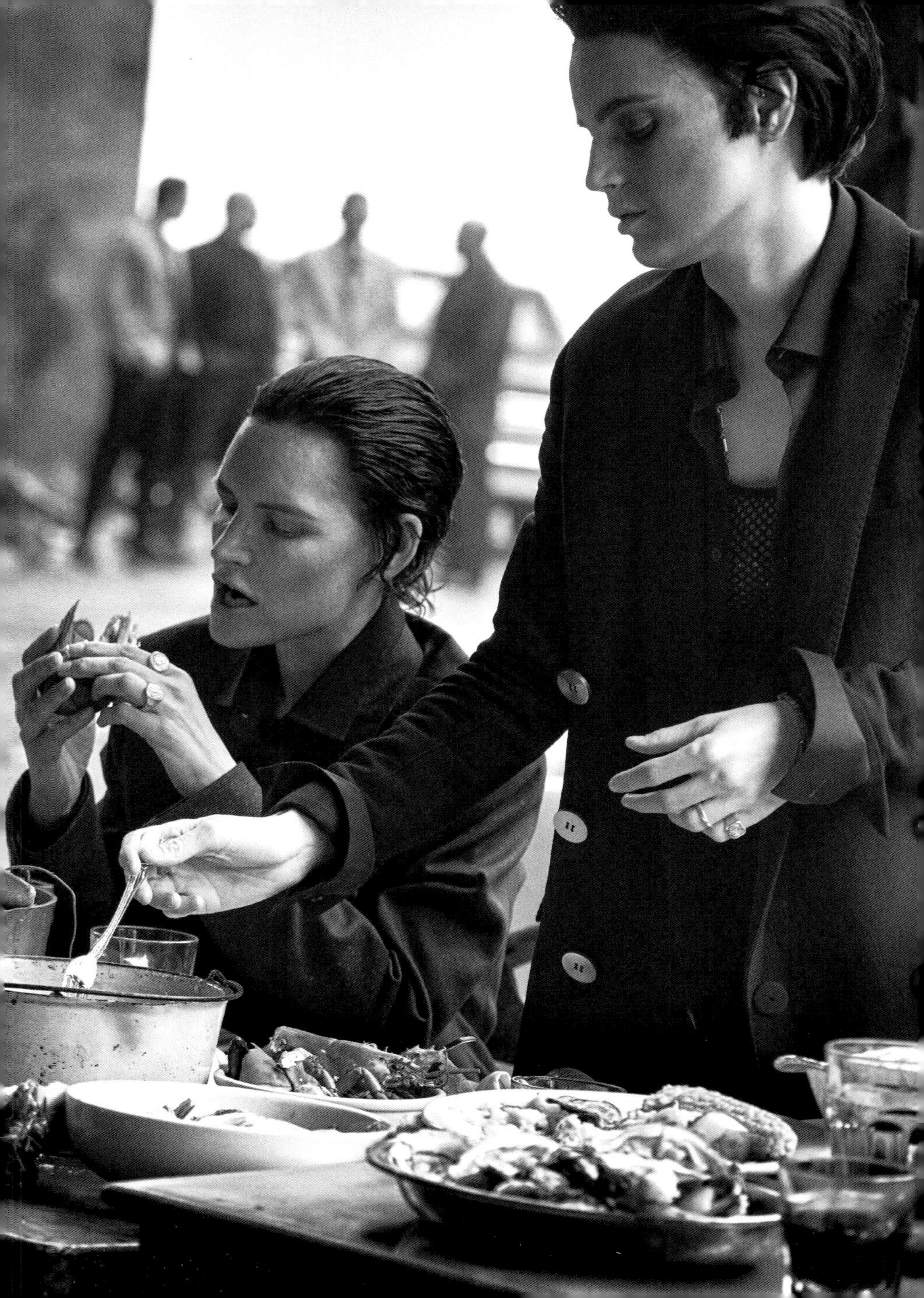

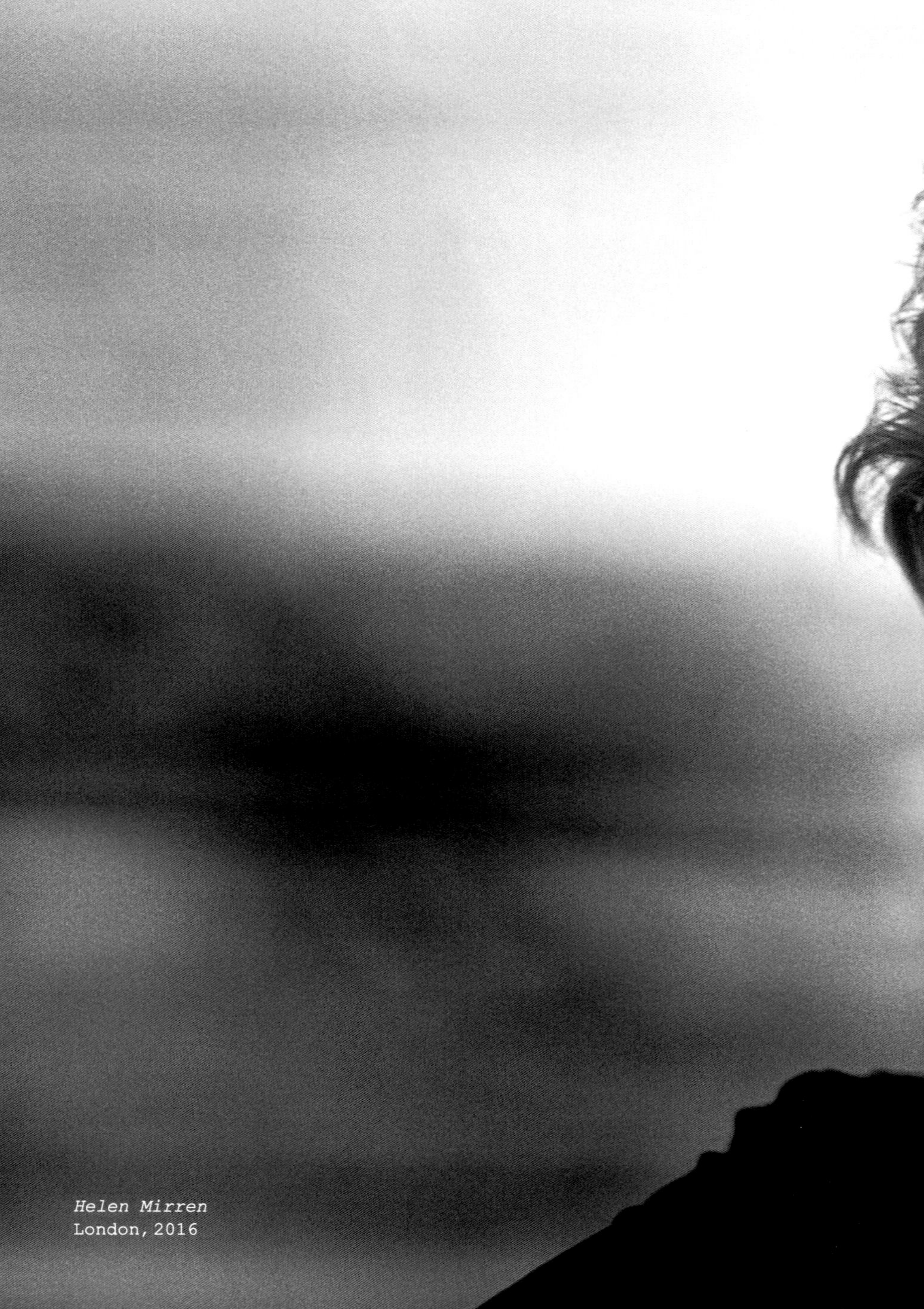

Helen Mirren
London, 2016

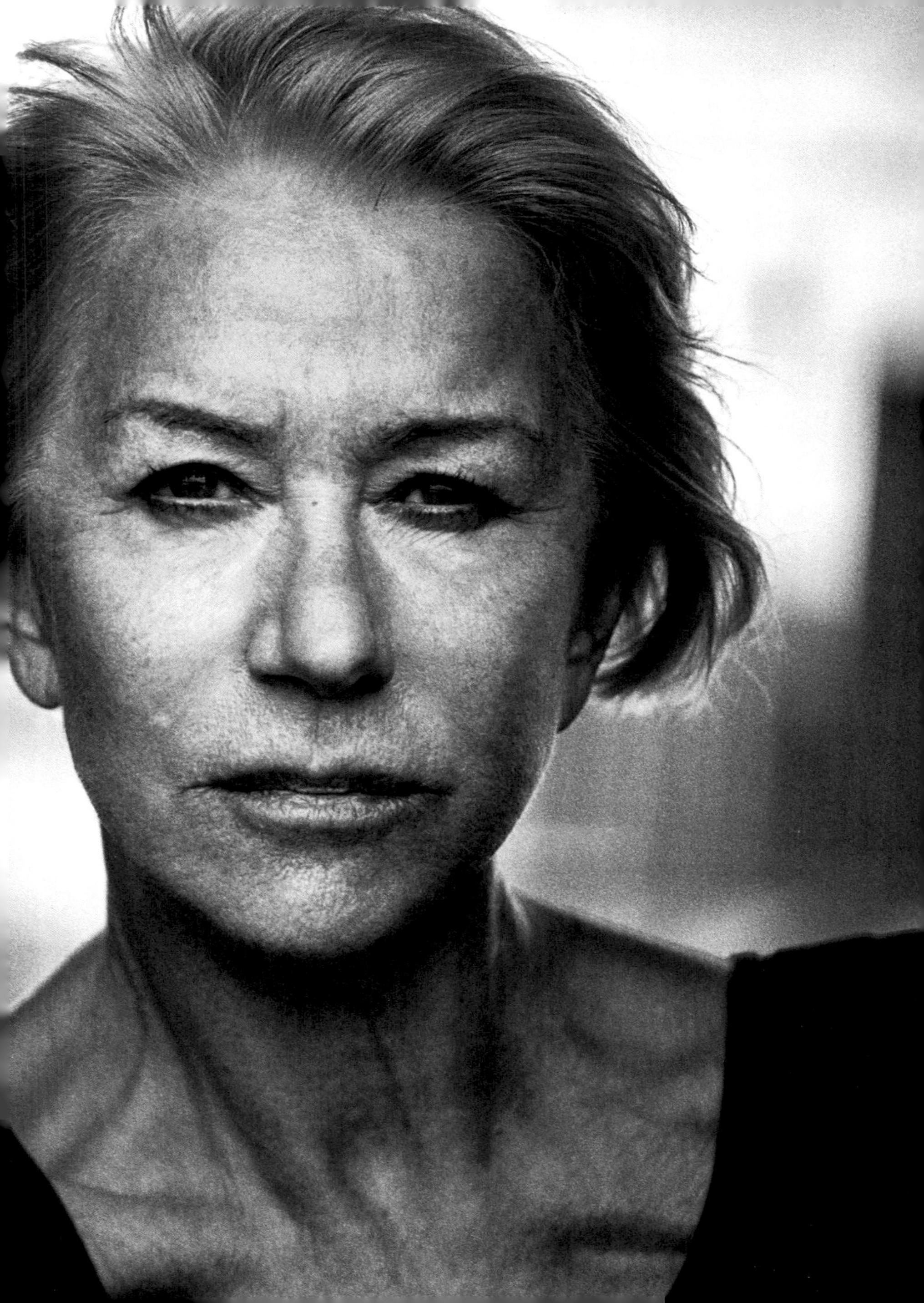

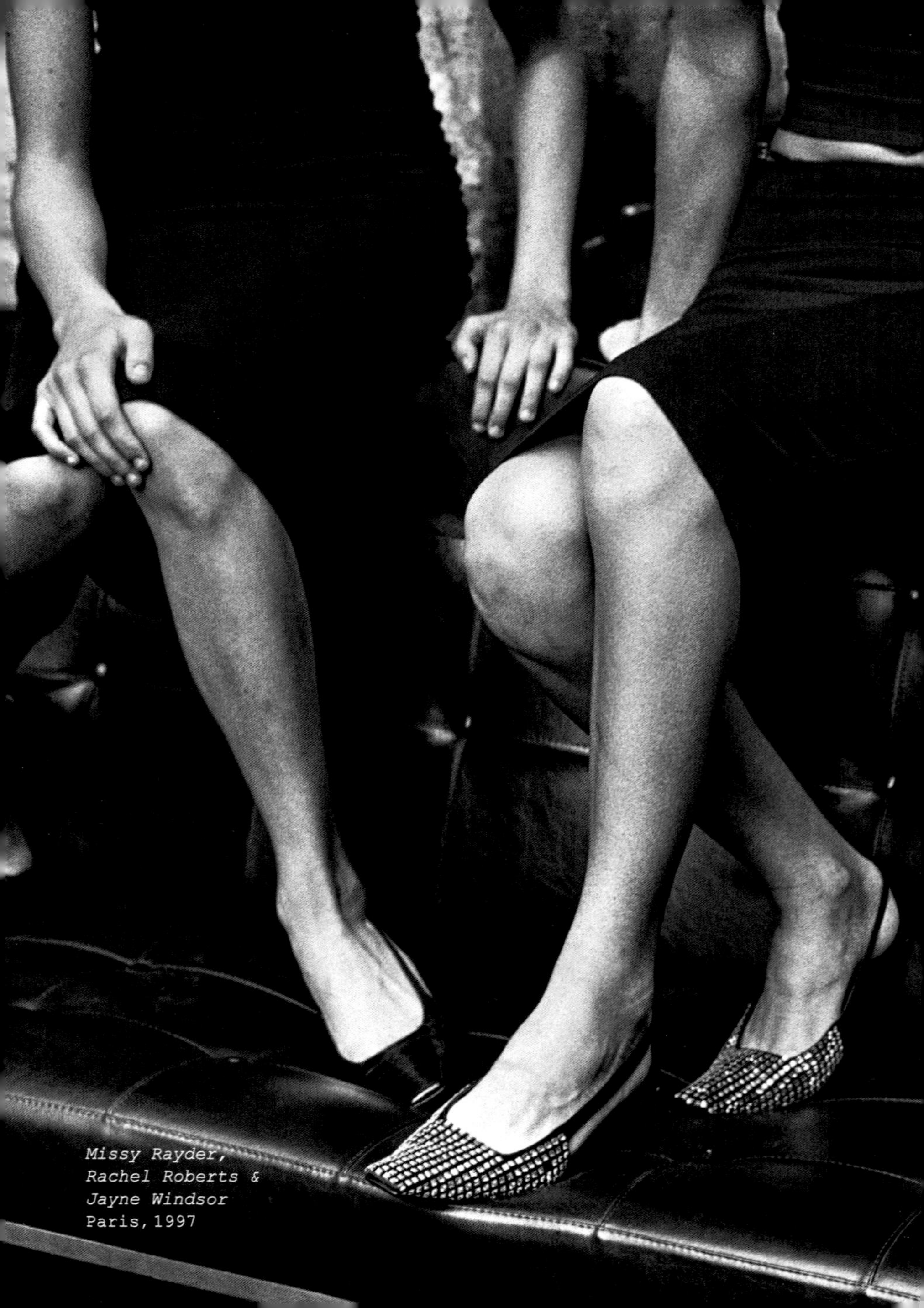

Missy Rayder,
Rachel Roberts &
Jayne Windsor
Paris, 1997

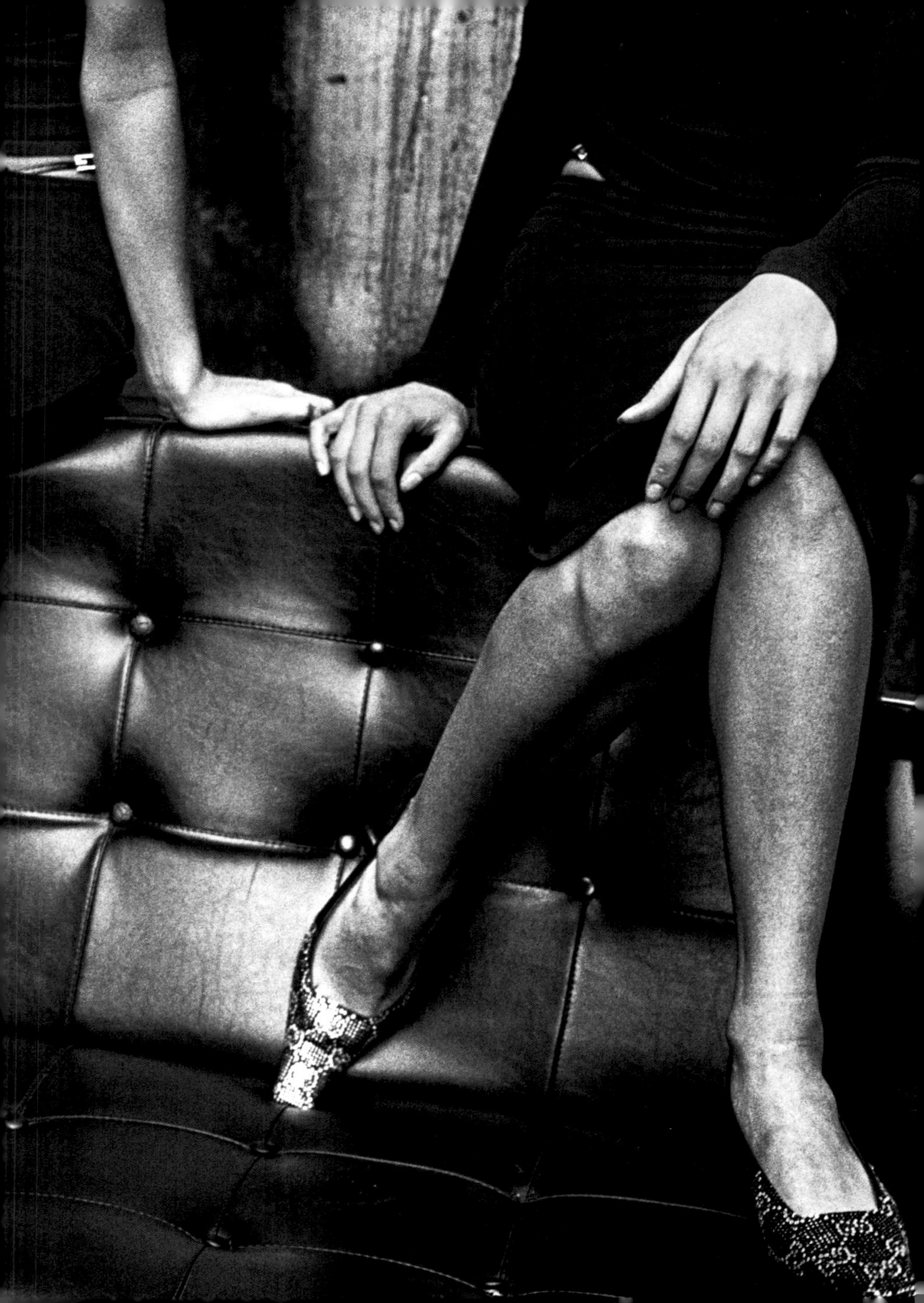

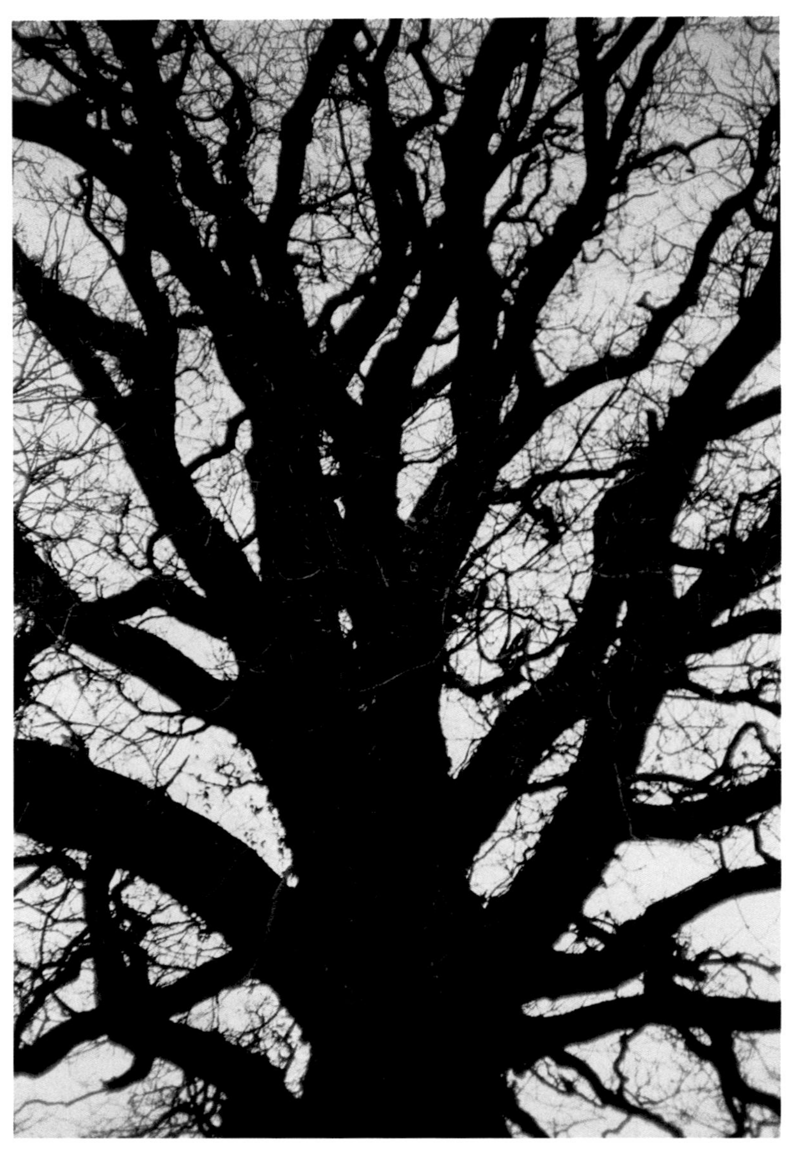

Force of Nature
Dorset Coast,1985

In memory of Peter Lindbergh

by Wim Wenders

What were Peter's greatest talents?

Asking that question, I'm not talking about photography, that goes without saying, that was his craft, his profession, finally his art, for which Peter Lindbergh became world famous. But ... where did all that come from? It wasn't just "there" as a stroke of genius, it had a source in his life. I include all of you who knew Peter and worked with him in my question, so you can all answer it for yourself: "What were his greatest gifts?" I try to define what comes to my mind.

I sometimes watched him work, on beaches in Normandy, in the streets of New York, in industrial ruins in Berlin or on rooftops in LA, and what strikes me most in my memory now, Peter, is how much you were always laughing, and how that joy came from a soul entirely living in the moment, immersed in a constant joyful present. And everybody on the set was totally involved in your world.

The recording instrument for that magical present tense was your camera, Peter, and it wasn't measuring time in seconds, or fractions of seconds, but in exposures, and it went incredibly fast sometimes, click-click-click-click-click-click-click and sometimes more hesitantly, click — click ... With your camera you were generating and shaping a present tense.

Fully being there in every moment, that is already a huge accomplishment, but taking others along with you into that time zone, and stretching those moments, not only for yourself, but for those around you to some kind of tiny joyful eternities, that is an incredible gift! You had it in you to make that carelessness contagious and include others in that lightness of being.

That was the bliss in which your photography blossomed and in which the most impossible things became possible. By pulling others into this state, you gave them the rare chance to let go and free themselves of that net that life so often throws over us and makes us become actors of ourselves.

In the bliss of your look and in front of your camera, people weren't just beautiful, not just supermodels, not just icons, but women (and sometimes men) in all their glory of freedom, of equality, of sister- and brotherhood and thus, yes, of a different beauty.

Nobody else, it seems to me, had that liberating gift, could control at the same time a whole machinery of electricians, of wardrobe and make-up artists, grips and prop men and make it all look like the easiest thing in the world.

Inside that magic presence you created little pockets of solitude in which you could also be alone with a person, just you, the other, and your camera, in the now, in that joyful experience of the sheer moment.

But that was not all.

Your other great gift, Peter, was your generous friendship. You were such a good friend! Yes, that is an art, too! More than ever!

You were a good friend to many of us here, made so many of us feel that you were happy to see us, and that was never an act, never phony, never just a show. You gave us all the most heartfelt unique "Peter hugs," and to feel your big solid body in those embraces was a unique experience, because we physically realized how giving, sharing, and ... kind you were.

Let me say this word again, because it has become so rare today and almost lost: you were such a kind man, Peter! Your kindness and generosity were genuine, they were your favorite state of being.

All of that was condensed in that wide awake pair of eyes behind those almost invisible glasses over that big smile shining through that stubble on your face.

Those eyes were always sparkling with joy, and when our gaze met them, that joyfulness jumped over and started to work in us. We're all not strangers to such joy, to such kindness, to such knowledge of the present tense, we have it in us, but we have mostly forgotten it. It is the child we all carry in us, but you preserved it, Peter, you kept it alive and intact. You hadn't lost the ability to draw from that well of childhood. That was the open source in your art and in your life. Just remembering this child shining through your eyes will always bring a smile onto our faces.

One of the last times
I saw you, Peter, was
early in the morning. I
tiptoed through your stu-
dio to leave the house,
and there you were, lying
on your sofa, sleeping,
all dressed, with your
open computer resting on
your stomach.

I had left you, late the
night before, in your studio when you had shown me
some series of photographs
you had taken recently
and that you were fond
of. Those were pictures of
Peter Handke, and you were
so glad about your encoun-
ter, and the other series
was a photo session with
that wise rebel child Greta
Thunberg. You also en-
thusiastically described
how you met her. And then
we said good night, and
I knew you still had long and
lonely hours in front of you.
That was the reverse angle of
your joyful shooting sessions:
those long nights of going
through thousands of raw photographs and selecting quietly,
seriously, painstakingly, fully
concentrated, alone.

Those eyes remain closed now
that saw and loved so many of us
here and that gave all of
us so much light and lightness.

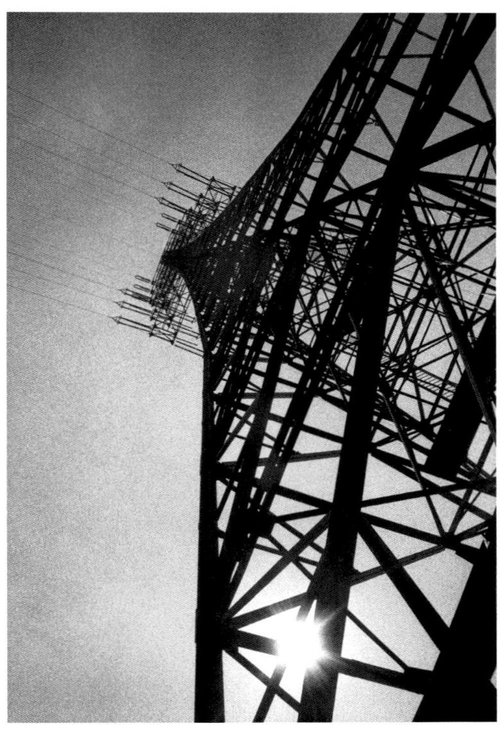

These eyes taught millions to
see beauty not only as a product
of fashion, but as our innermost
human propensity for freedom,
kindness, a sense of identity,
and joy and for the right of in-
habiting the child in us.

We're all grateful that you were
and are and always will be in
our lives, Peter.

*Church of Saint-Sulpice,
Paris, September 2019*

Force of Men
Duisburg, 1984

Peter Lindbergh
in conversation with Felix Krämer

This interview was conducted over several hours in June 2019 at Peter Lindbergh's studio in Paris. In the previous meetings, an enthusiastic exchange about the exhibition had already taken place. During the two years he spent preparing the show, it developed into a project close to Peter Lindbergh's heart. There were many unforgettable moments — from that first mutual brainstorming session to the spreading out of hundreds of pictures on the floors of both my office and his studio, down to the in-depth discussions about what it means to curate an exhibition of your own works. Throughout the continuously warm and cheerful cooperation, nothing was more unimaginable than that we would have to open the exhibition without Peter Lindbergh. To the very end, he worked on the show with great passion. This unique energy and enthusiasm is palpable in Peter Lindbergh's photographs, which changed the world. FELIX KRÄMER

Felix Krämer: It was at our first meeting that we started discussing whether the planned exhibition was to be a retrospective or not. We both felt that this would not be the right format. It soon occurred to us that you should be the one choosing the works and that we would show the photographs which are closest to your heart.

Peter Lindbergh: Your idea for me to curate my exhibition immediately appealed to me. At first I thought it would be no problem at all. How wrong I was! It's like being in a life and death struggle! [He laughs.]

Krämer: The intensity with which you took on this task has truly impressed me. Every time we met up to talk about the exhibition, the passion and seriousness that drives you became ever more apparent.

Lindbergh: The greatest challenge is that each one of the selected photographs must be able to stand up to whatever thoughts it may inspire. What is more important, content or photography? Does reality come before interpretation? What part does the truth play or can we simply tell fairy tales? Are we responsible or not? What is fashion photography? What should it be? Where can we find ourselves, our creativity, our own identity and our own expression? With every decision for or against a photo, whether to include it in the exhibition or not, one is faced with these questions. I've now reached a point where there is no longer a place for innocence and where these questions have to be answered. The more you look for clarity, the further it slips away and you realize that you can really only control small "contents." Then, once you've reached the champions' league, you just have to let go, hand over control and stop giving interviews [laughs], in order to reveal major content, which you only just partially grasp yourself, and which evades, somewhere deep down, any exact reproduction. Trying to describe this complexity would cause you to lose 80 percent of the content — it would be *Lost in Translation*, to quote the title of Sofia Coppola's film.

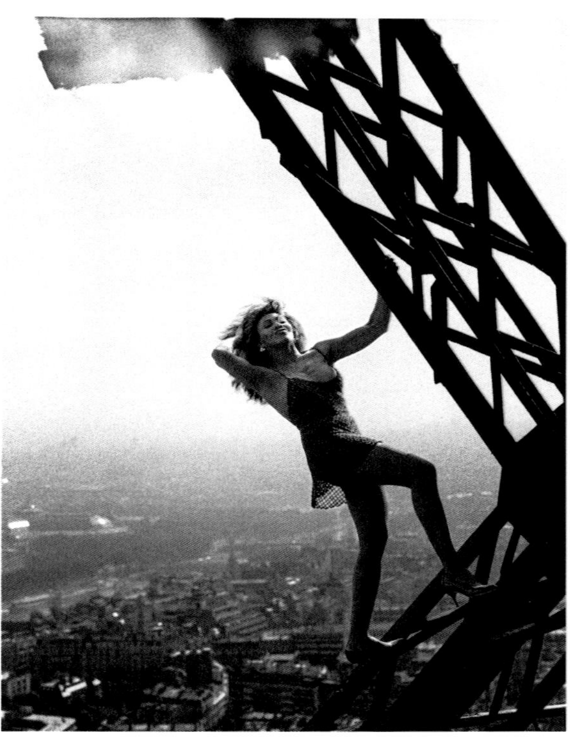

Krämer: Can you describe what sets this exhibition apart from your previous ones?

Lindbergh: Actually, all the exhibitions I've done so far were realized in cooperation with a curator. In those cases, a concept was proposed and we exchanged ideas about it. The results were very impressive shows. But now that I have to master this task alone, depths open up that I think about intensely and that sometimes even frighten me. I am confronted with

Tina Turner
Paris, 1989

the question: Who are you really and where do all these pictures come from? And of course: Why this way and not any other?

Krämer: Could you perhaps give me an example?
Lindbergh: Right at the beginning, the exhibition shows a group of large-format pictures, each about three by four meters in size. I had my difficulties with the selection of these photographs. There is really nothing more intense you can do with your works. I feel totally responsible for each and every photograph in my exhibition and that is fantastic! I had nothing to hide behind. Suddenly I knew, that's it! Playing chess is easy in comparison.

Krämer: So at the beginning of the project you had no idea in which direction it would be going?
Lindbergh: No, initially I thought it would be more of a process in which you stick to the rules or even try to do the exact opposite. I am aware that this sounds crazy, but it happens that feelings, character traits, emotions rise up from the unknown, they come to light and become manifest. In the end, I made the decisions instinctively, following my gut.

Krämer: If I understand correctly, you're saying that when cooperating with curators one has to sometimes make compromises. Our project, however, takes place on a different level — which is also reflected in the title you've chosen, *Untold Stories*. To yourself, you have to answer for this presentation totally differently than

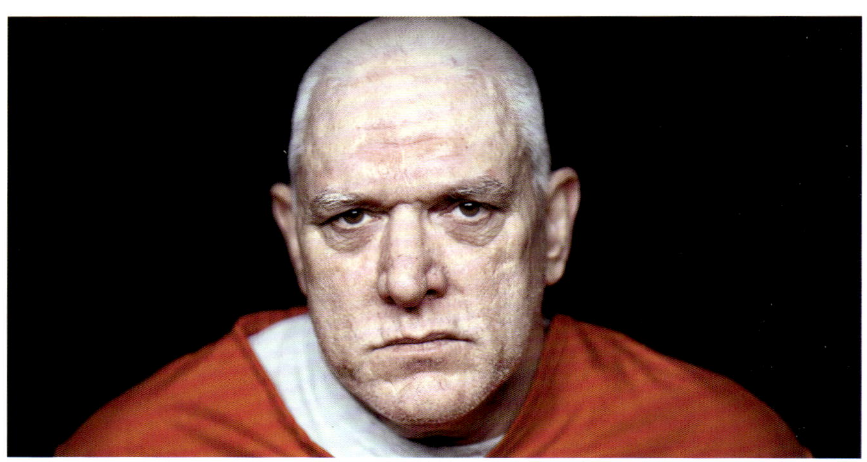

Testament: Elmer Carroll
Florida, 2013

you would for an exhibition with external curators.

Lindbergh: There were times when I thought that this project would never be finished; that it was something that just could not be completed. Every time I went on a trip I would return to the selection for the exhibition with completely different inspirations and ideas — and of course with new pictures, too. Sometimes I could not even comprehend what I'd done before and started all over again.

Krämer: In other words, your view of your photos has changed during the preparations?

Lindbergh: Yes, absolutely. You keep starting from different points and suddenly you see new connections. There are many references I had previously not thought possible, especially with the photos that we are showing as blue-backs at the start of the exhibition. In this section I tried out many different combinations: a thematic selection, a narrative of its own — both utterly dull — or exclusively commissioned photos. None of these ideas worked very well. In retrospect, it's difficult to retrace how I arrived at the final point as there were many influences. After all, insecurity is an important factor because you're always looking for and finding new perspectives. And in doing so you discover new paths.

Krämer: The exhibition is divided into three chapters. At the beginning and the end there are two large-scale installations. In the main section you are showing what you consider to be the most important photographs from your entire body of work, loosely chronologically, and you present them in new contexts.

Lindbergh: When starting to prepare the exhibition, it initially felt similar to when I got a commission to do the photography for an entire edition of *Vogue* in the past — 120 pages in one fell swoop. Upon first reflection, a theme and a precise structure might seem the right approach. However, I very much prefer to take on the challenge of telling a story over 120 pages or in 120 works that does not follow a pattern, but that is nonetheless full of variety and does not turn out to be boring. If you succeed, you enter another dimension: you can experiment freely, find new contexts and reveal them. In the second part of the exhibition, I experiment with my photos and show iconic works as well as works that were never exhibited before, in pairs or in groups, which also makes astonishing interpretations possible.

Krämer: The show concludes with the 2013 one-sequence-shot *Testament*, which is also being presented for the first time. Elmer Carroll, a death row inmate, is being filmed while facing a one-way mirror for 30 minutes without moving. The film is very haunting and reveals a hitherto unknown side of your work. At the same time it triggers important questions.

Lindbergh: In *Testament*, I wanted to confront the viewer, in a nonjudgmental manner, with the image of the prisoner, while not giving any details of his deed. I studied over 300 court cases. The themes that *Testament* revolves around for me, and which are taken up again and again elsewhere in my work, are introspection, expression, empathy, and freedom. Ultimately, the film deals with the impossibility of being really and truly free.

Krämer: Two years ago, when I approached you with the idea of mounting an exhibition, I said to you that I thought you weren't actually interested in fashion. Your answer really pleased me: "Finally someone has said it." Prior to our first meeting, I thought long and hard about whether I should even ask you the question, because I knew that it would either result in a good conversation about your photos or put an end to the whole project then and there.

Lindbergh: The idea of me curating the exhibition myself opened up the possibility of thinking about my photos in a more comprehensive way, in a context other than fashion. Previous presentations of my work concentrated quite strongly on the fashion aspect. The aim of this exhibition is to open up my photos to different interpretations and perspectives. Mind you, I am not trying to say that my pictures are not about fashion photography, as that would be incorrect. I insist on the definition "fashion photography," since, for me, this term does not mean that you have to depict fashion — photography is much bigger than fashion itself, it is a component of contemporary culture, like music.

Krämer: Of course fashion plays an important part. But the more I study your work, the more I discover an ambivalence that has nothing to do with the depiction of fashion.

Lindbergh: Yes, because nowhere is fashion conveyed directly. That is important to me. I am not interested in specific collections or trends, which is why I have not attended a fashion show for the past 25 years. I've always wanted to preserve my freedom of thought and not allow myself to be absorbed by fashion. Fashion photography's purpose is not primarily to show fashion. Instead, fashion photography is its own cultural contribution, in the same way that fashion is.

Krämer: In my opinion it does not make a lot of sense to think in these categories. First of all, your works are fascinating, because they are strong pictures that have shaped our visual perception and continue to shape it to this day. The label you put on it — whether it's art, non-art, fashion photography, photography — basically makes no difference. Each generation decides for itself what it believes is relevant

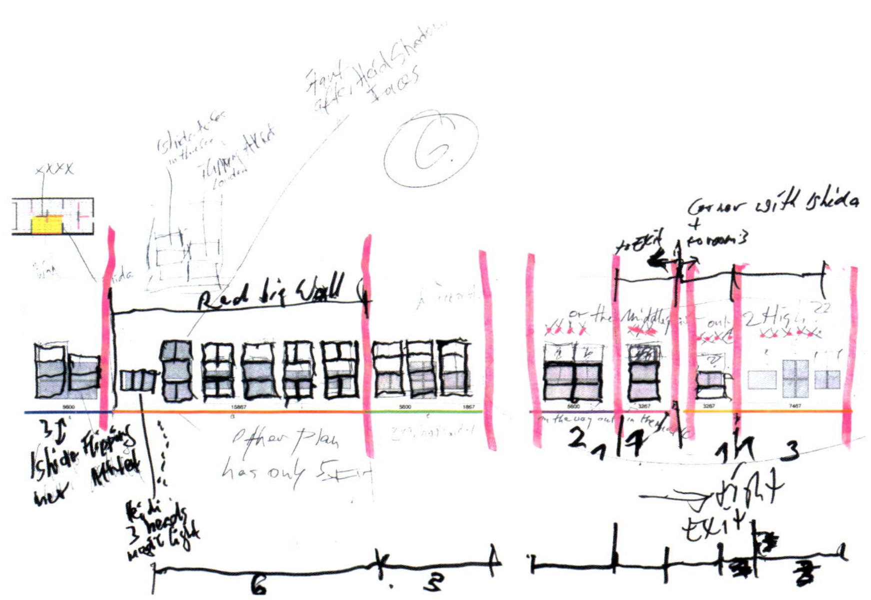

anyway. In the end, the picture has to be convincing.

Lindbergh: I absolutely agree with you, but it is an issue that constantly comes up all the same. To many people, categorization is important. Even the question as to whether photography is art is one you hear regularly. Plus, in the case of fashion photography, it has to be taken into account that allegedly it couldn't be art anyway as it is commissioned work. Just recently, I had a conversation about the need of art to be free, which would imply that fashion photography or any commissioned pho-tography could never be art. If one were to think this through, then all museums would soon have plenty of free space as so much would have to be cleared out. Art history is full of commissioned work; Titian, for example, did everything he could to get a com-mission. Photography is photog-raphy and that should be enough.

Krämer: In the 1980s, when you started to concentrate on fashion photography, this attitude was very different from that of your colleagues and it was quite a strong statement. Most of them tried to photograph fashion in such a way that it would appear as glamorous as possible. I presume that your artistic background contributed to your different, very individual view of fashion. This view is often inspired by art history, whether it be your allusions to the French sculptor Aristide Maillol, the director Fritz Lang or the choreographer Pina Bausch from Wuppertal, who also happened to be a close friend of yours. Presumably these references are partly intentional, partly not; how does it work?

Lindbergh: These inner images exist in my head, next to many other things, and mostly I pick out the references very deliberately. It is the situations and the commissions that determine when the connotations come to light. In 1981, I met the head designer of Comme des Garçons, Rei Kawakubo, who brought a breath of fresh air to Paris with her minimalist, conceptual fashion. The first time I looked at the clothes she'd designed, I was seriously shocked. What I saw was something entirely new. Soon afterwards, various commissions for Comme des Garçons came along. Kawakubo gave me totally free rein and, unlike many clients, her mind was not set on a fixed idea. In that period, Fritz Lang's film *Metropolis* played an important role for me. At the same time, I thought a lot about Duisburg, the city I grew up in. In the resulting pictures, I did not aim to show what Comme des Garçons or the specific collection stand for; I was just taking pictures freely, which worked well for both the label and the clothes (see ill. pp. 18/19, 26/27, 54, 140). So this confirmed that fashion photography is not just about depicting something, but that other paths can be taken in order to create relevant pictures. Everyone, in the course of their lives, sees a world and stores it internally. That's where the impulses must come from. Ultimately you react to everything you have perceived and experienced, as a distinct individual.

Krämer: Time and again you have picked up the themes of Duisburg and the Ruhr region in your work. After your studies at the Werkkunstschule, the art college in Krefeld, you lived in Düsseldorf from 1971 until 1978. What role did this city play in your career? How strong was your exchange with the Düsseldorf art scene and the art academy?

Lindbergh: Initially, I trained with the commercial photographer Hans Lux in Düsseldorf, and then in 1973 I opened my own studio. For five years I did nothing but advertising photography in Düsseldorf — electronics, tobacco, anything I got a commission for. During this period, I established a good foothold. There was actually no contact between myself and the art academy and with Bernd and Hilla Becher, who only took over the photography class in 1976. The art academy itself was out of my league. Even after my training in Krefeld, and after my first exhibition there, at the Galerie Denise René-Hans Mayer in 1969, I still did not feel like an artist. Other than the Becher students, who were very much shaped by their teachers, I can't really tell you where it is I actually come from. I went through many stages, I saw a lot and experienced a great deal, and at some point it all came together.

Krämer: What I find interesting is that Bernd and Hilla Becher as well as their students have a very conceptual approach to photography. You, too, frequently work within concepts and very specific narratives.

Lindbergh: Time and again, during shoots, I notice that it helps if you reduce everything to one idea or one aspect that will serve as a starting point. But I do not have a compelling concept that I pursue, no clear position in all these networks that would have helped me to establish who I am. Part of my work remains a secret to me. And through this exhibition project in particular, I see my photographs in a completely new light. I am constantly surprised

myself. When I saw my photos on the wall in the exhibition model for the first time, it gave me a fright, but also in a good way. It was overwhelming to be thus confronted with who I am.

Krämer: What role does black-and-white photography play for you? I believe it is crucial for the intensity of your pictures?

Lindbergh: As paradoxical as it may sound, to me, black and white is often more authentic than color. Portraits in particular appear stronger by the reduction. Ob-

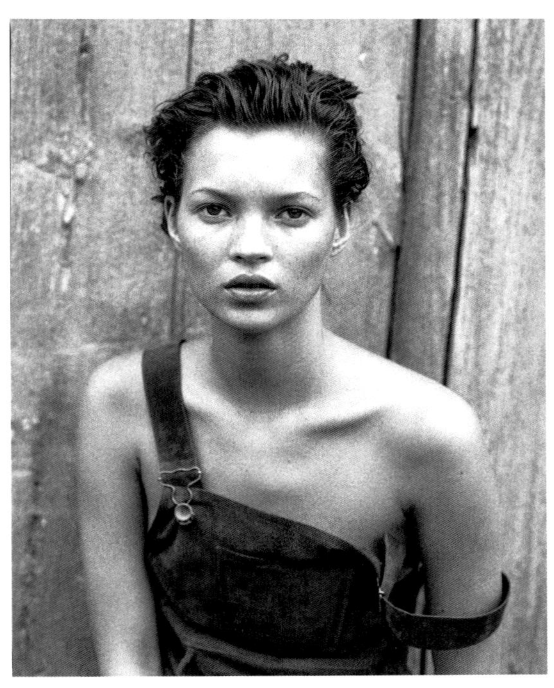

Kate Moss
New York, 1994

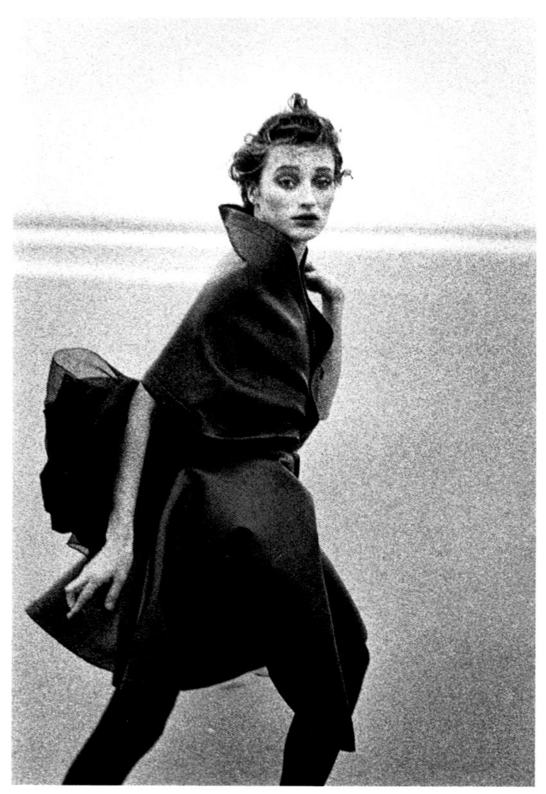

are some pieces that I actually find stronger and wilder in color.

Krämer: What would you say was decisive for you to establish yourself as a photographer, what helped you find your own style, your own visual vocabulary?

Lindbergh: My theory is that first you have to exist. Sometimes, other photographers tell me that their photos look like anybody could have taken them. I then ask whether they even know who they are themselves. Most of them lack an understanding of what I mean, but how can they expect to take their own photos if they cannot even answer this question? I, too, was not born as Peter Lindbergh and, especially at the beginning, it was a difficult road. There were moments when it really felt like I was only advancing at a snail's pace. Suddenly you then do something that's a success and people start to listen to you. It can take ten years, but that is how you slowly start to exist. If you want to be taken seriously as an artist you have to do what feels right for you and not answer to others.

viously, this inner conviction that black and white is somehow closer to reality is completely wrong. But maybe it shows just how much I have been influenced by the American photojournalism of the 1930s and 1940s, by photographers such as Dorothea Lange, Walker Evans, and many others. In recent years, I have also discovered color photography more and more for myself, and in the meantime there

Krämer: As I see it, various aspects are relevant to you, which initially appear to be contradictory: on the one hand, the moment of freedom is very important to you; on the other, there is also a form of control, especially when we look at how precisely your shoots are planned in advance. In principle, two types of settings are predominant: some large sets are staged almost like a Hollywood film; then again you also work in very intimate situations where it is just you, your compact camera, and the person who is being portrayed. In both scenarios, are you interested in the tension, the moment that can't actually be planned?

Lindbergh: The two approaches are really not that different. I often feel as though the photos are taking themselves. This may sound a bit vague, but there are situations in which you have to summon up the courage to submit to the events and resist any form of control. It is at such a moment that the magical powers appear, when you hand over the control to the magic. Sometimes you put in the most enormous effort — several trucks, cranes, storm machines, extravagant decorations — and it feels like nothing at all. Then you realize that a person simply standing in front of a wall says a whole lot more. In both types of settings it all comes down to one single moment — in that respect they are very similar. If you can't find that moment, hara-kiri is the only option. Then you have to start all over again.

Krämer: Can you describe how you come across the moment?

Lindbergh: A lot falls into place almost by itself. The photograph occurs in a second that you cannot anticipate; it just happens. Perhaps you don't even notice it. It is only afterwards that you look through the photos and find the one shot that is right. Sometimes you have to stop looking into the camera for two minutes so as to let go of what you actually had in mind. Sometimes you are forced to take photos without knowing what will happen — a lovely challenge. It is important to be prepared for the fact that, from one second to the next, an enormous poetry can unexpectedly lend enormous legitimacy to a situation that has got out of control.

Krämer: Being able to recognize the right moment for the picture, and then actually taking it, is not self-evident. In each generation, there is only a handful of photographers who, with their creativity and inner vision, can produce a picture that has not existed before, that will change and enrich the world just a little bit. Is creativity a rare stroke of luck?

Lindbergh: As I see it, we all have this form of creativity at our disposal, but most people just can't get access to it because it is hidden somewhere in their gut. After all, everyone can see, everyone can hear, everyone feels. But not everyone can translate this into a language. The freer you become — regardless of how it happens — the wider your perspective becomes, too. Perhaps you basically have to work on your freedom, on feeling free, because then you can get much further without being restrained. There is an apposite quote from the Japanese Zen master Shunryu Suzuki that means a lot to me: "To express yourself as you are without any intentional, fancy way of adjusting yourself is the most important thing." You need to find a sort of yearning, a longing — then you can get closer to your true self.

Krämer: Ultimately, in other words, it's all about looking. Taking pictures is one thing, but picking out the right one of the hundreds, maybe even thousands of pictures taken, recognizing what's right about it, is just as important. I can imagine that there are many photographers who take good photos and that it is the selection of these pictures that is the real challenge.

Lindbergh: This becomes evident in the fact that sometimes the best things happen by accident, totally unexpectedly. Some art directors are surprised that I look through my pictures myself so as to find the right image, and that no one does a preselection for me. But other people can only attempt to get into my head. It is difficult for them to allow surprises and slip-ups, which in the end may be exactly what I was looking for. In my opinion that is the only way to progress.

Krämer: You have repeatedly discovered a potential in technical accidents, such as, for example, in this portrait of Milla Jovovich in which a beam of light falls across her face (see ill. p. 57).

Lindbergh: The photo is a good illustration of why other people cannot do this for me, because they'd see nothing in it but a flaw. Another example was a shoot with Tina Turner on the Eiffel Tower that resulted in only one really good photo (see ill. p. 47). It was the last picture we took: the face and everything just right. However, at the top of the negative you can see the remnants of some glue. We could have easily retouched the blemish, but I decided to leave it in the photograph. Even external influences like snowstorms can result in surprises. There's a lot that happens that you just have to accept and you can't plan for. For me, these situations are often a gift.

Krämer: What also fascinates me about your pictures is the interest in the individual. You observe very closely and approach the person opposite you with great curiosity. It's almost as though you get inside the person you're photographing.

Lindbergh: The relationship with the person I am portraying is a very special one. I have the impression that people bring themselves to the shoots and don't put on a show. They are not trying to be someone other than who they really are. Nowa-

days it almost happens
by itself.

Krämer: The way you
describe it, you have
a very special connec-
tion with the people
in your photographs.
Lindbergh: Of course
it depends on whether
I am meeting someone
for the first time on
set or whether it is
someone I have worked
with time and again
throughout the years.
Although it can cer-
tainly happen that I
connect very quickly
with a person I've
only known for a couple
of hours. The book
Shadows on the Wall
is, above all, about
the magic that suddenly
happens and that makes
everything possible.
Several actresses say
in it how well they
know me, how good they feel
around me, and how they feel they
can have a different relationship with me for that very
reason. Charlotte Rampling paid
me a truly great compliment:
she wants me to show that she
wants to reveal herself through
my eyes to other people, rather
than her doing it. Or Penélope
Cruz saying there is nothing
fake in my pictures and that I
capture the truth, the essence
of a person. What a compliment!
Good pictures only happen when
people are not too conscious of
the shoot situation, and open
themselves up.

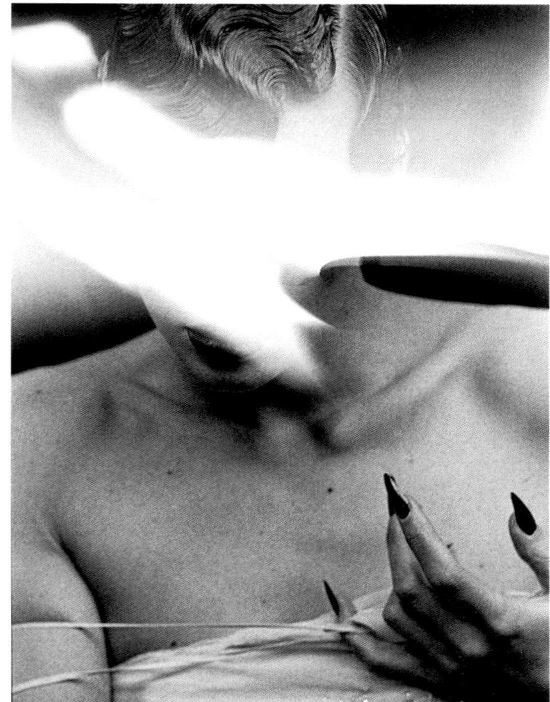

Milla Jovovich
Paris, 1998

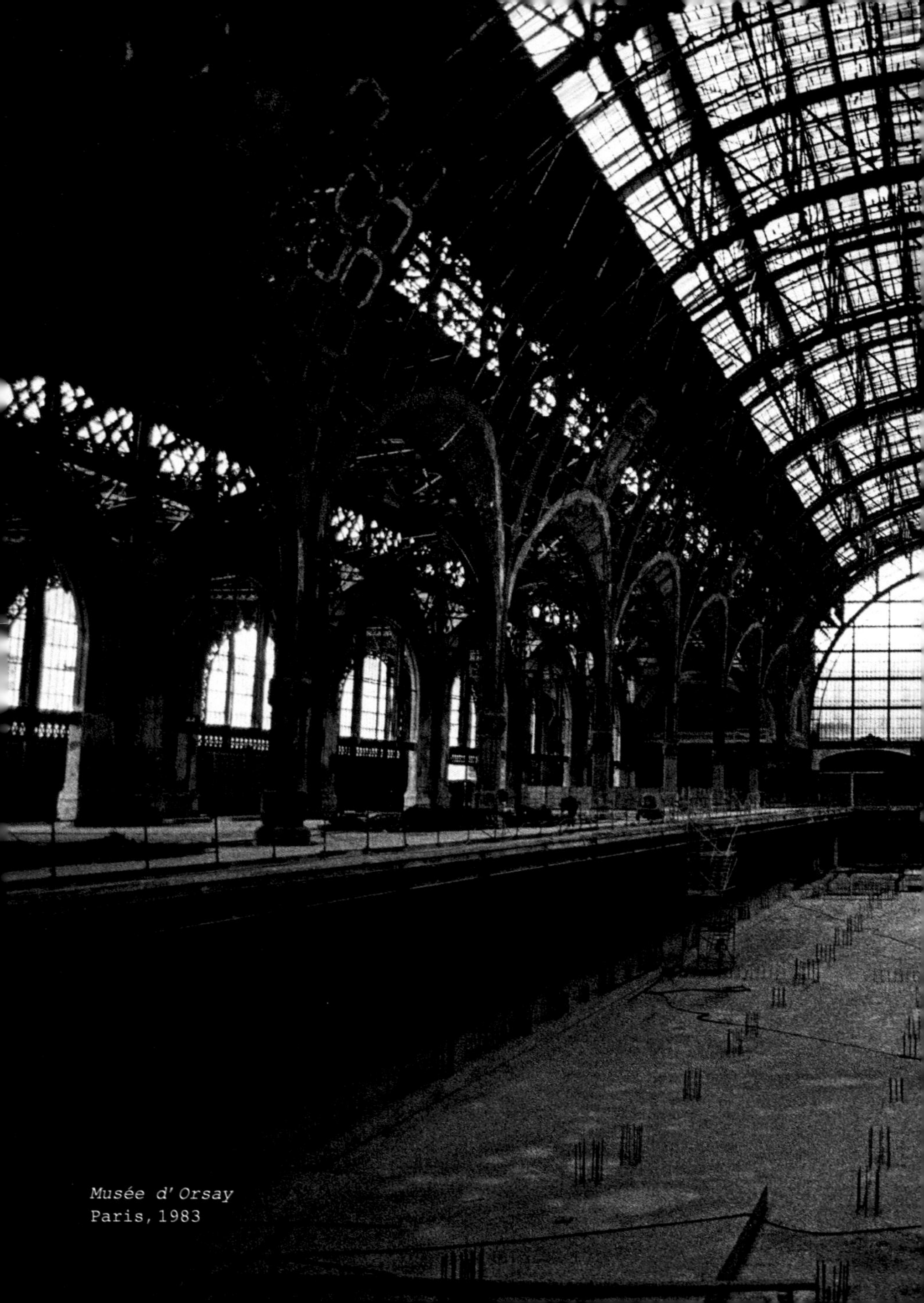

Musée d'Orsay
Paris, 1983

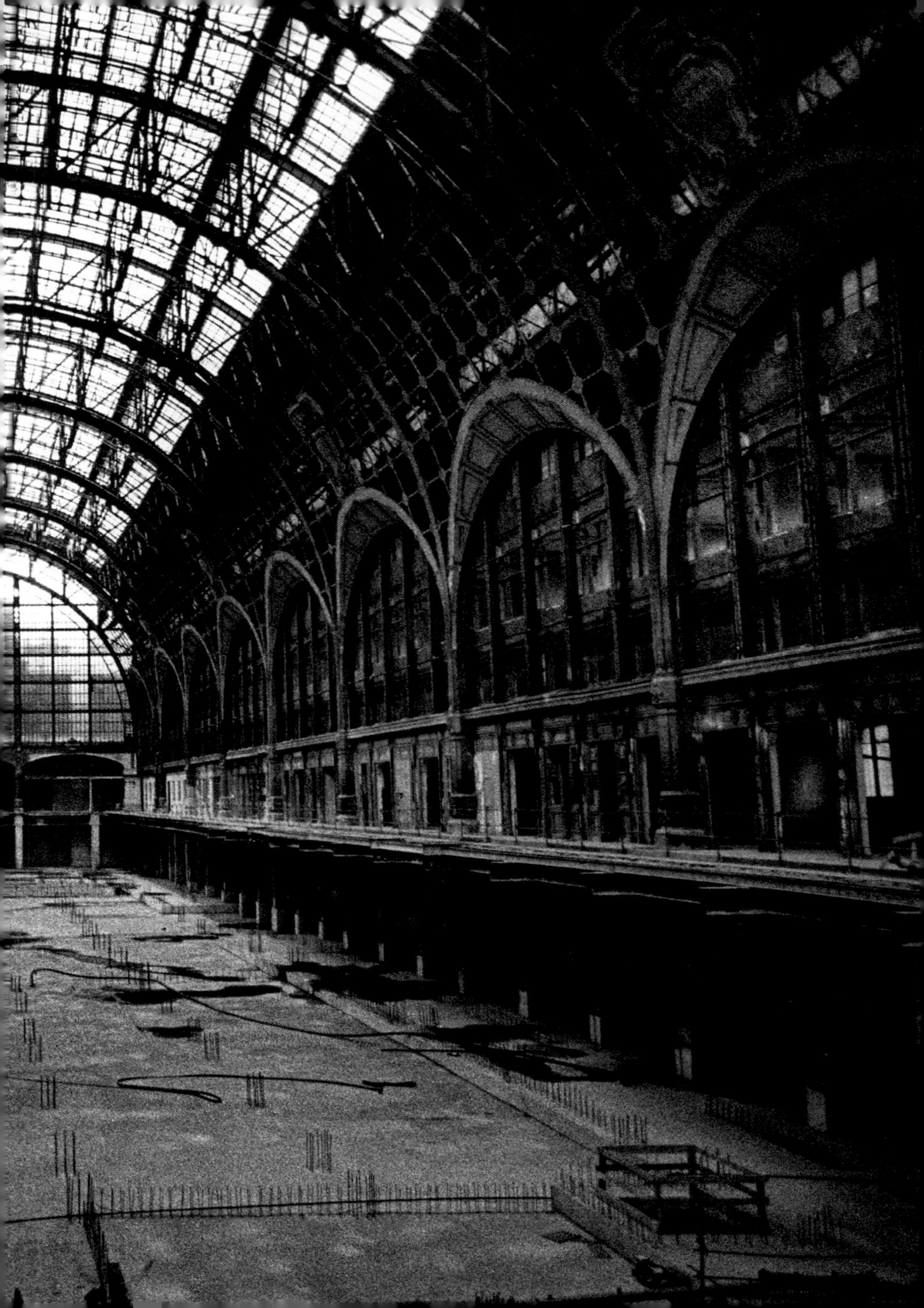

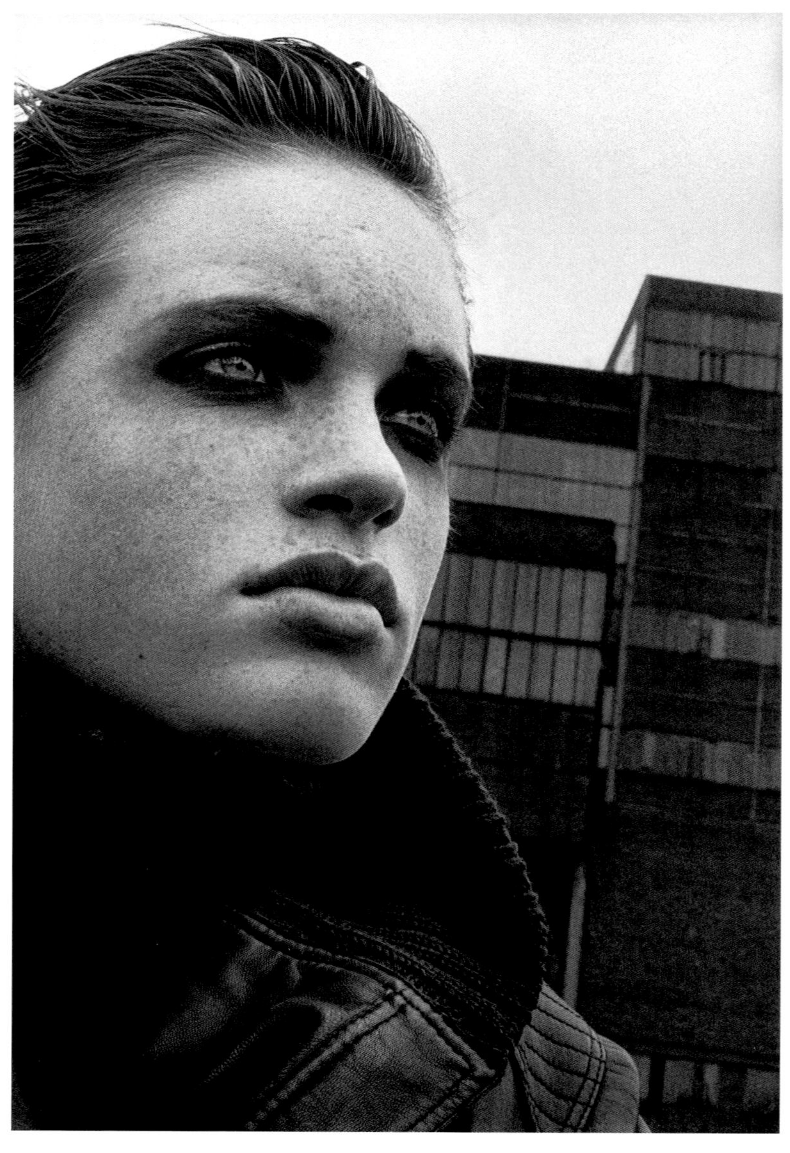

Kara Young
Duisburg, 1984

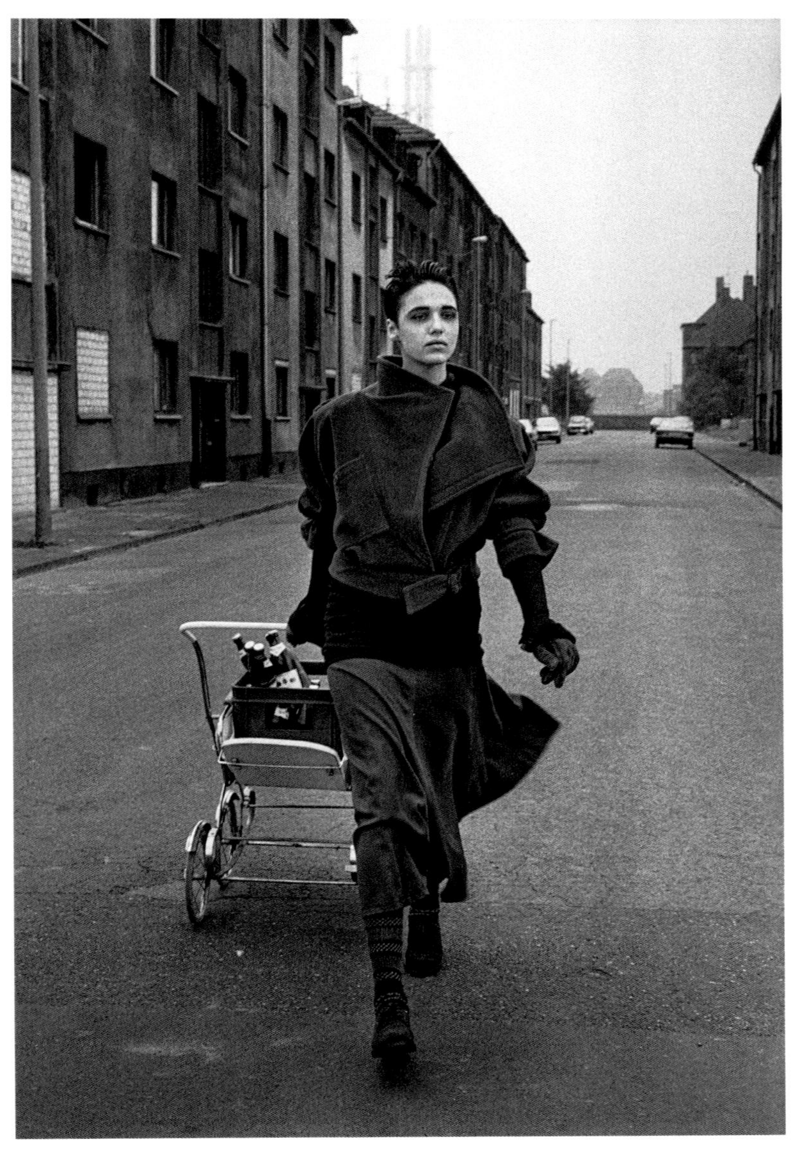

Amanda Cazalet
Duisburg, 1984

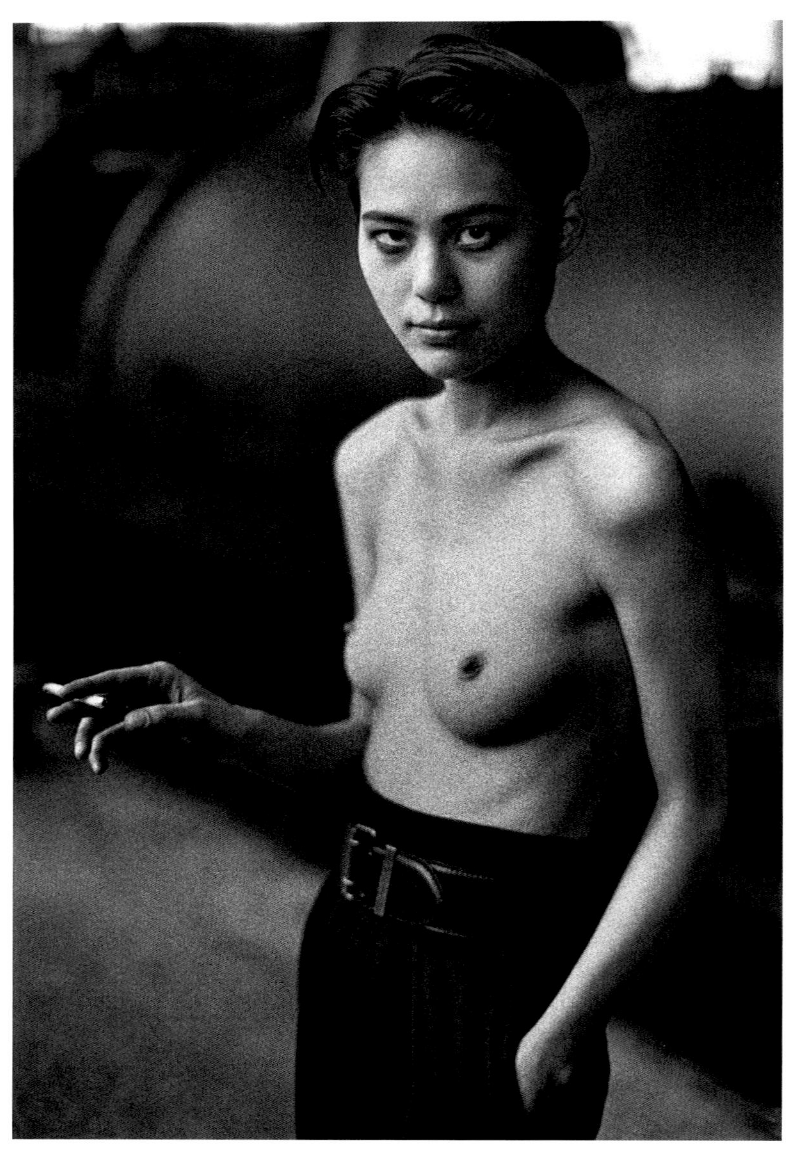

Ariane Koizumi
Duisburg, 1985

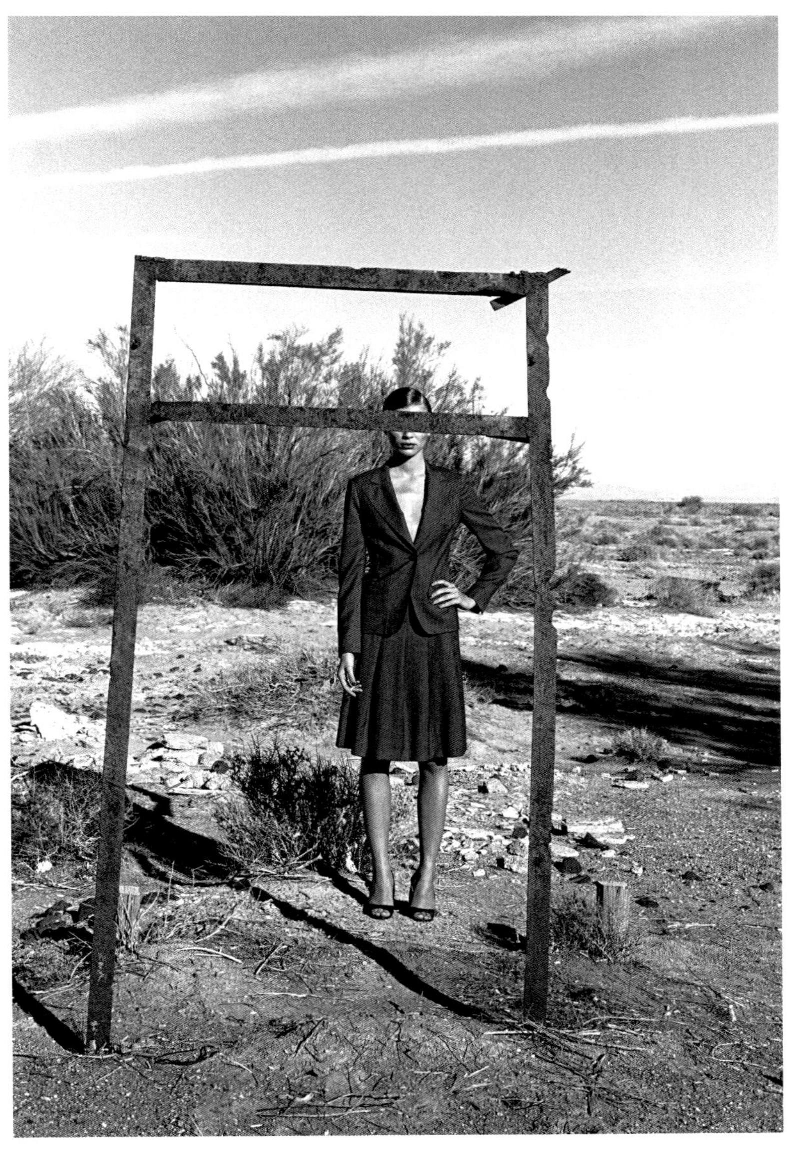

Esther Cañadas
Nevada, 1997

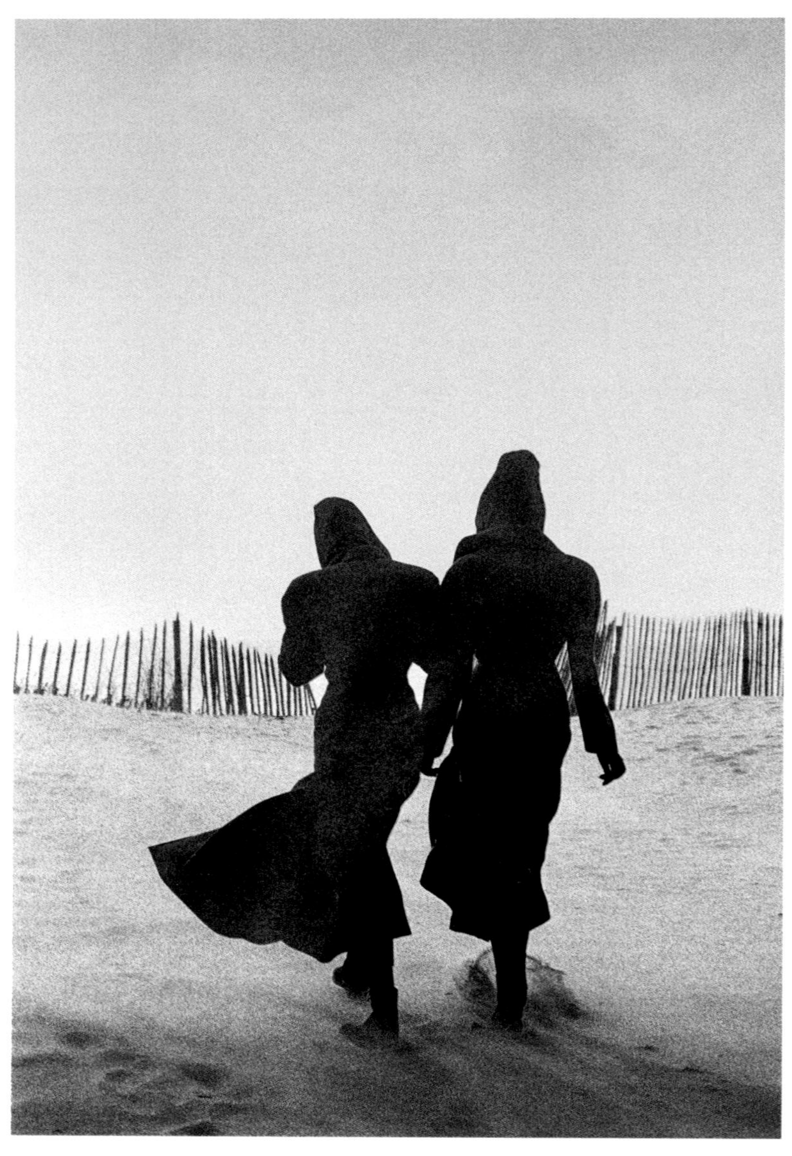

Tatjana Patitz & Linda Spierings
Le Touquet,1986

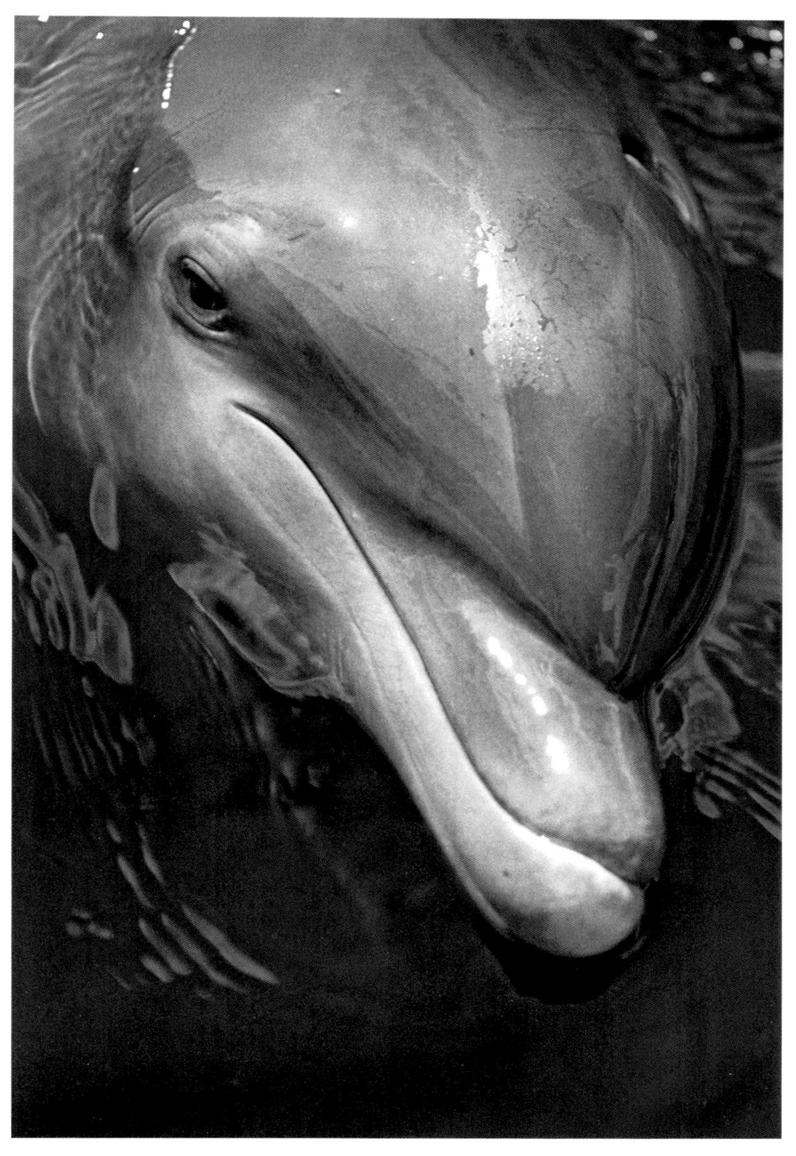

A New Friend
Florida, 1992

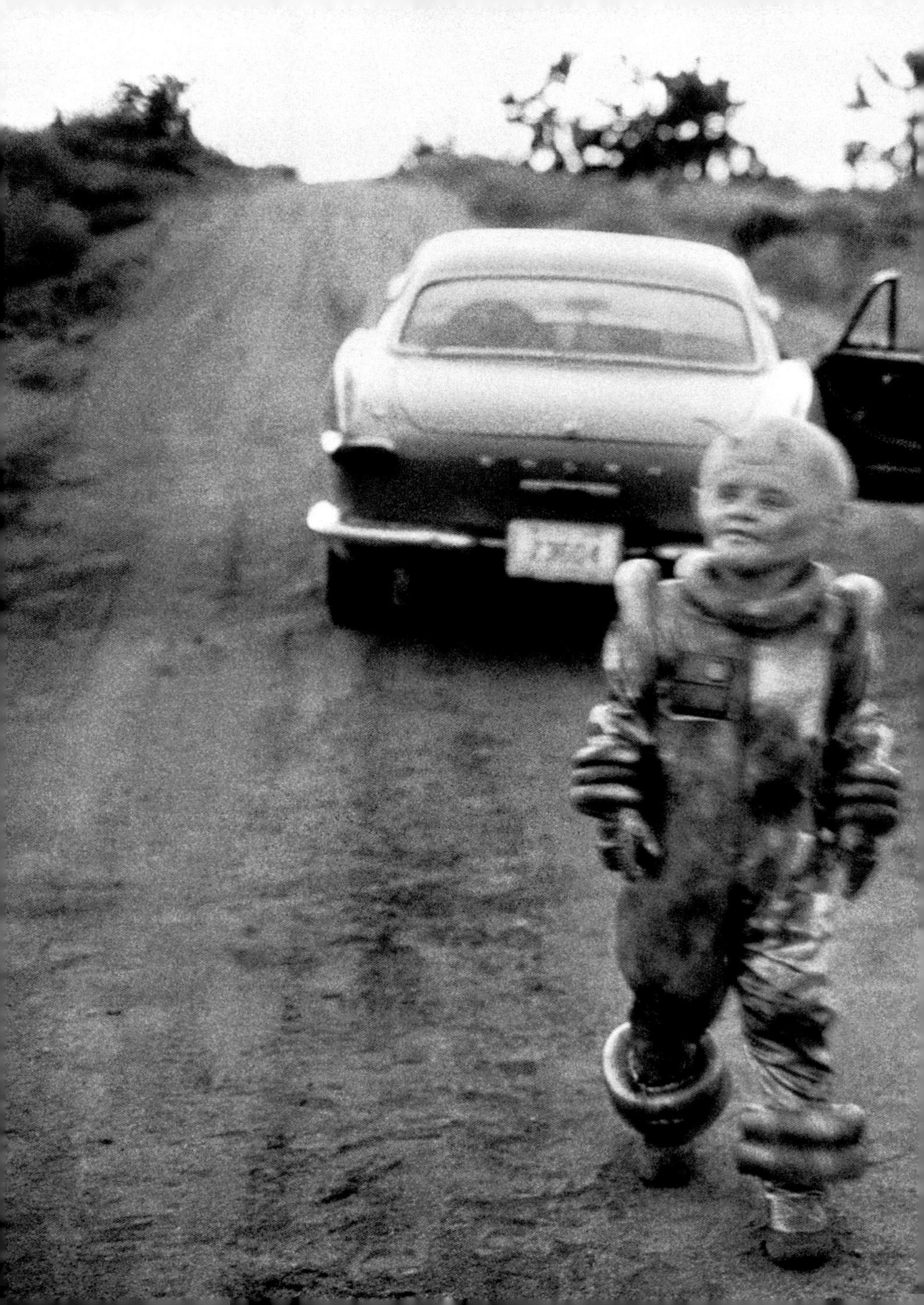

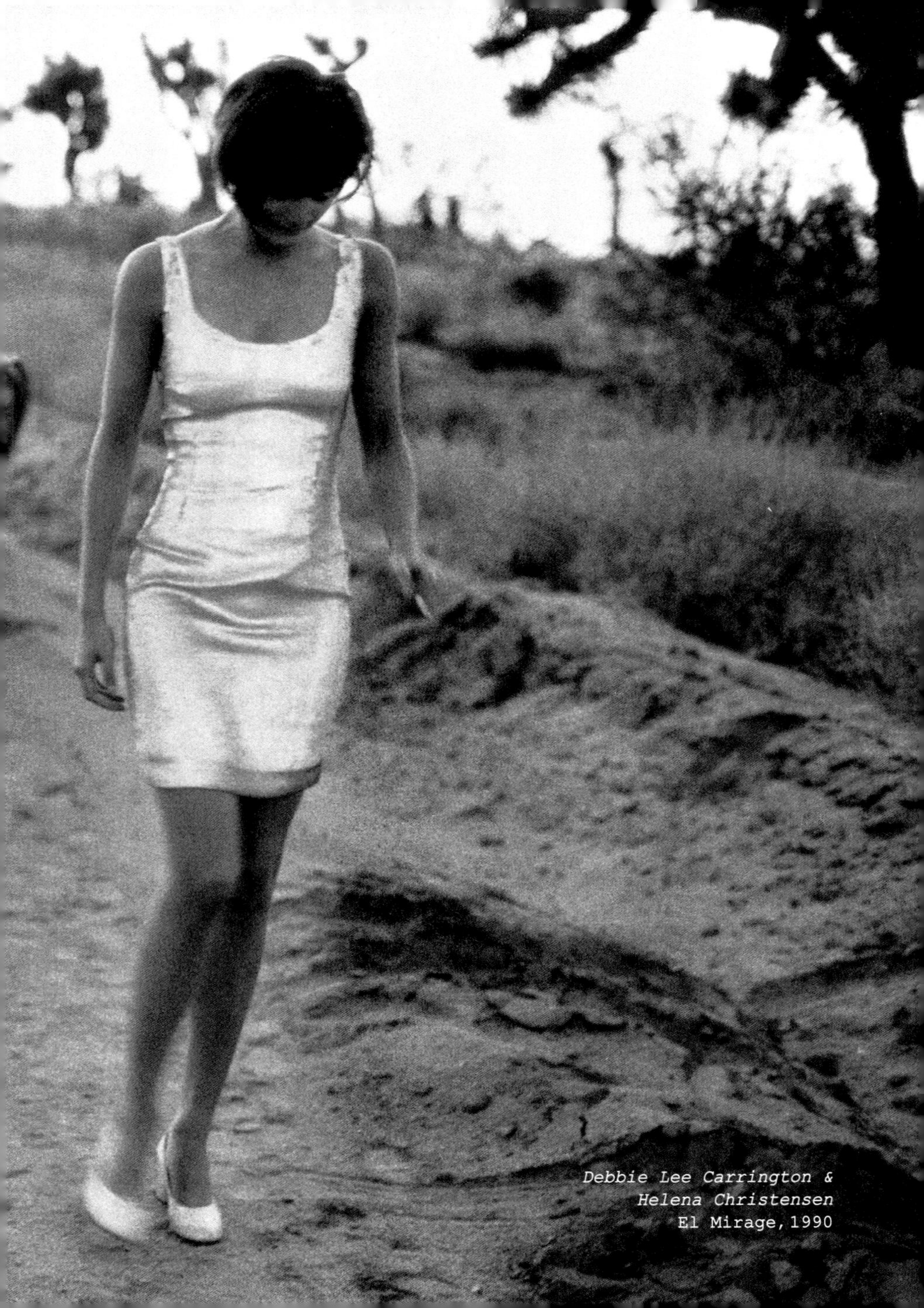
Debbie Lee Carrington &
Helena Christensen
El Mirage, 1990

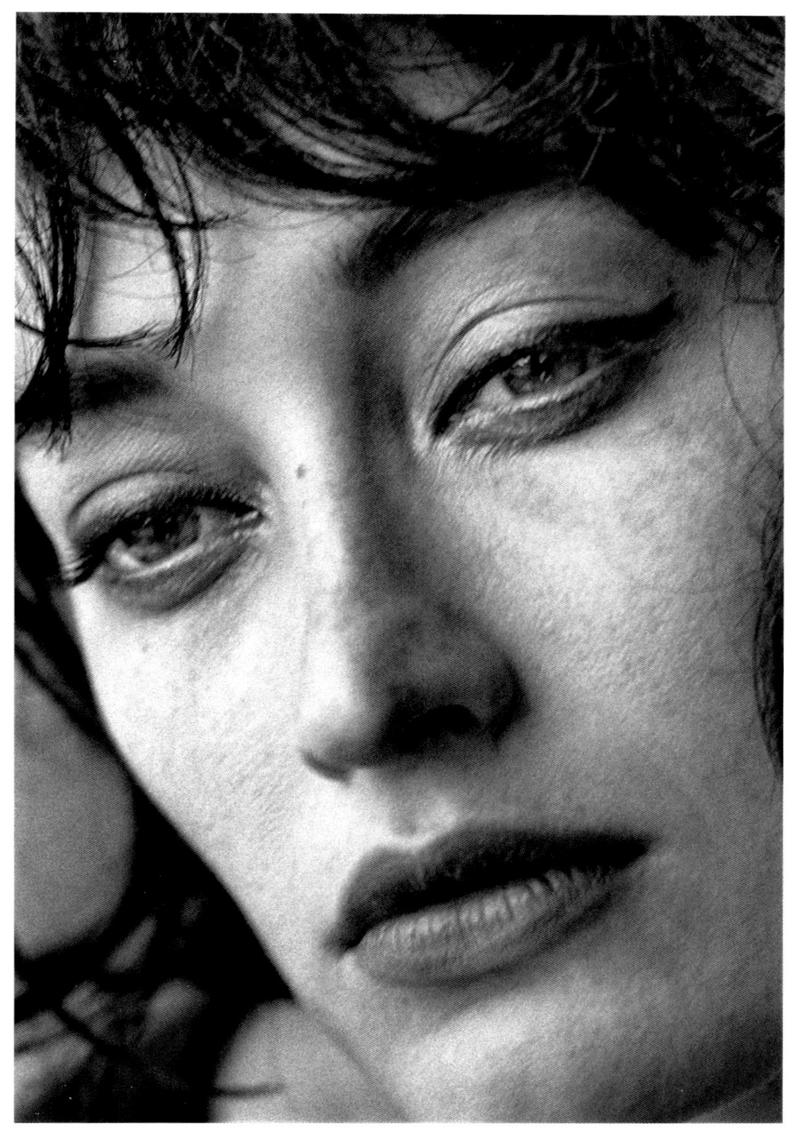

Marie-Sophie Wilson
Rome, 1991

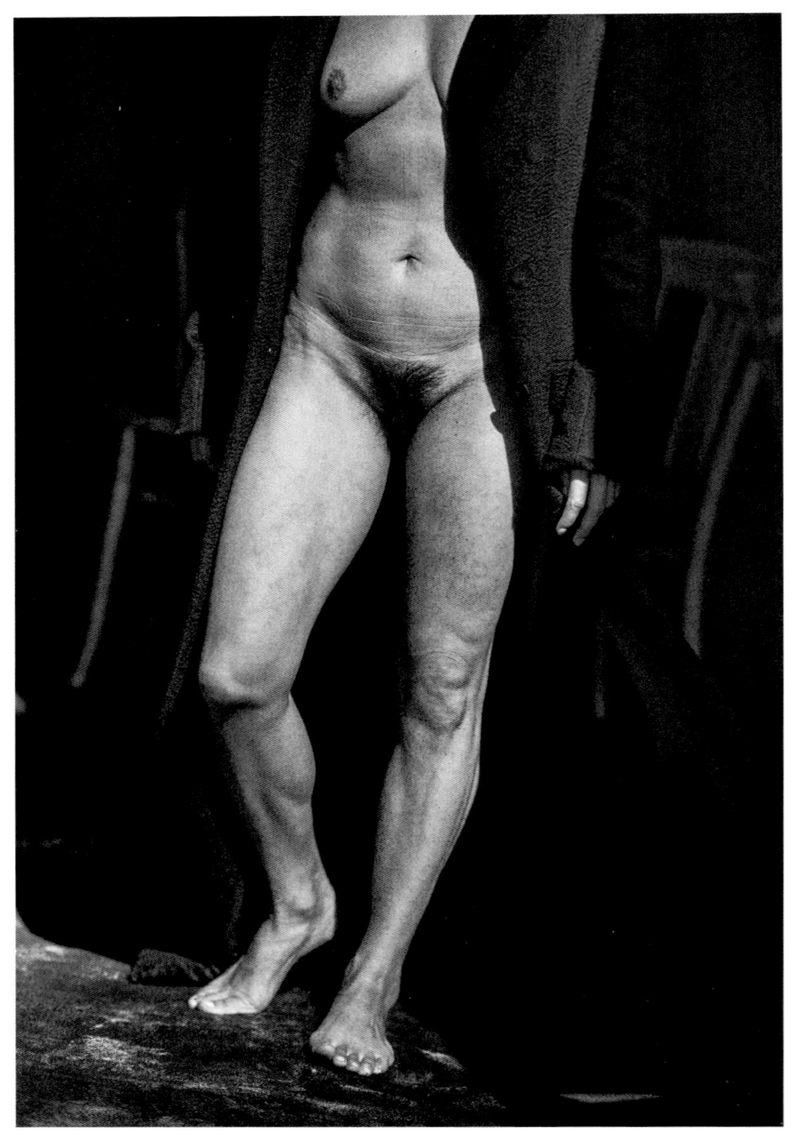

Eri Ishida
Salin-de-Giraud, 2017

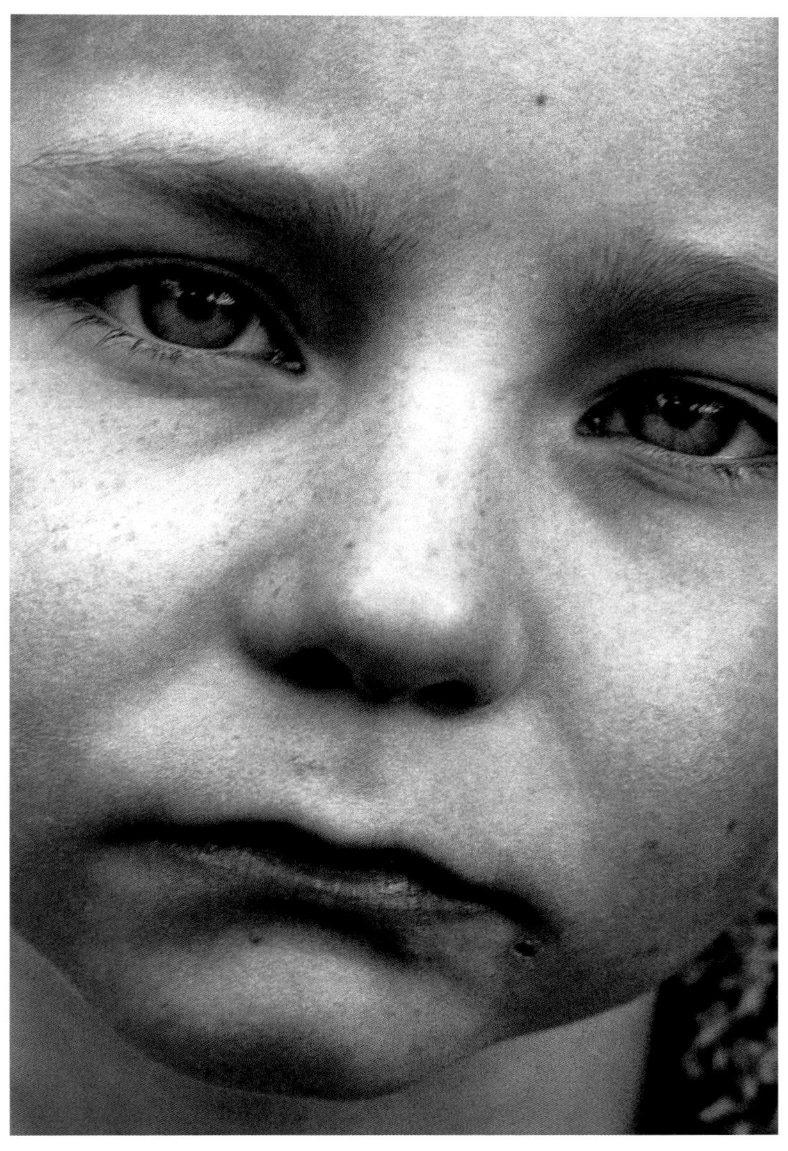

Beckley, West Virginia, 1998

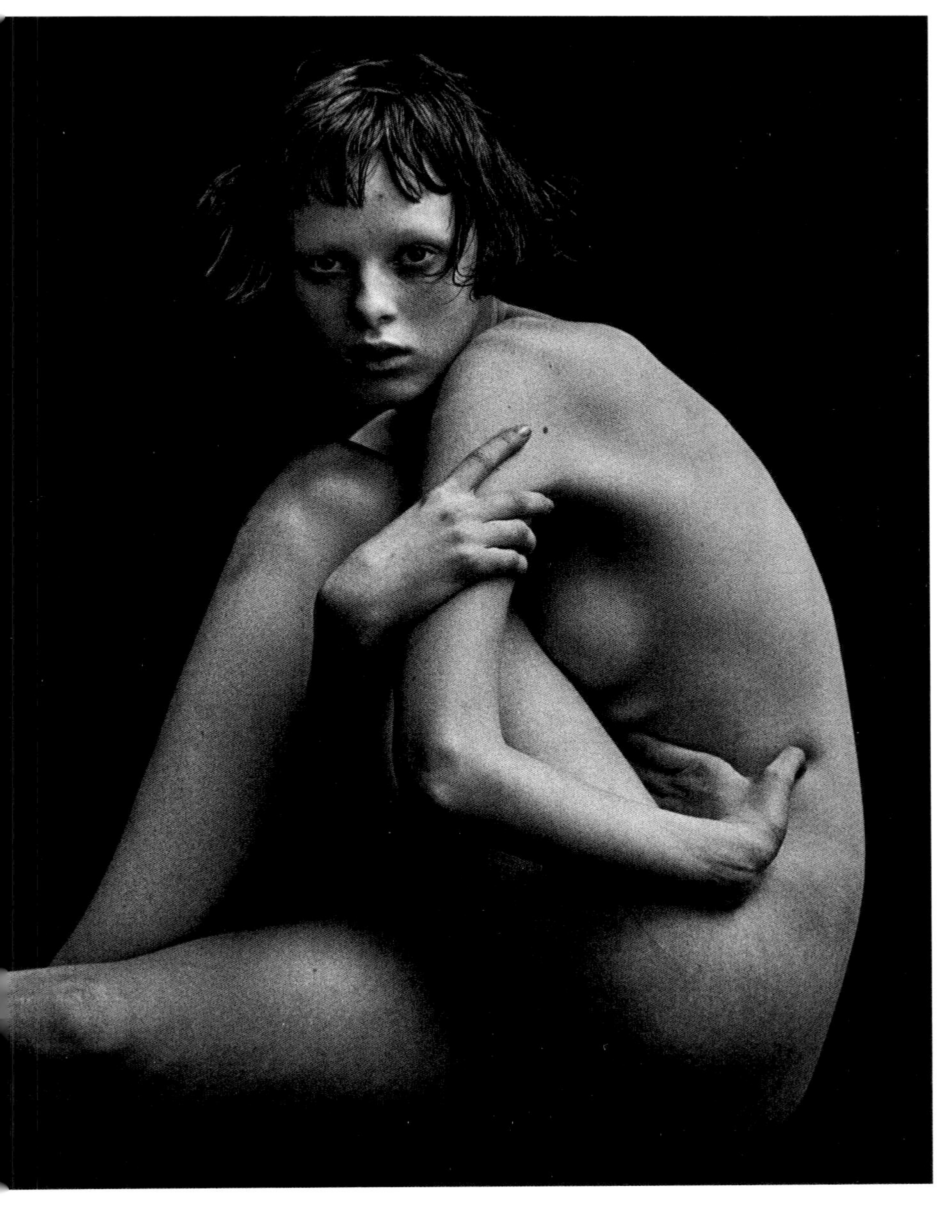

Karen Elson
Los Angeles, 1997

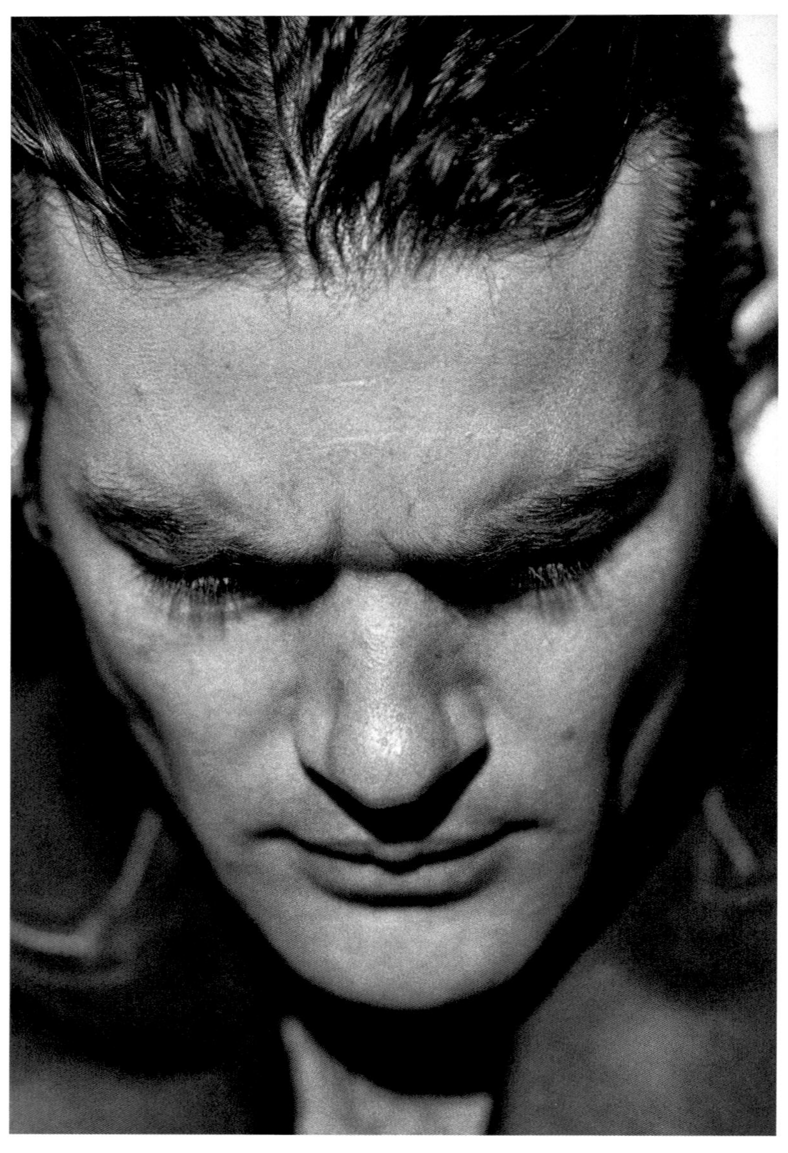

Antonio Banderas
Los Angeles,1995

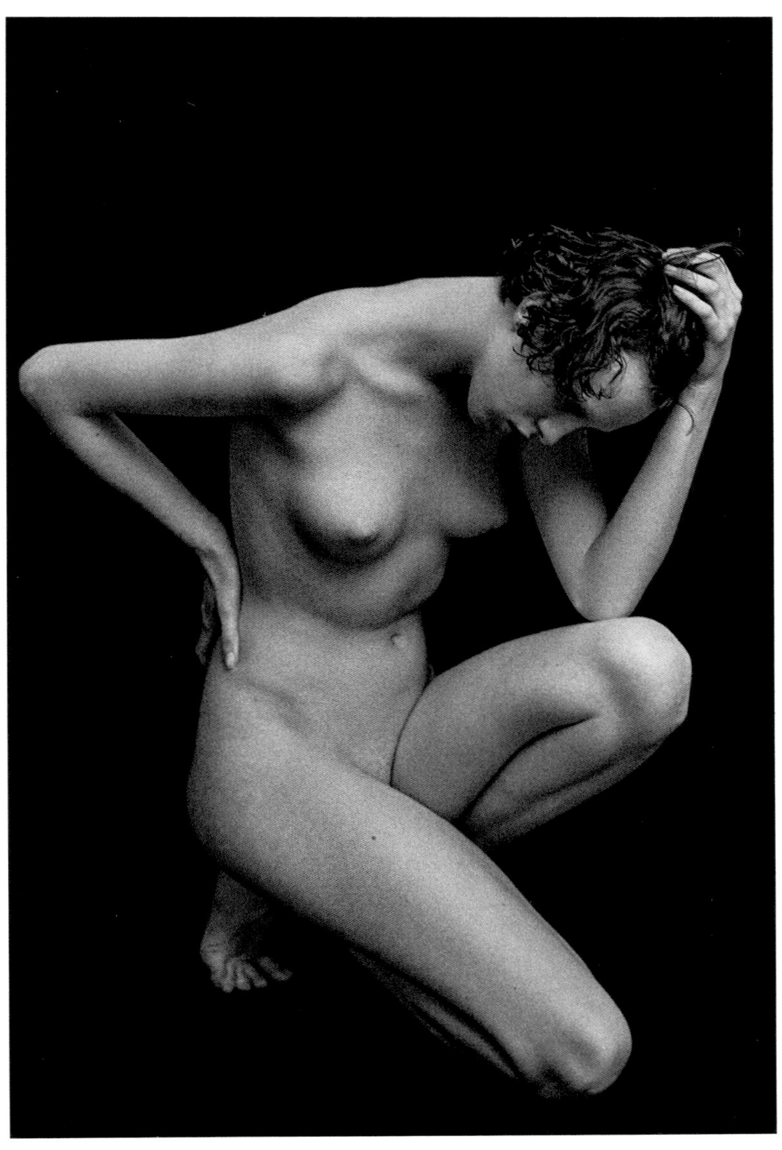

Karen Elson
Los Angeles, 1997

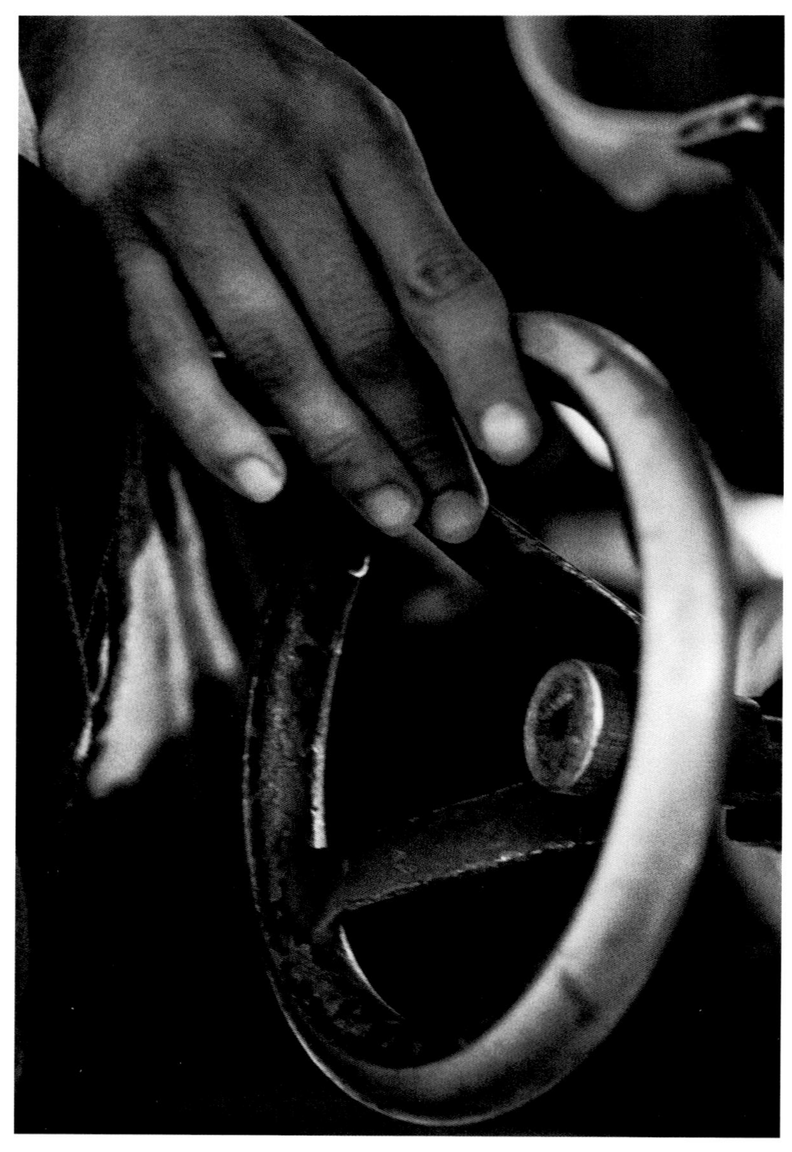

André van Noord
Parma,1990

76

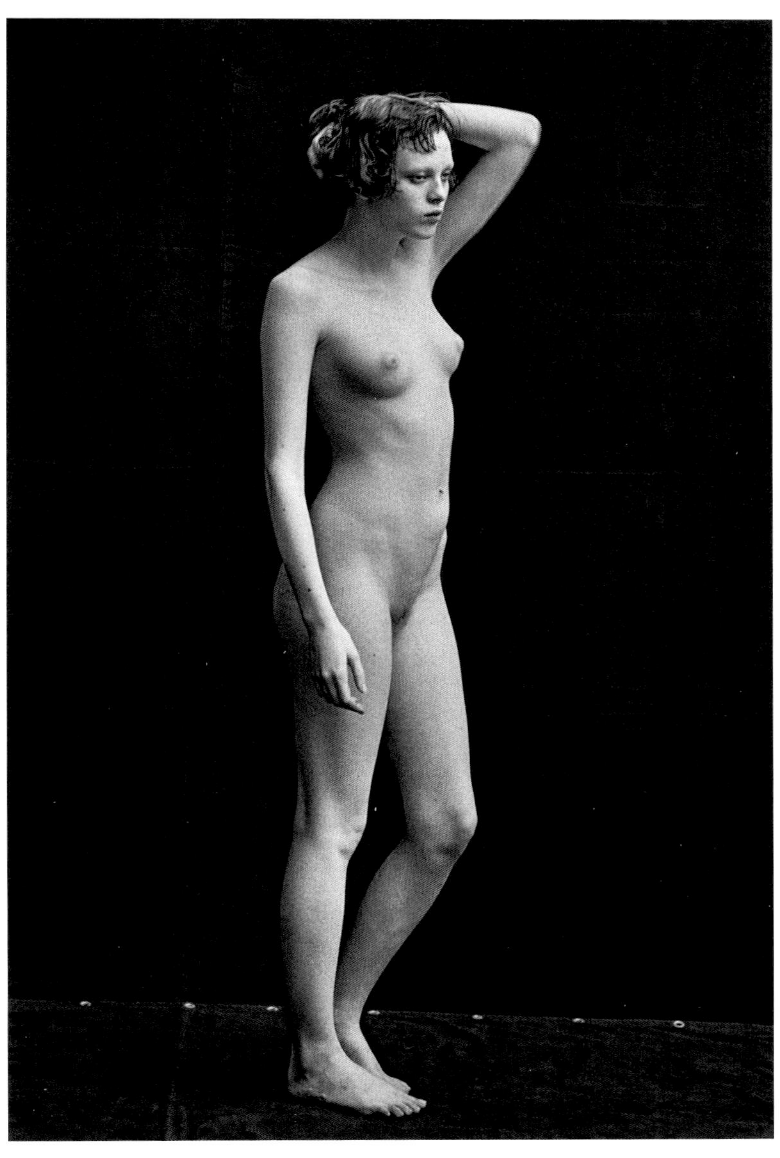

Karen Elson
Los Angeles, 1997

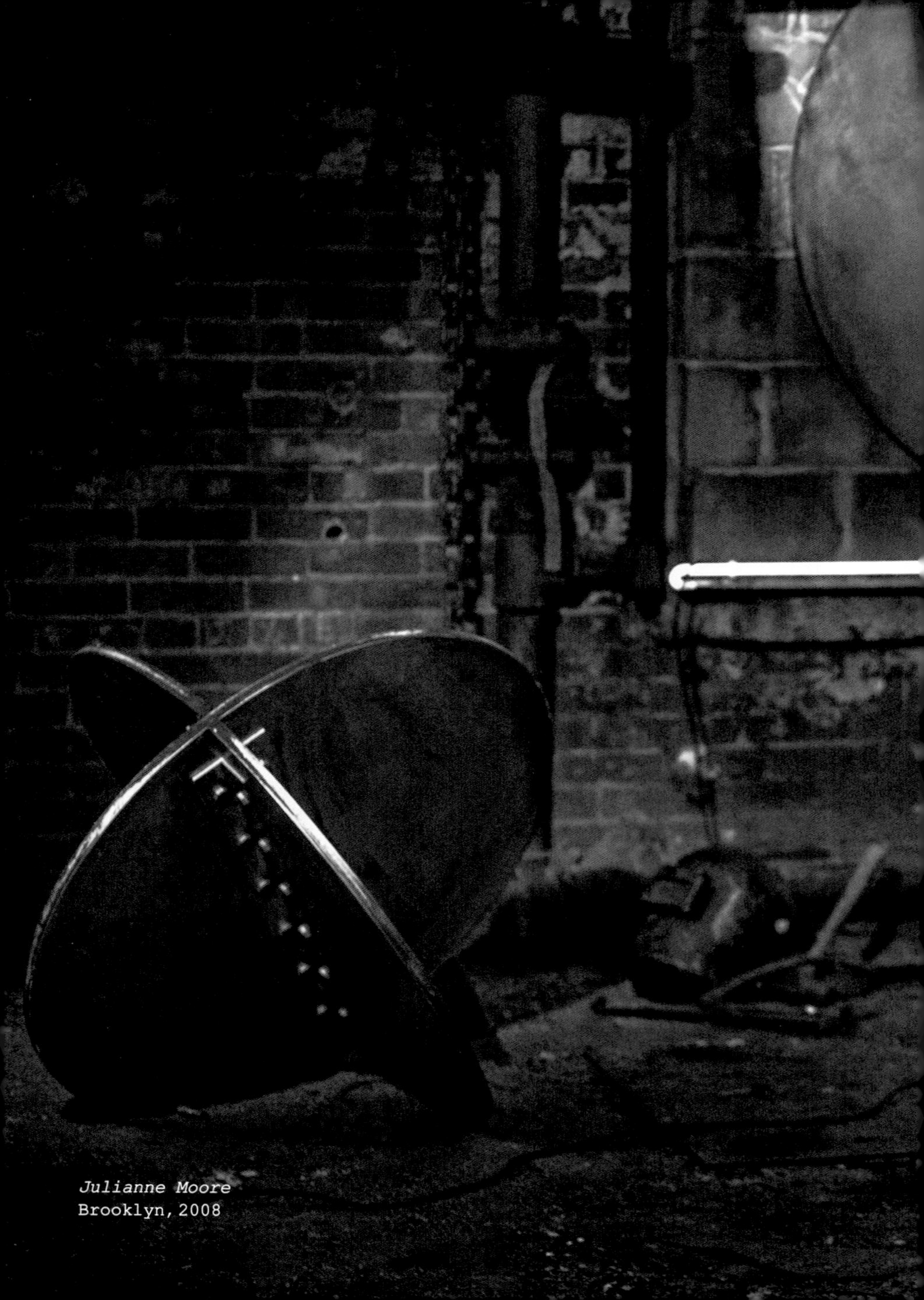

Julianne Moore
Brooklyn, 2008

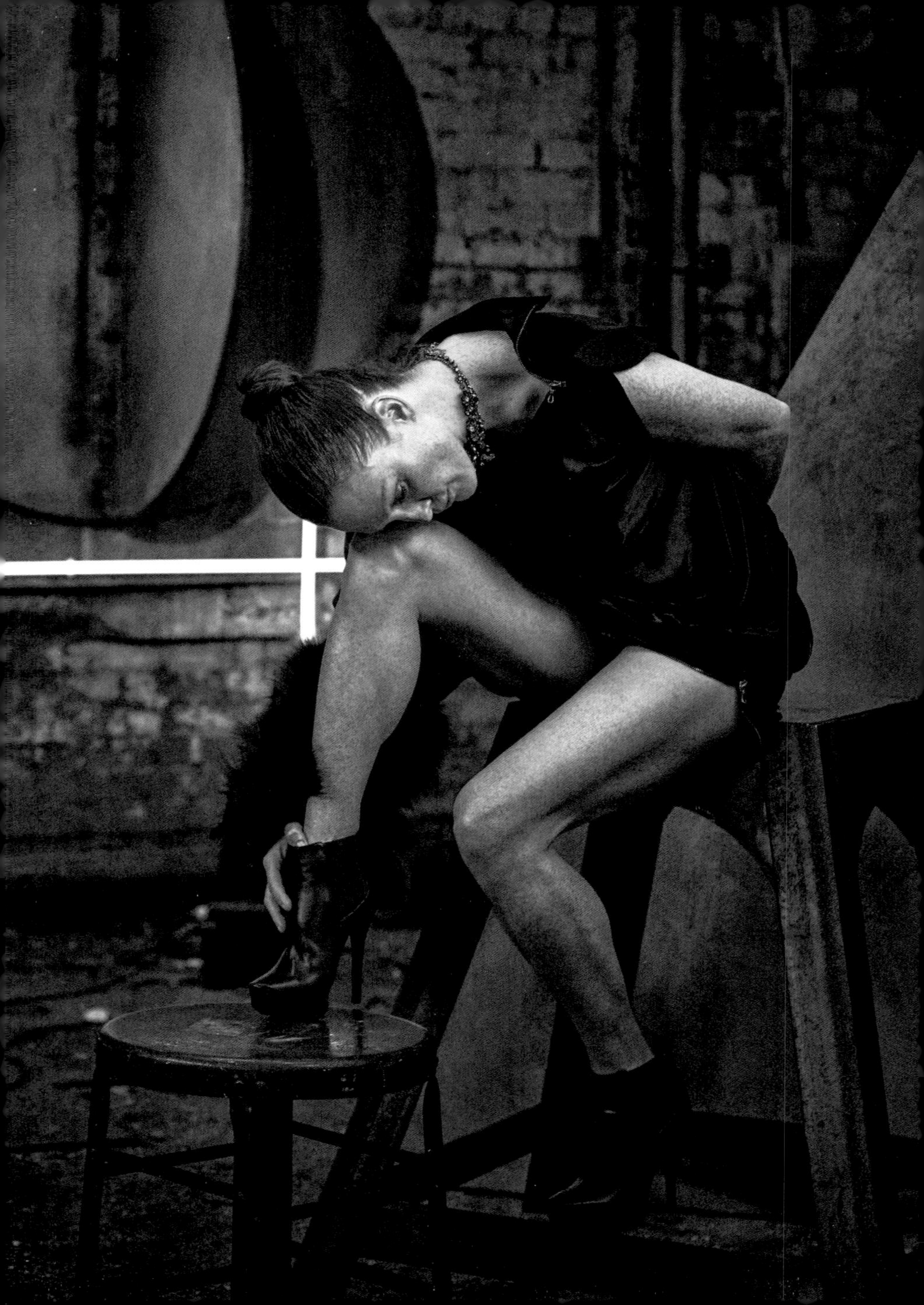

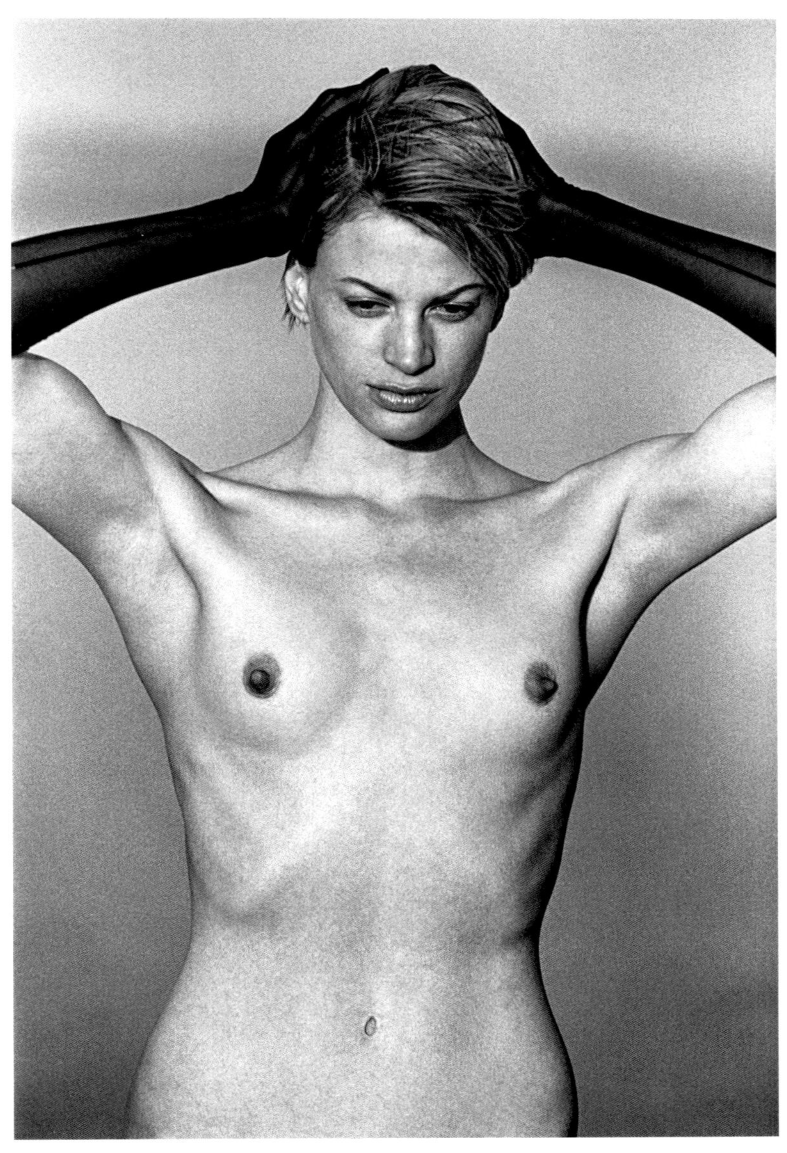

Kristen McMenamy
El Mirage, 1995

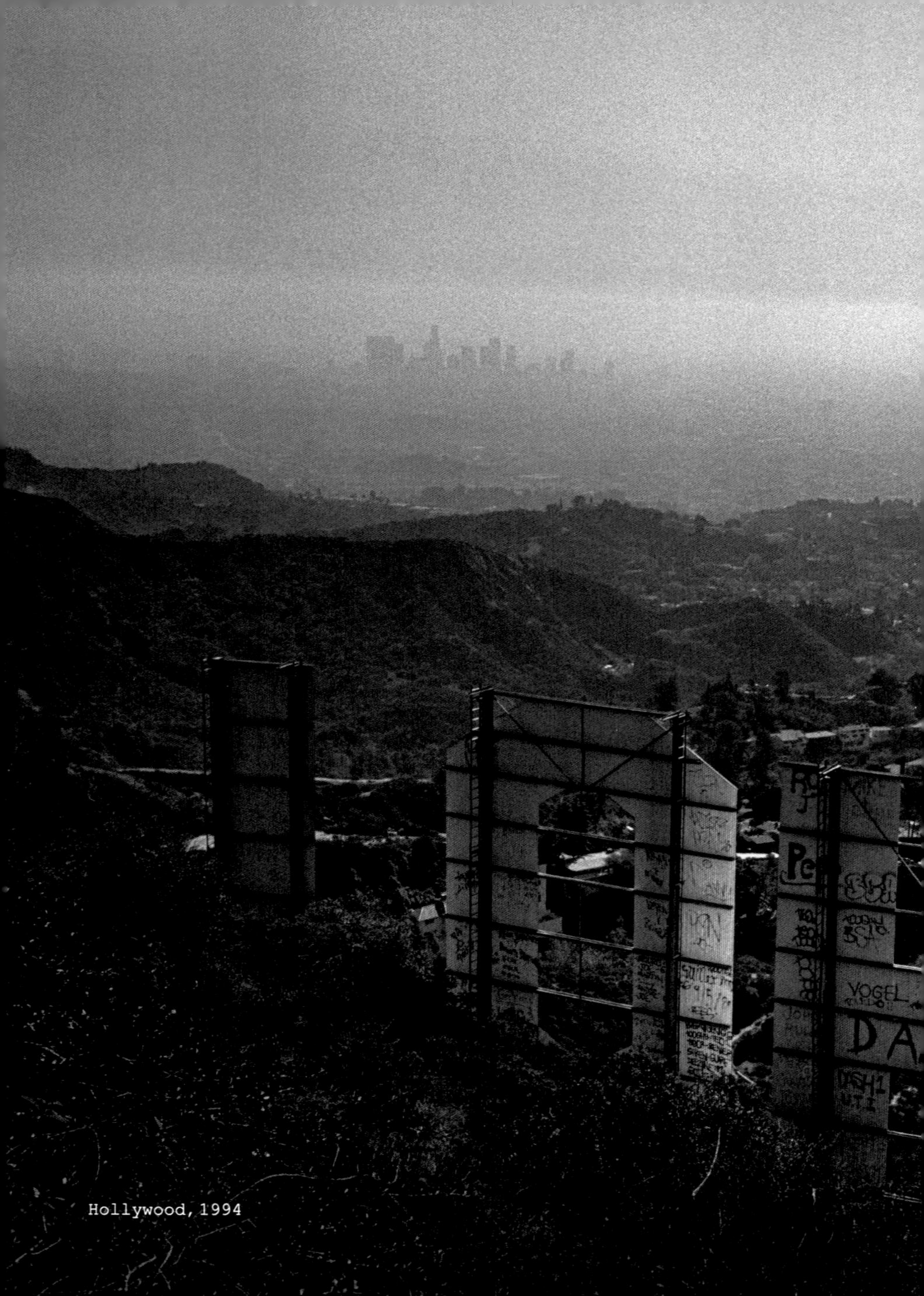
Hollywood, 1994

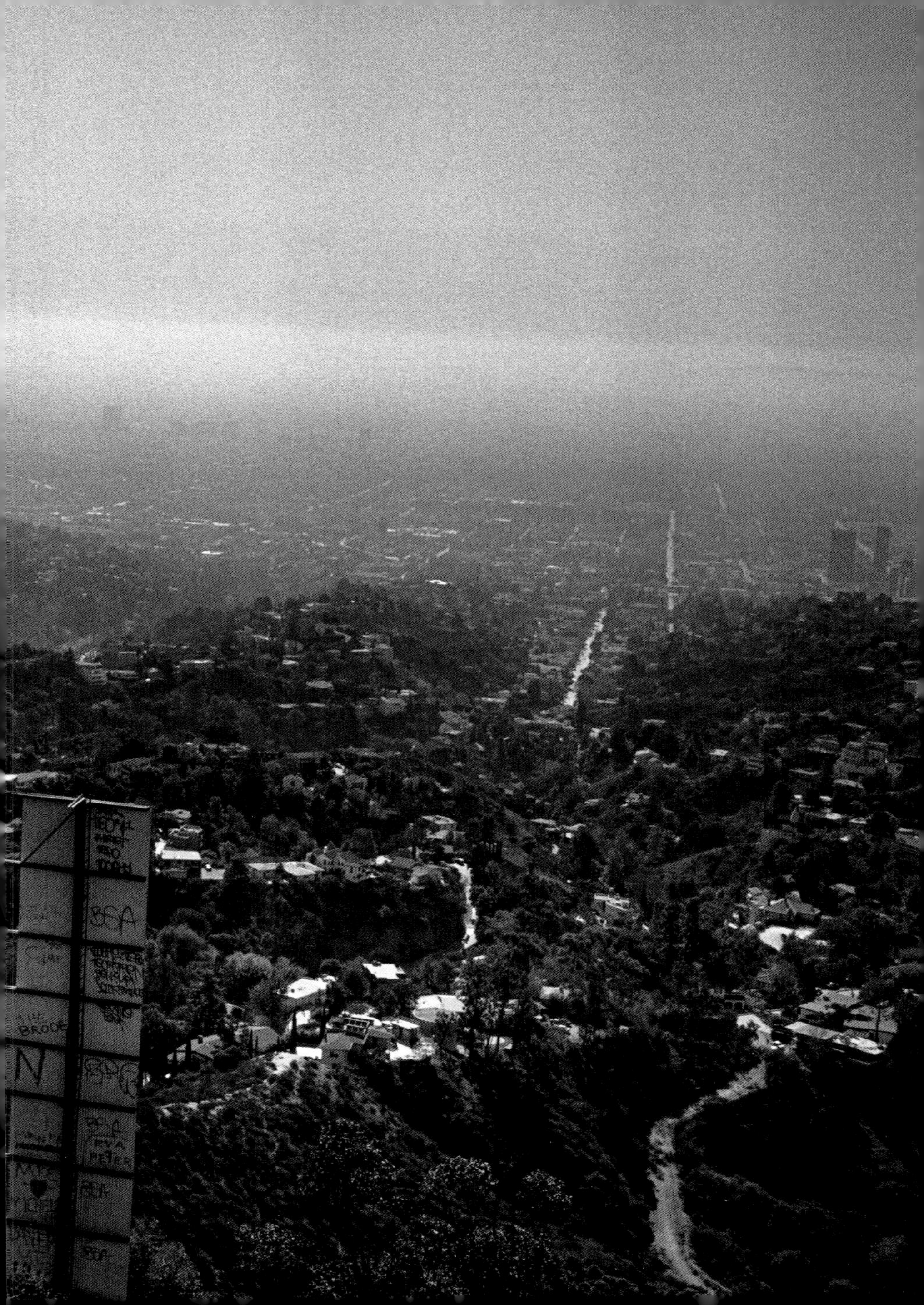

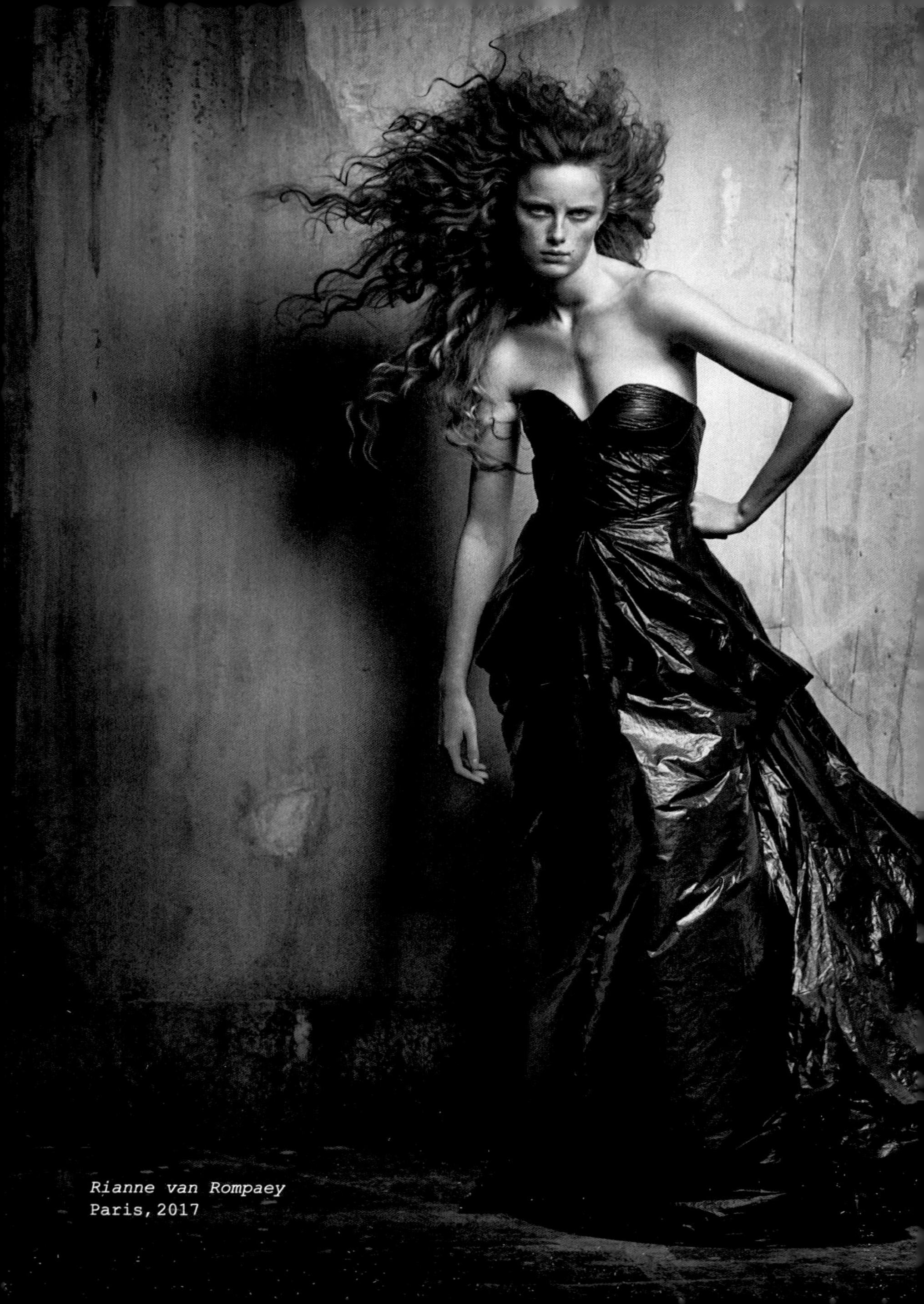

Rianne van Rompaey
Paris, 2017

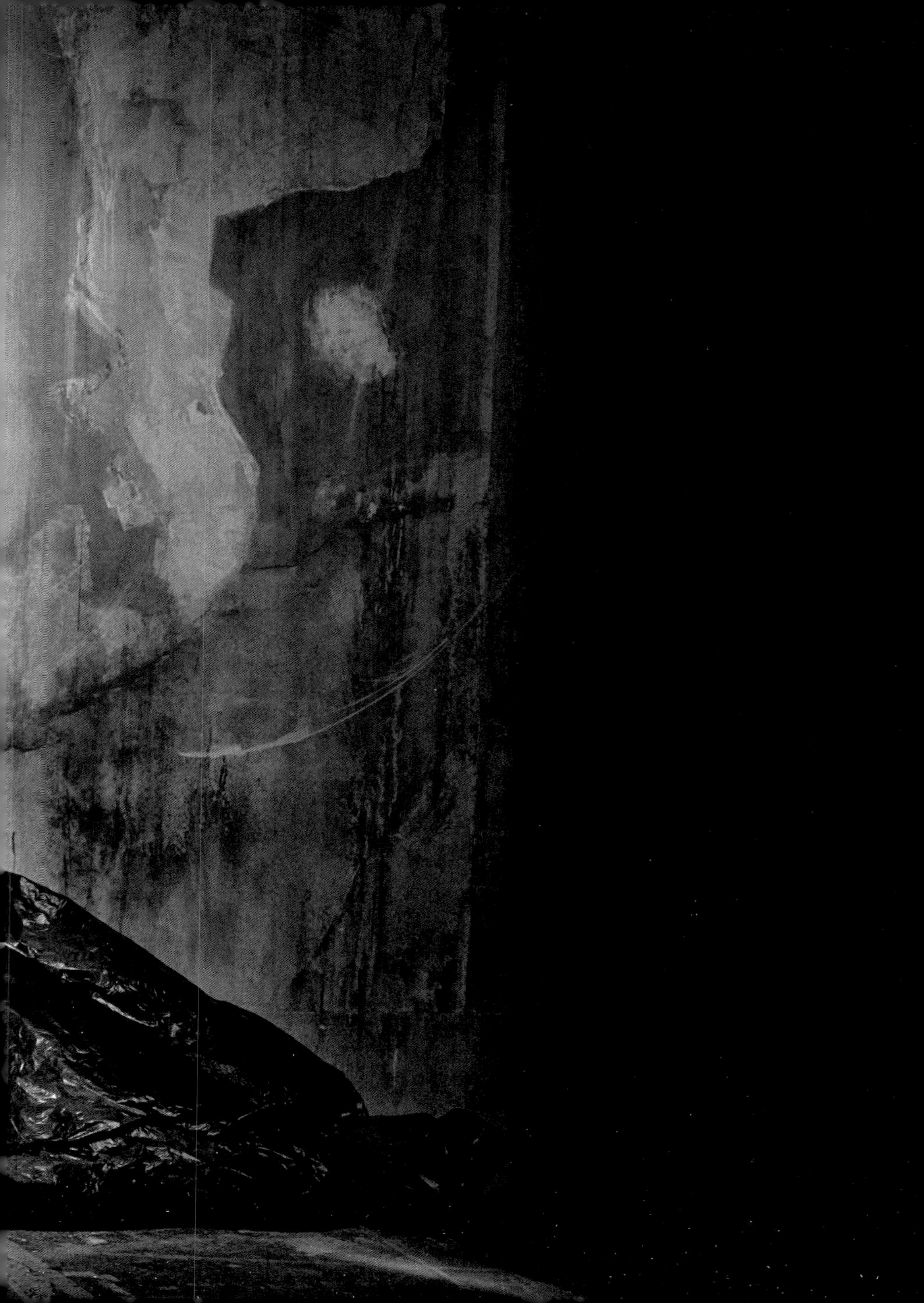

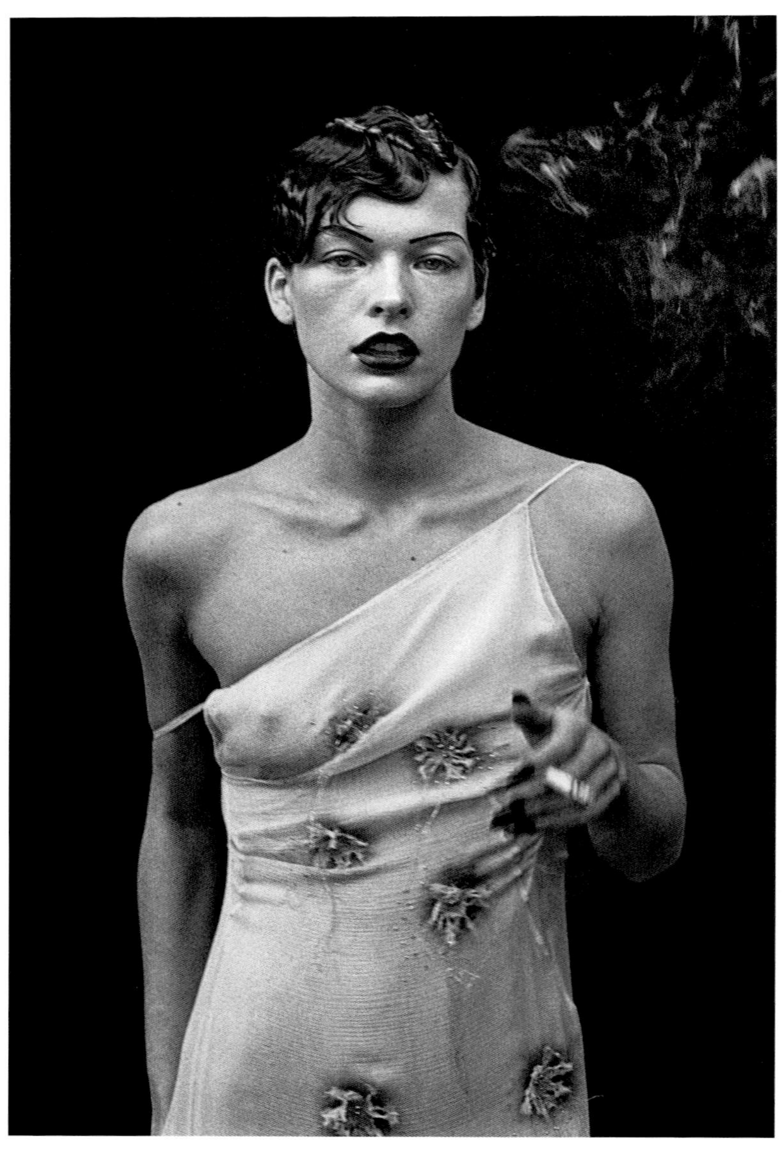

This spread:
Milla Jovovich, Paris,1998

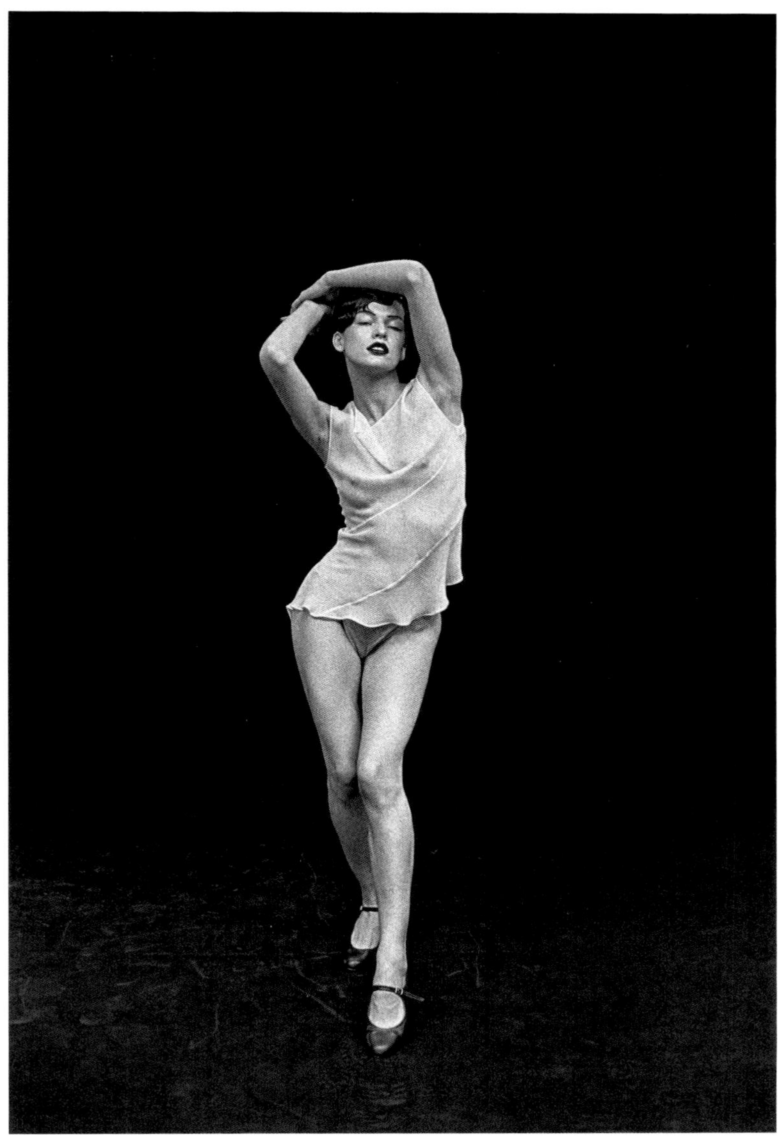

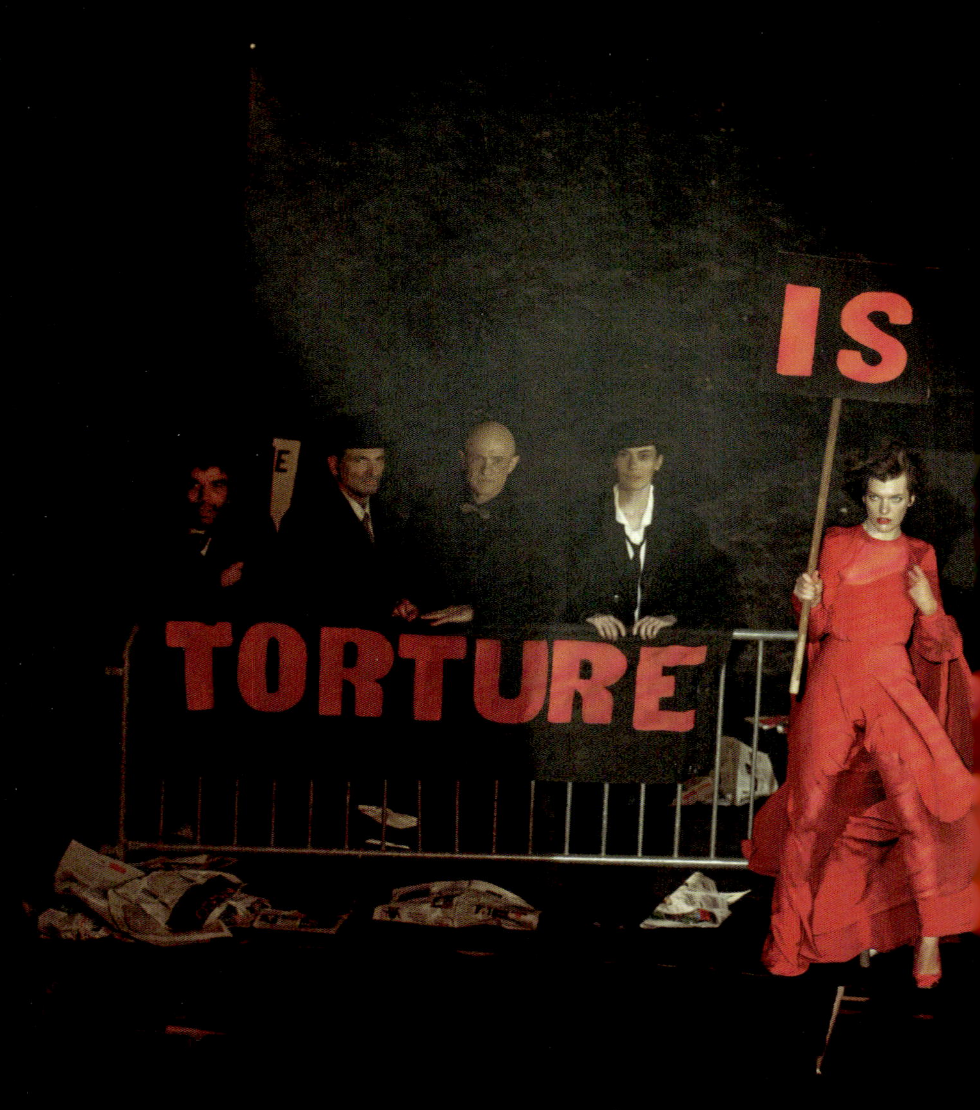

Milla Jovovich
Paris, 2012

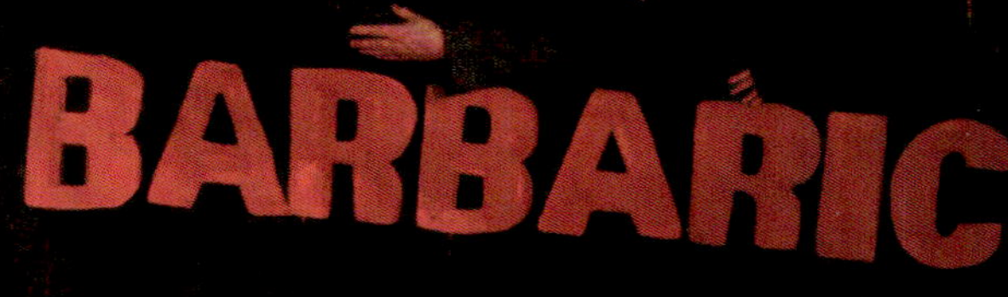
BARBARIC

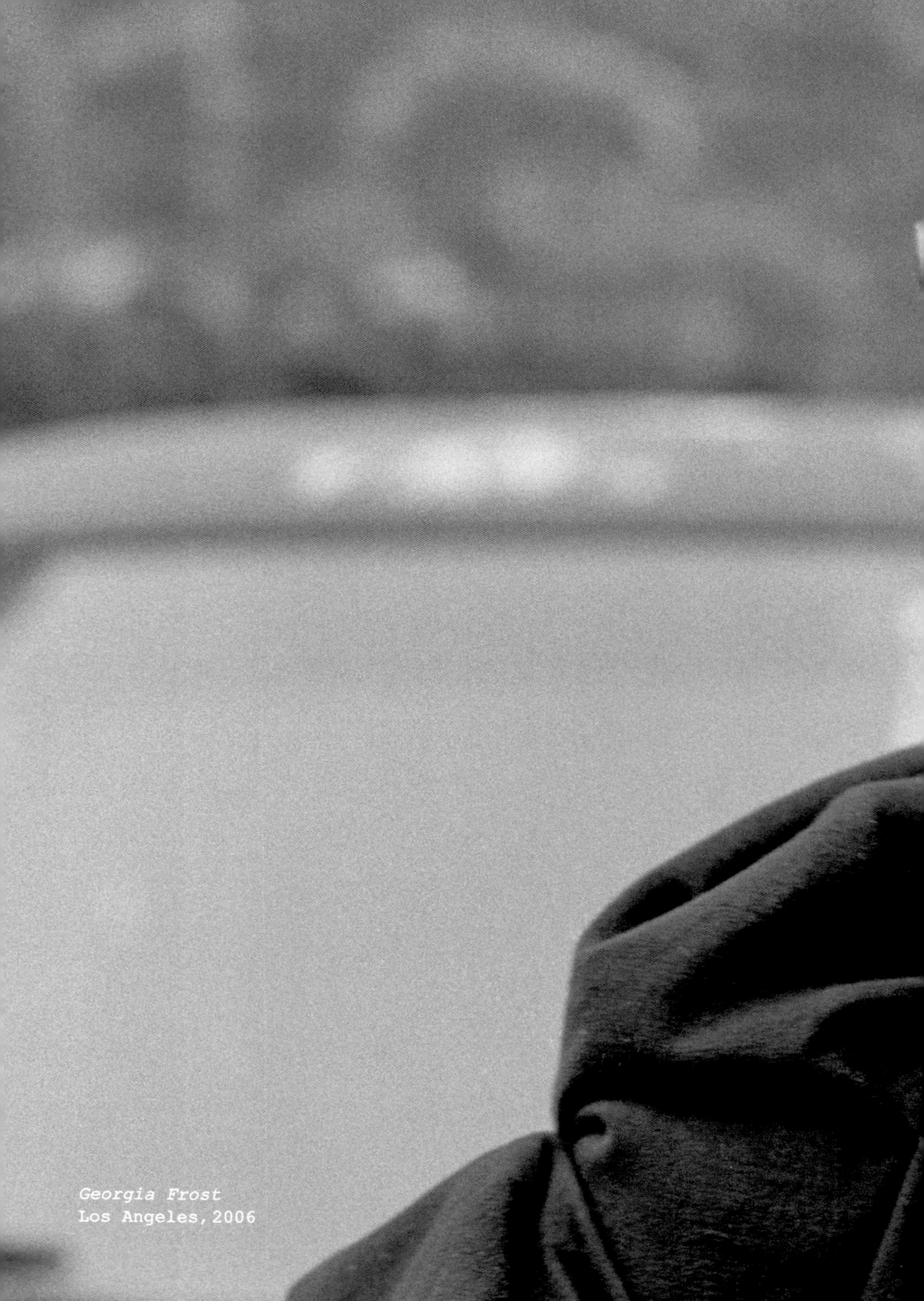

Georgia Frost
Los Angeles, 2006

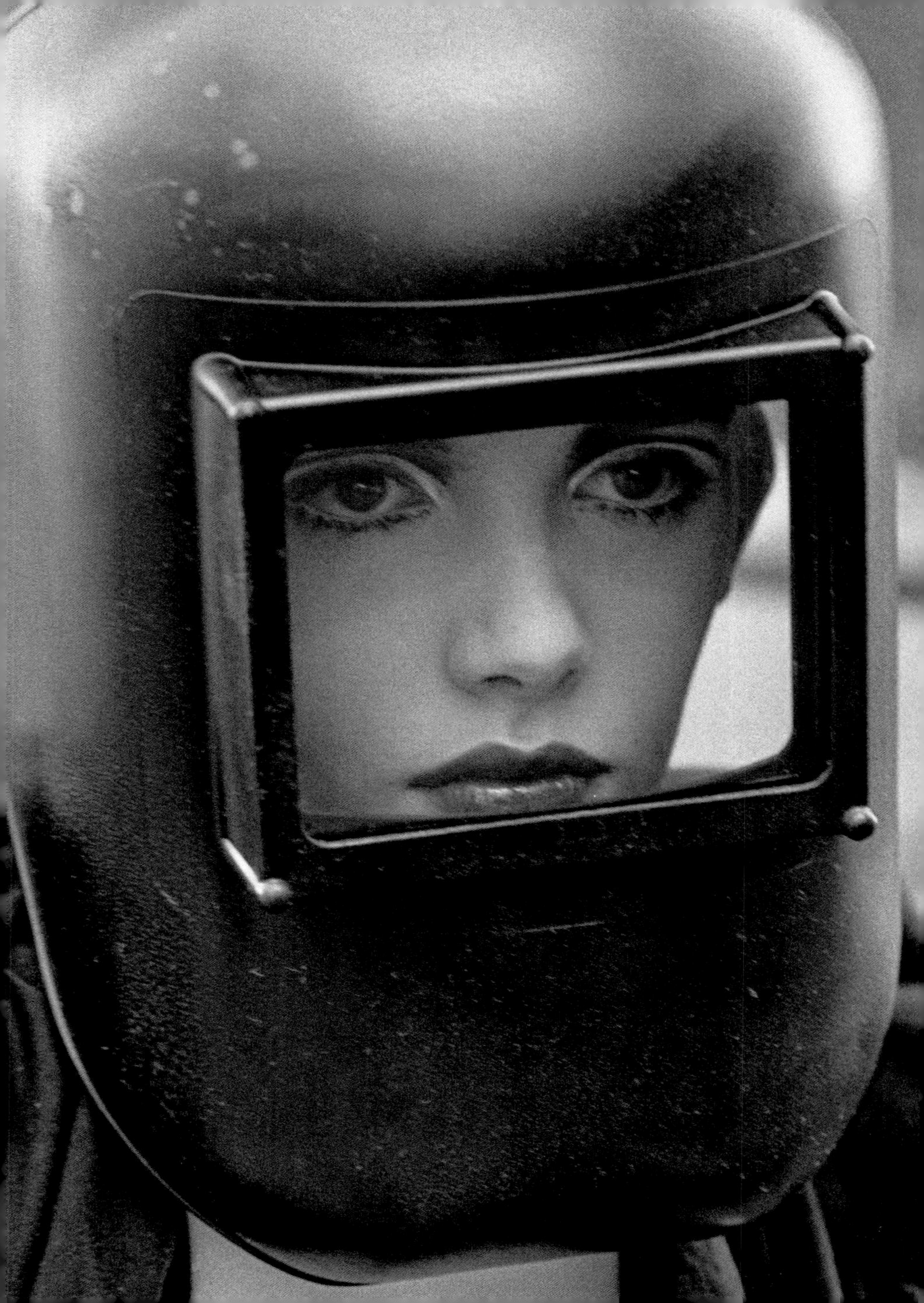

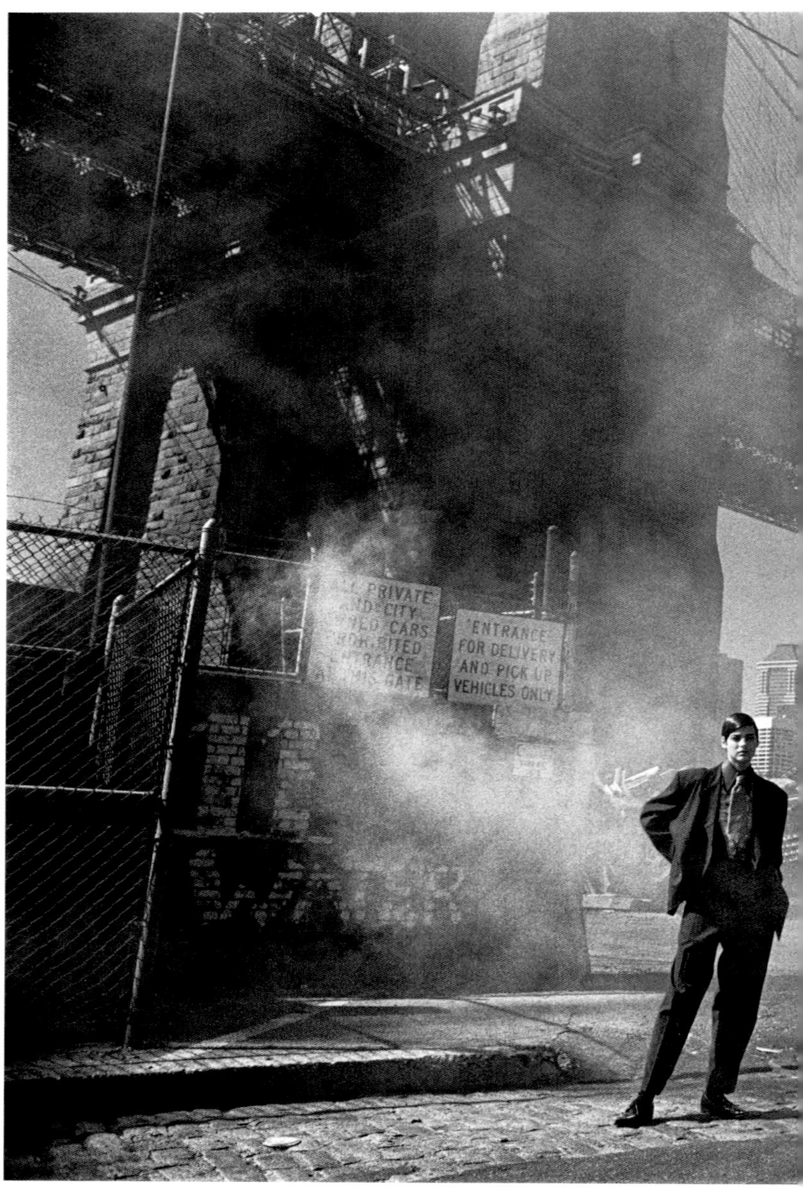
ALL PRIVATE
AND CITY
OWNED CARS
PROHIBITED
ENTRANCE
AT THIS GATE
ENTRANCE
FOR DELIVERY
AND PICK UP
VEHICLES ONLY

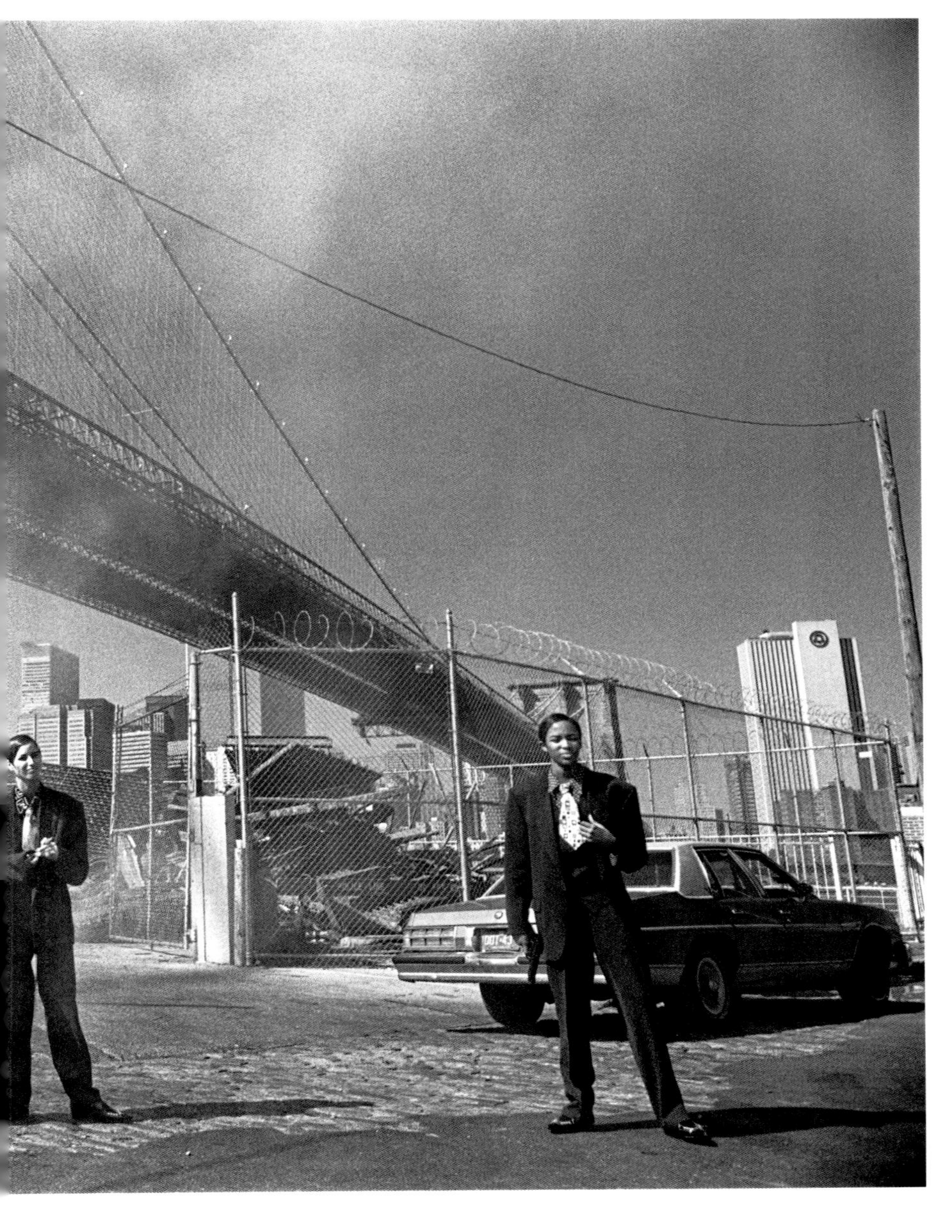

Linda Evangelista, Christy Turlington & Naomi Campbell
Brooklyn, 1990

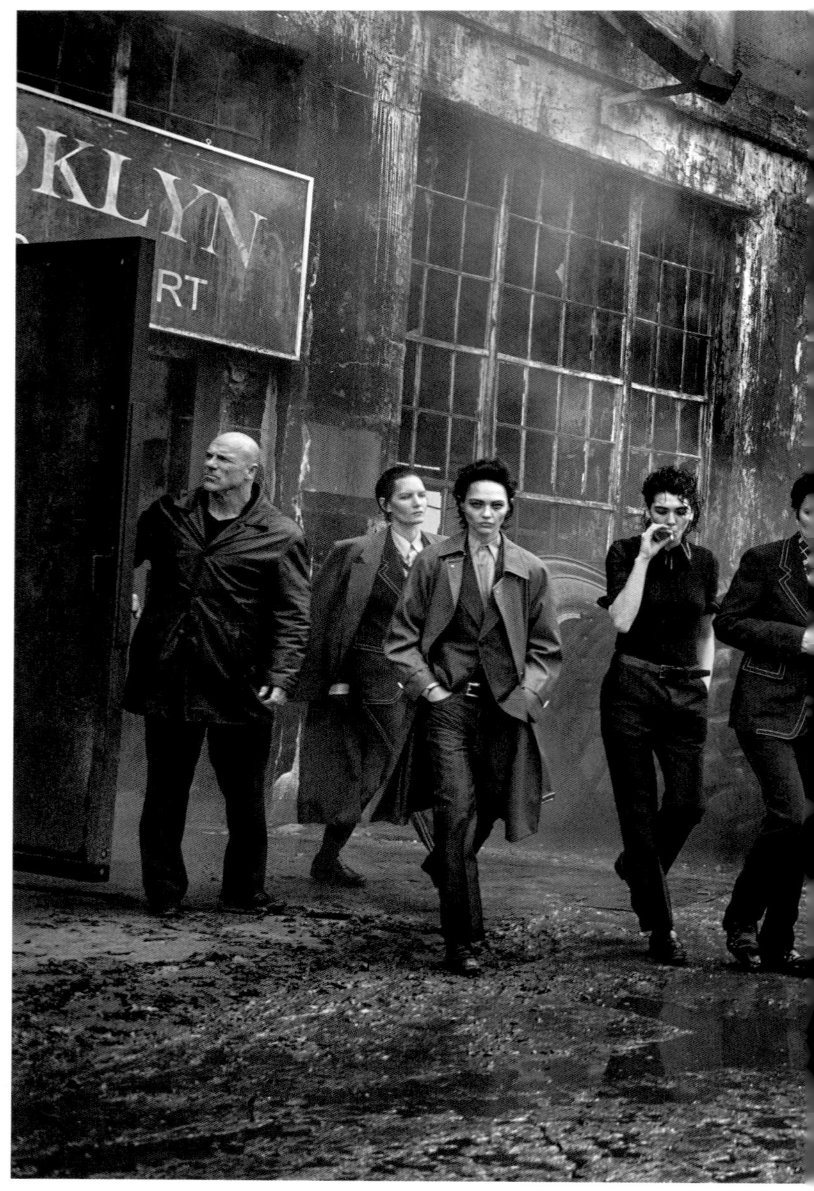
KLYN
RT

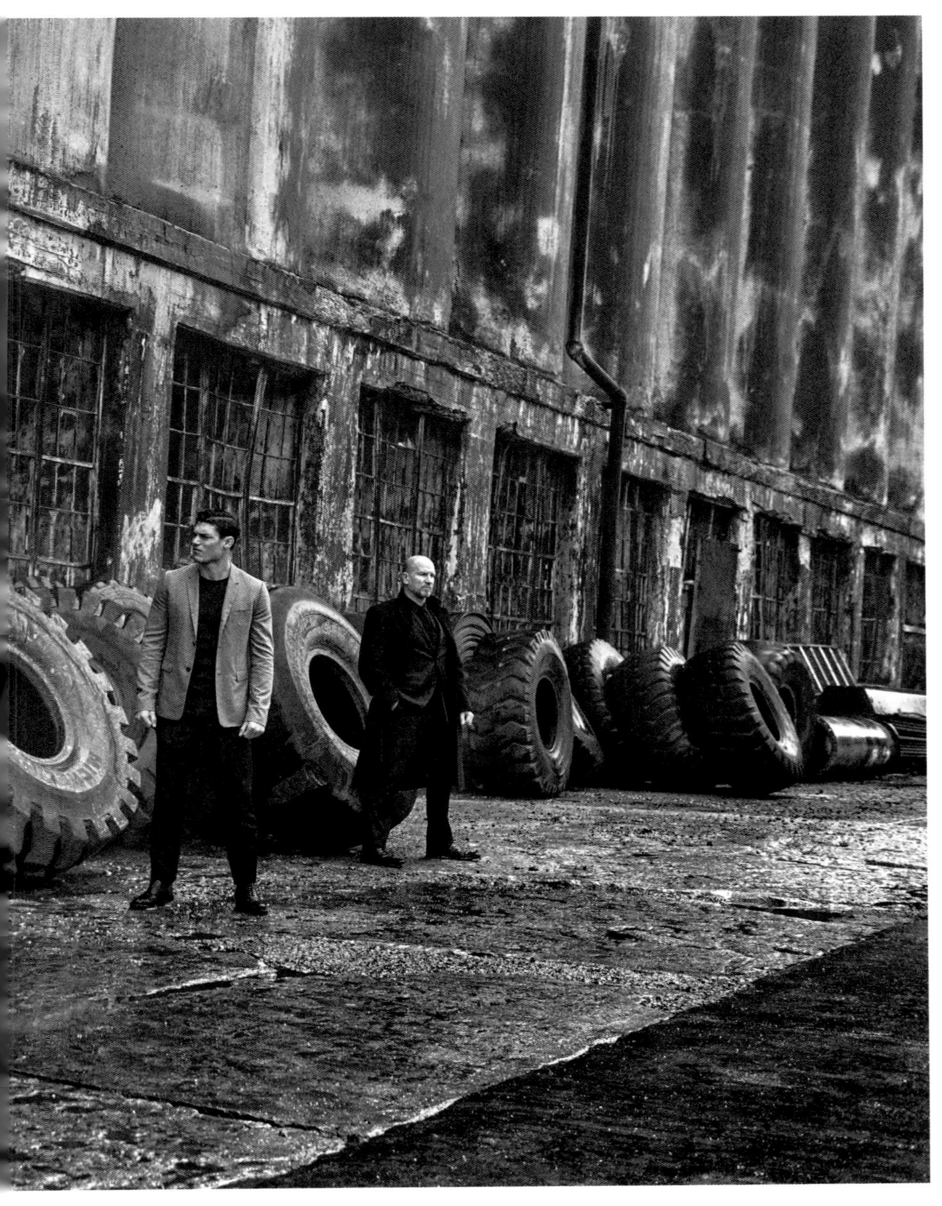

Kirsten Owen, Sasha Pivovarova, Steffy Argelich & Guinevere van Seenus
Brooklyn, 2015

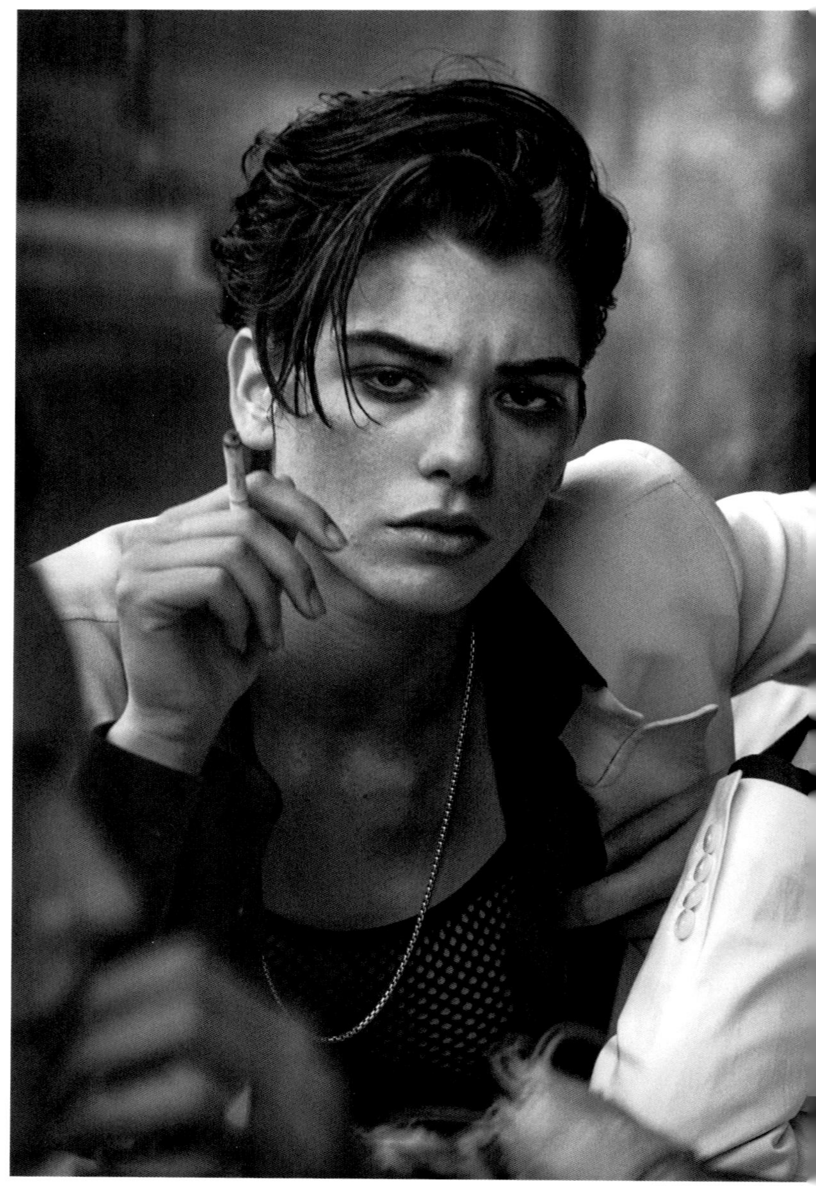

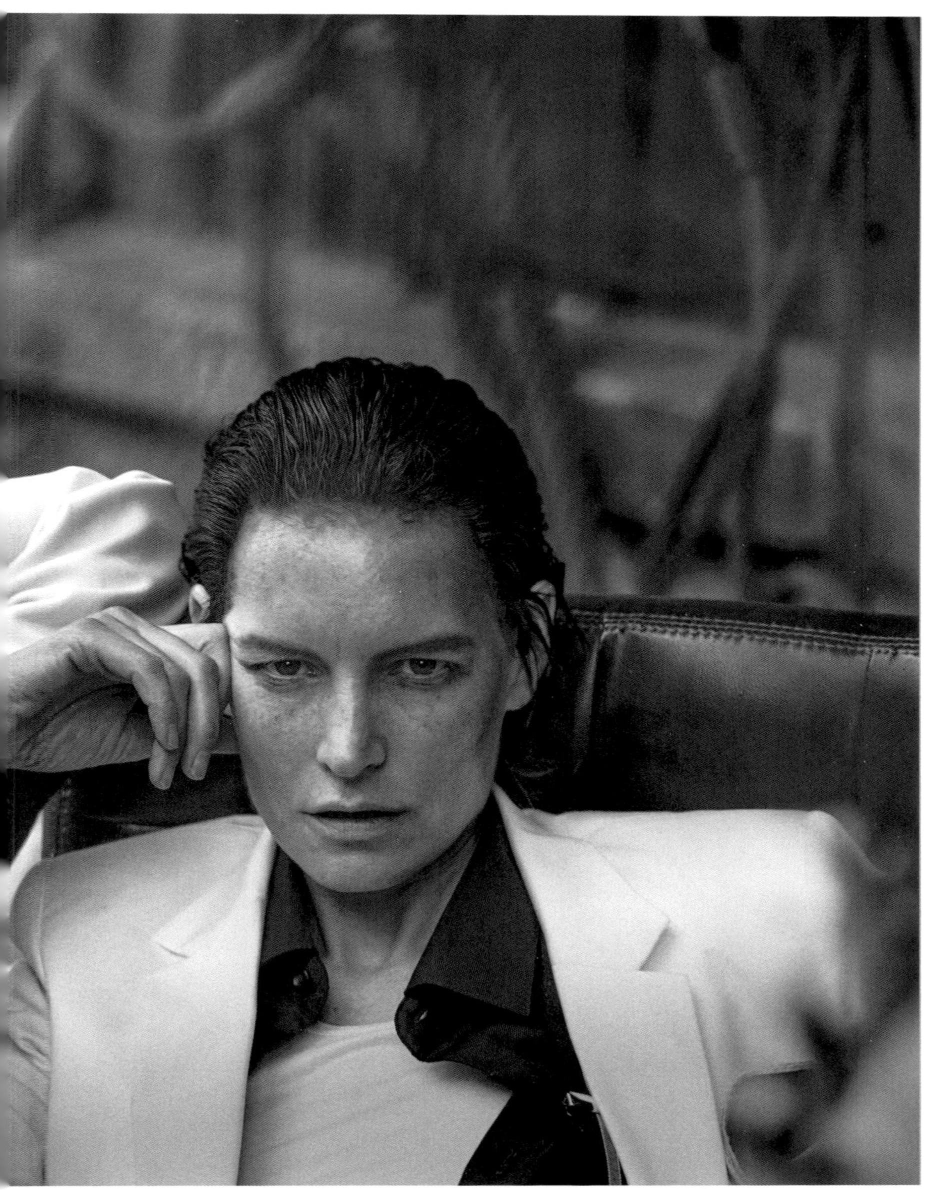
Steffy Argelich & Kirsten Owen
Brooklyn, 2015

Naomi Campbell
Ibiza, 2000

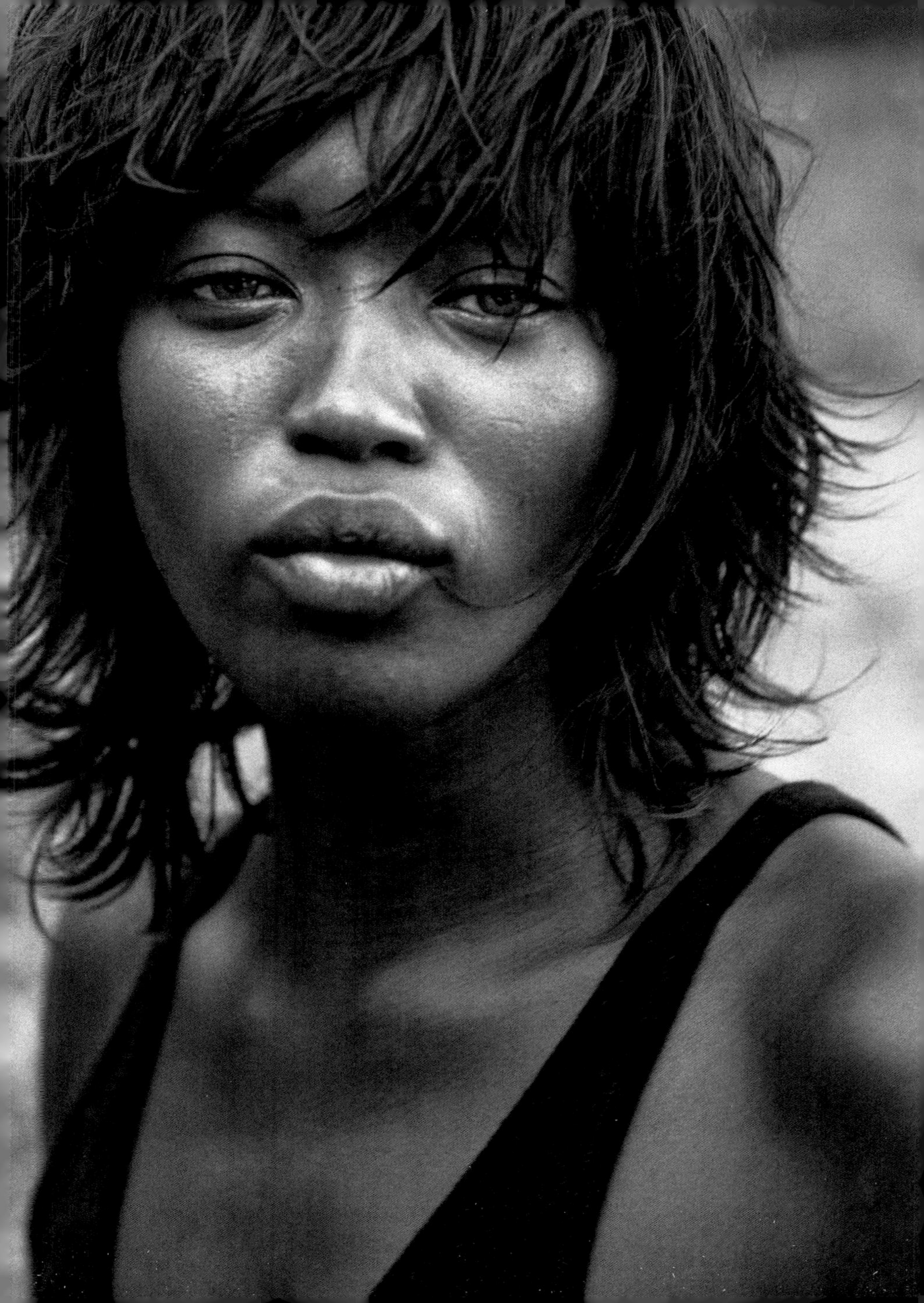

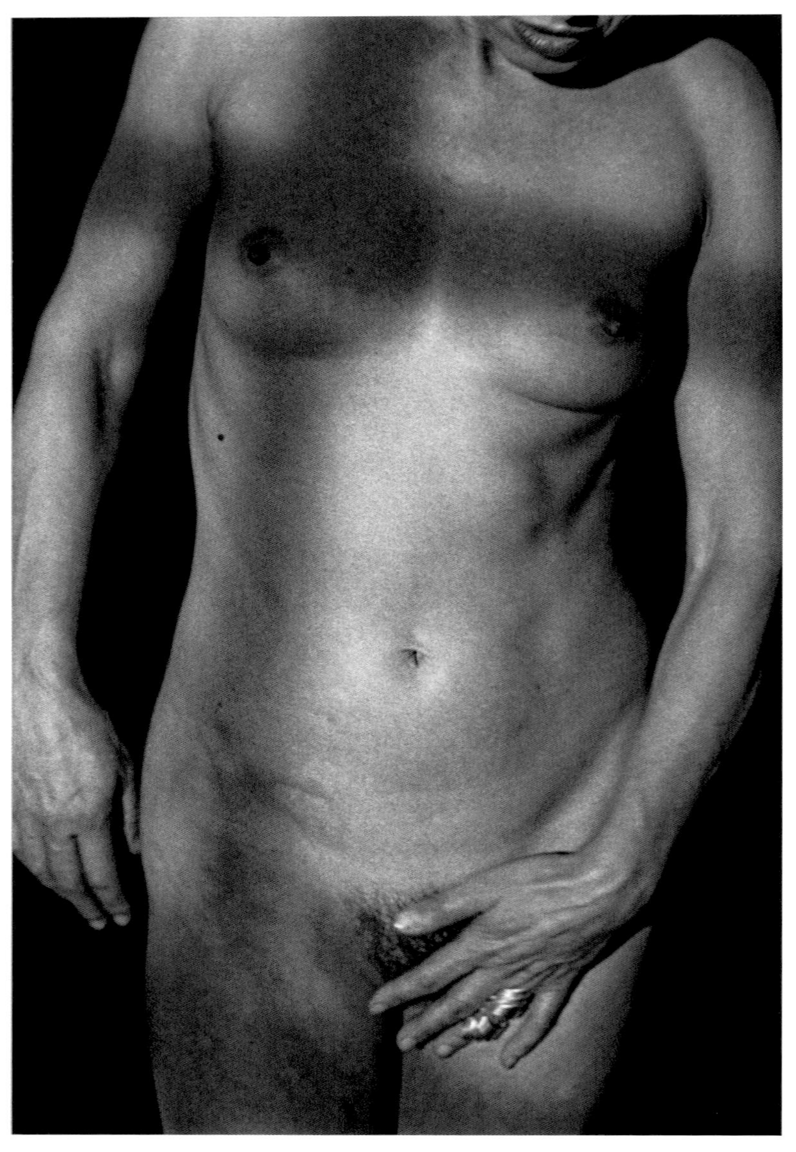

Uschi Obermaier
Los Angeles,1994

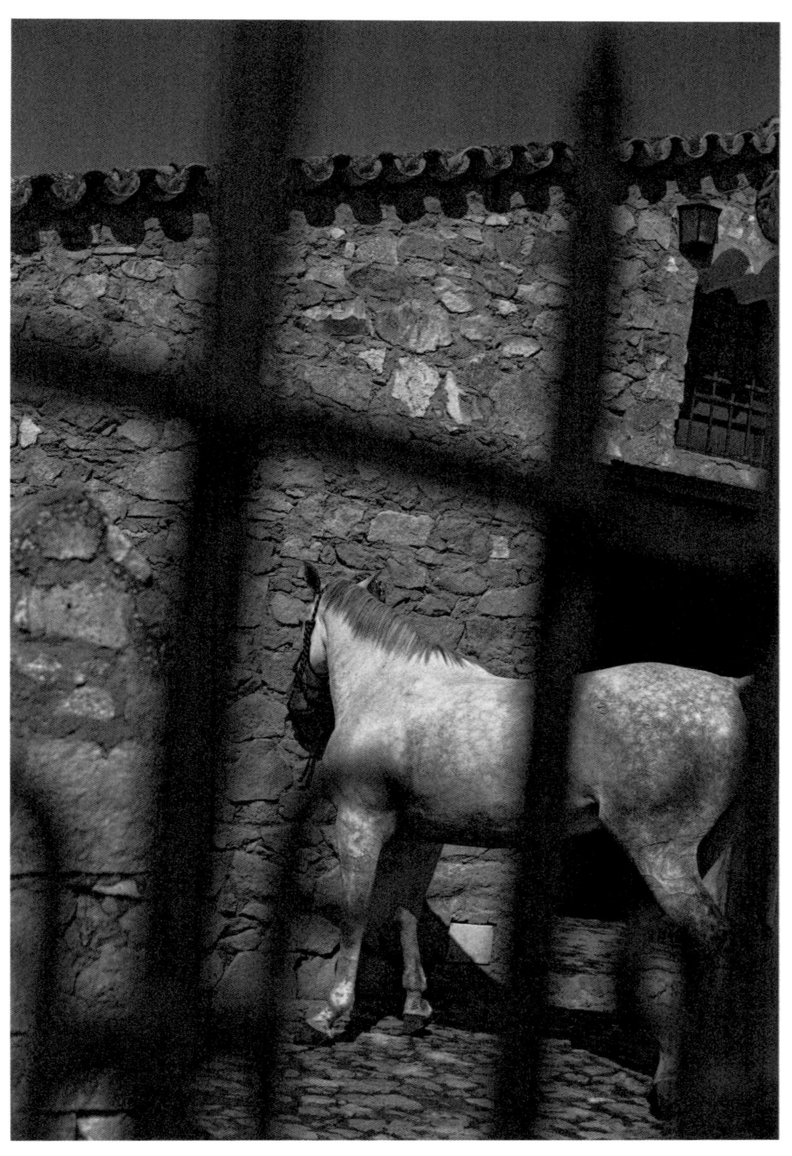

Finca Lo Álvaro
Sevilla, 2010

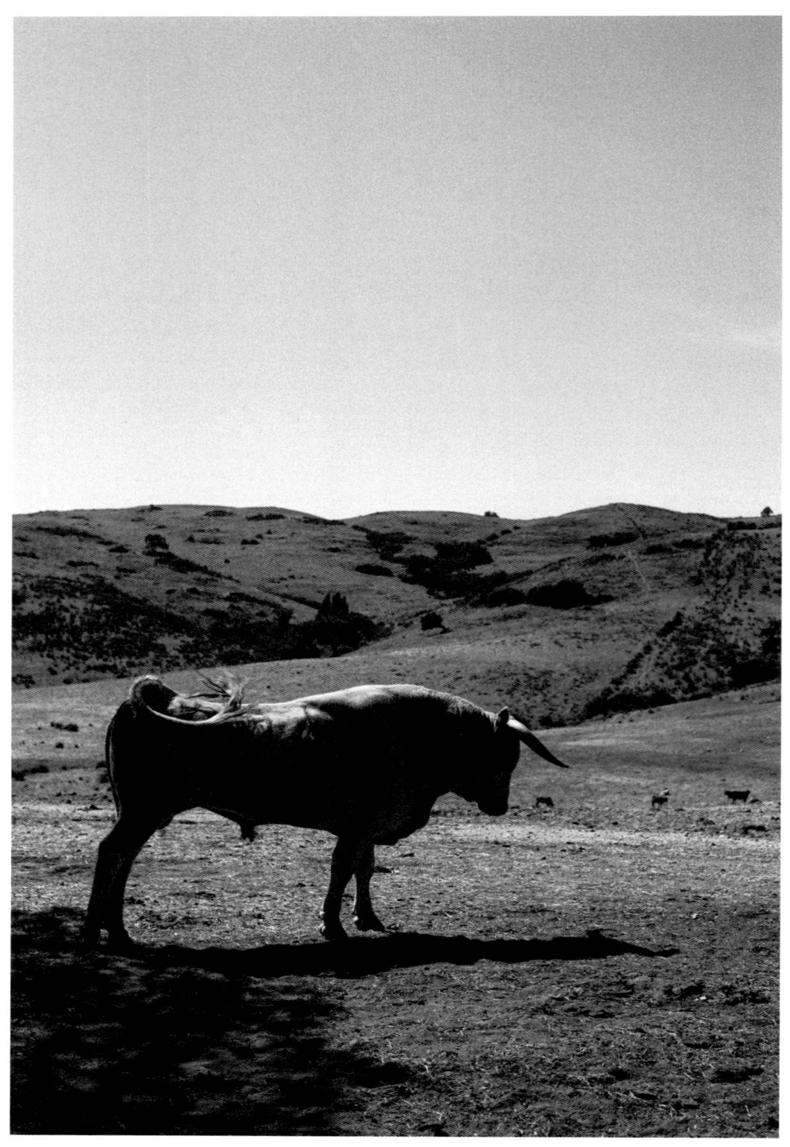

Finca Lo Álvaro
Sevilla, 2010

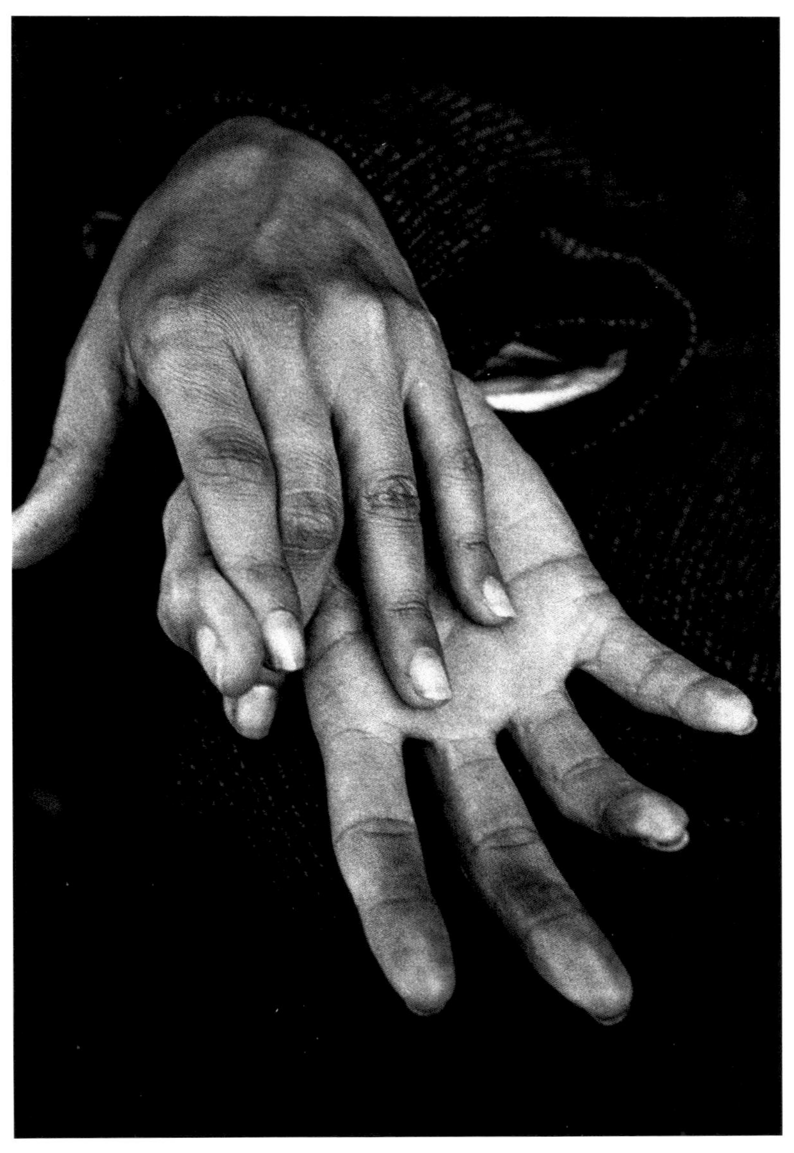

Lorraine Bracco
Los Angeles, 1990

Pharrell Williams
Los Angeles, 2014

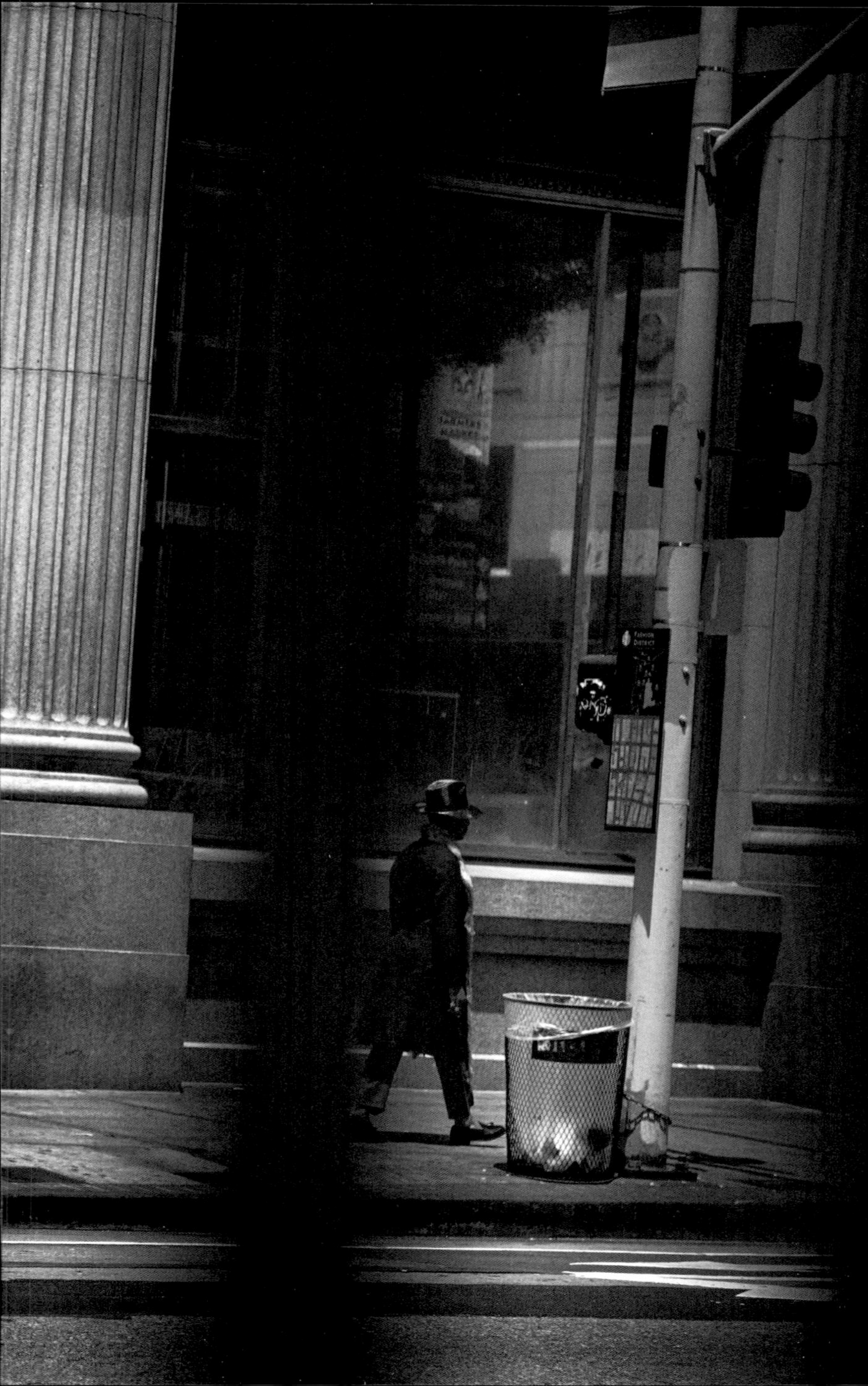

Eri Ishida
Salin-de-Giraud, 2017

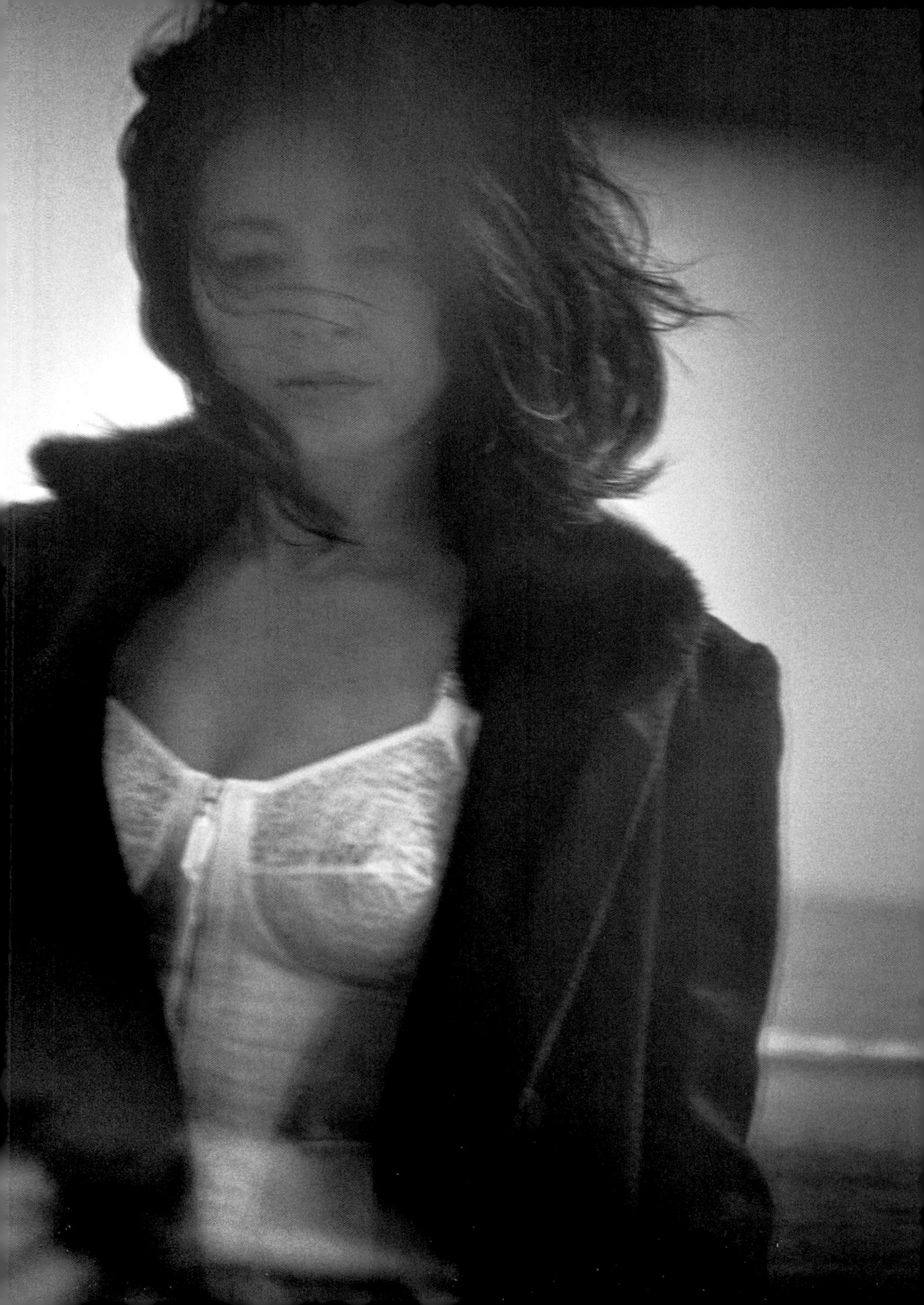

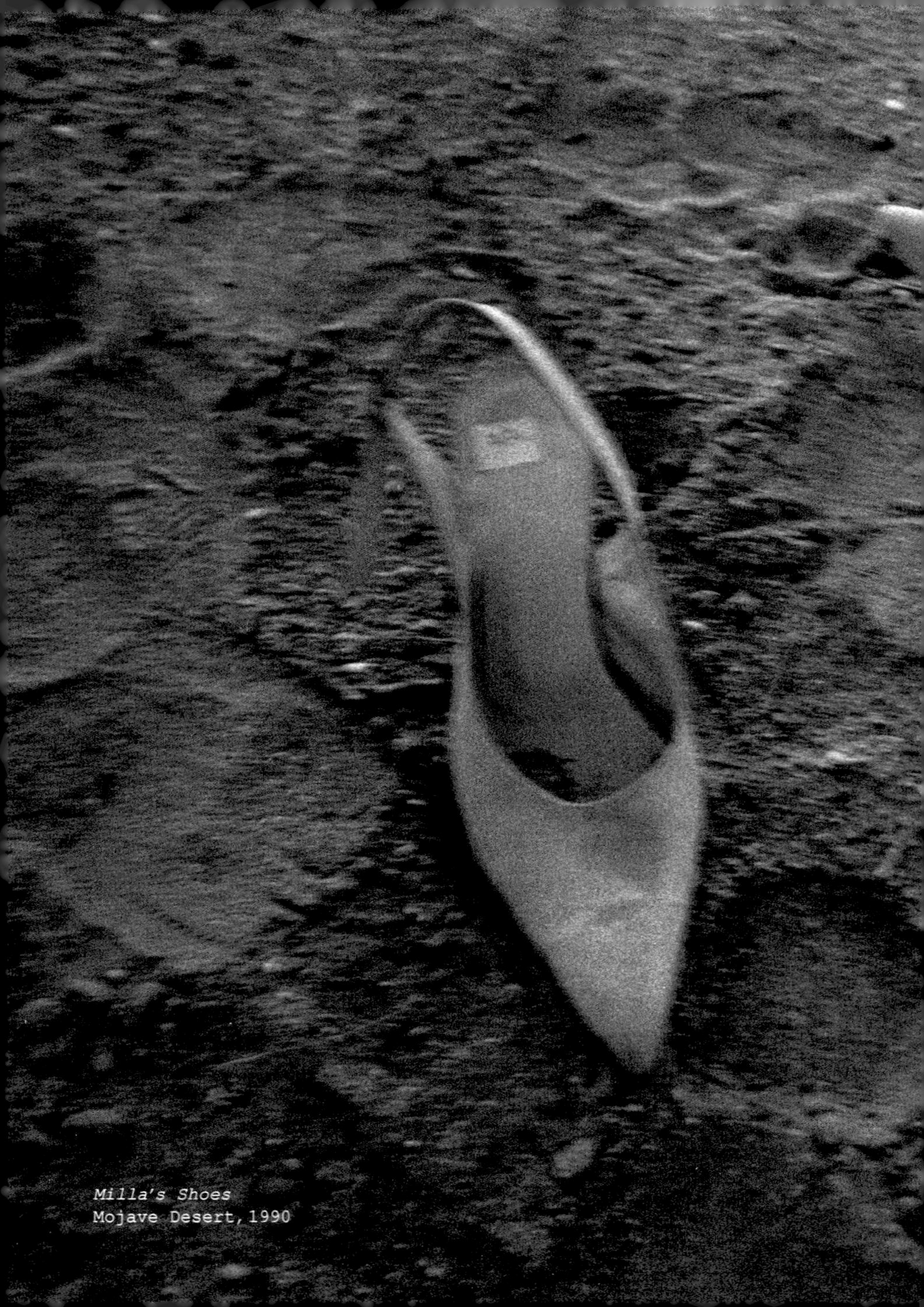
Milla's Shoes
Mojave Desert, 1990

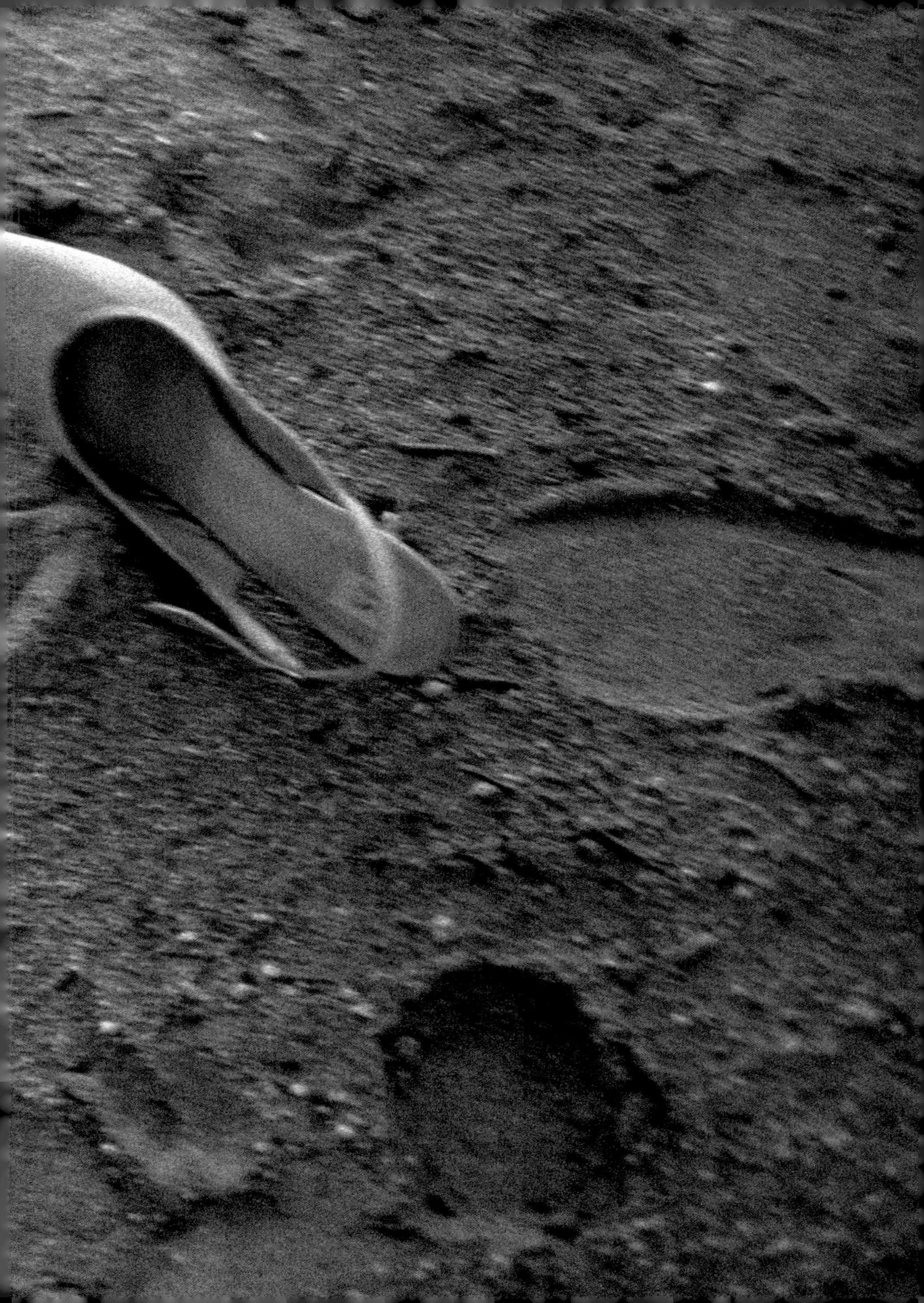

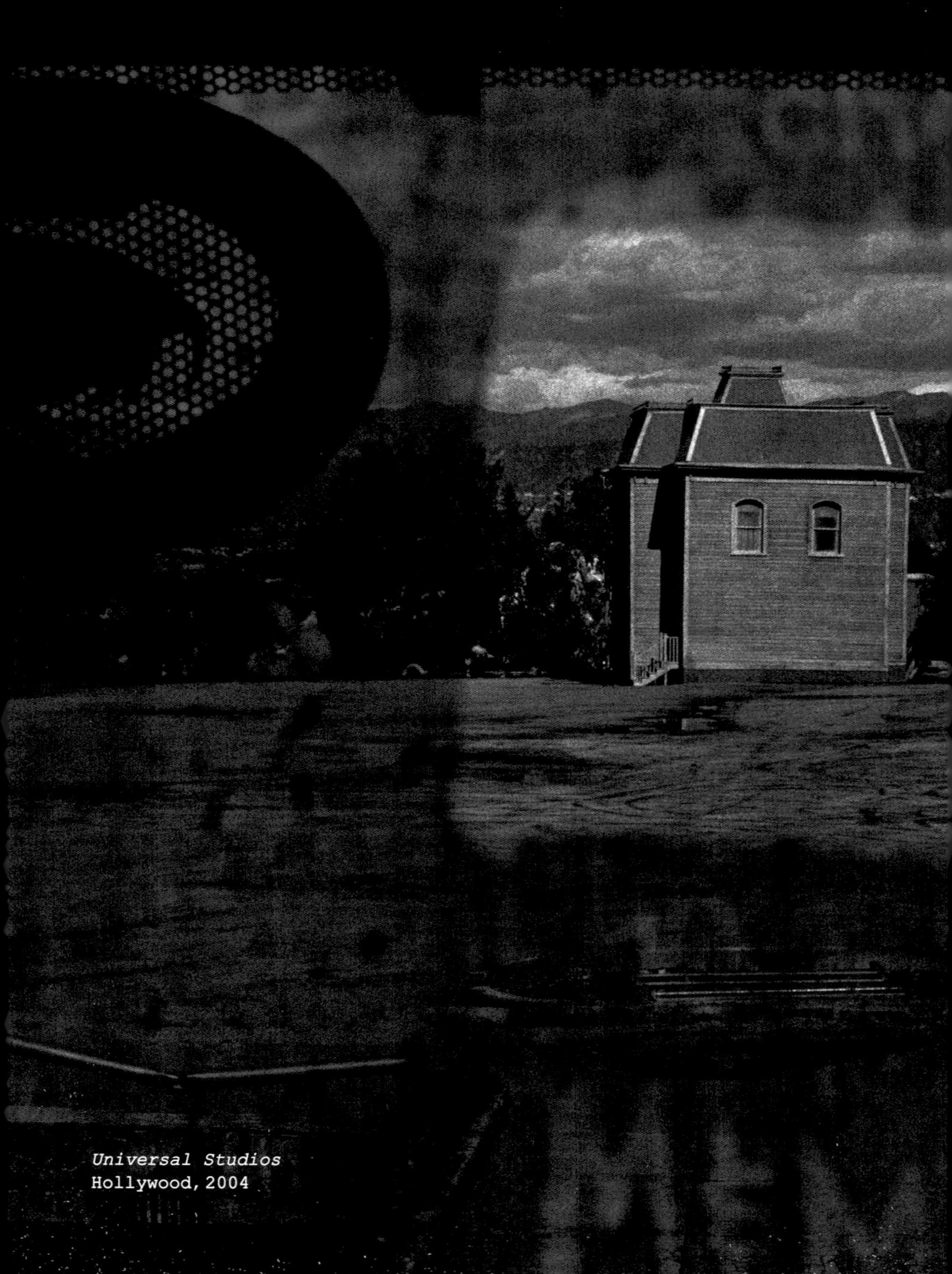
Universal Studios
Hollywood, 2004

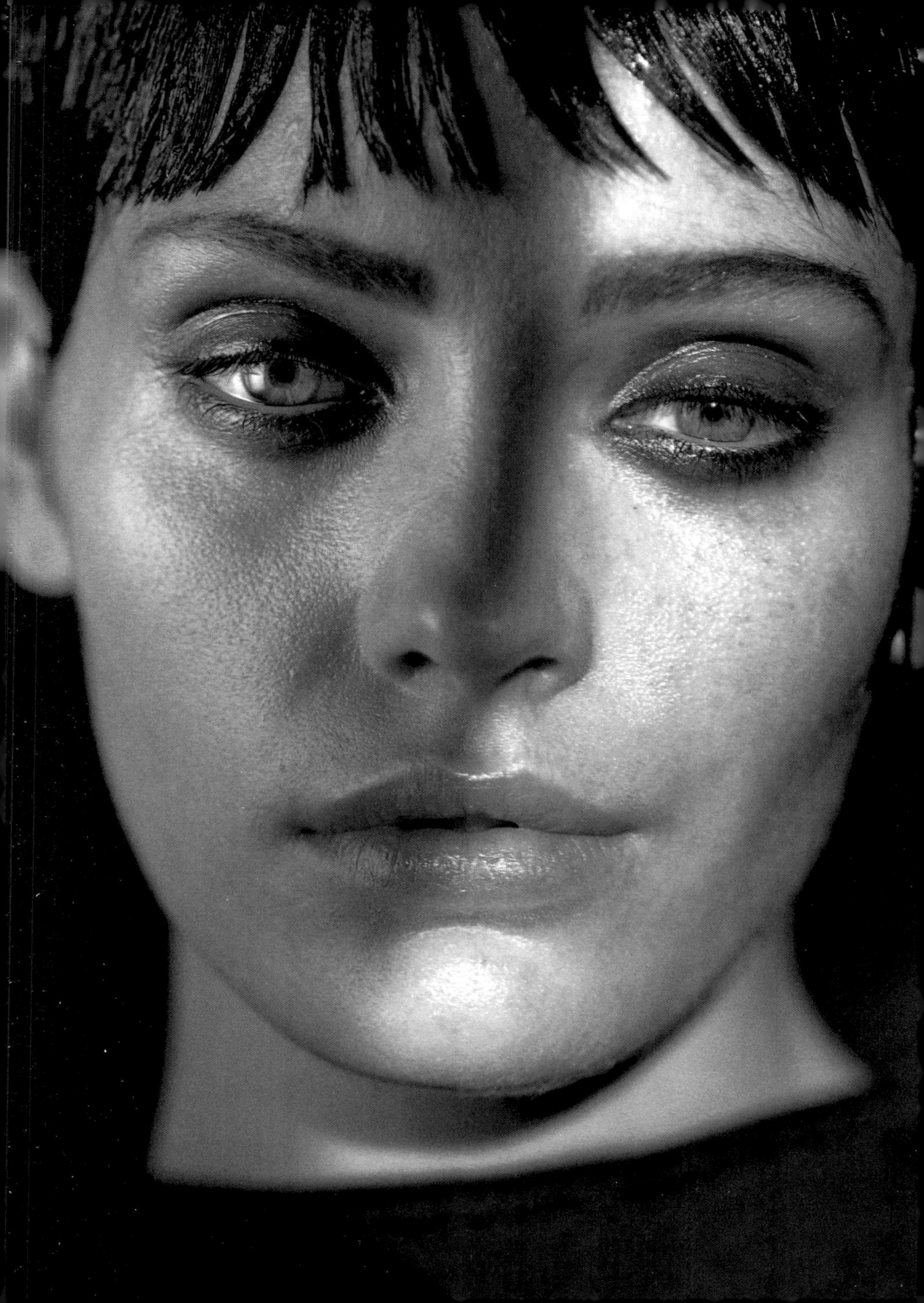

Hannah Whelan
London, 2012

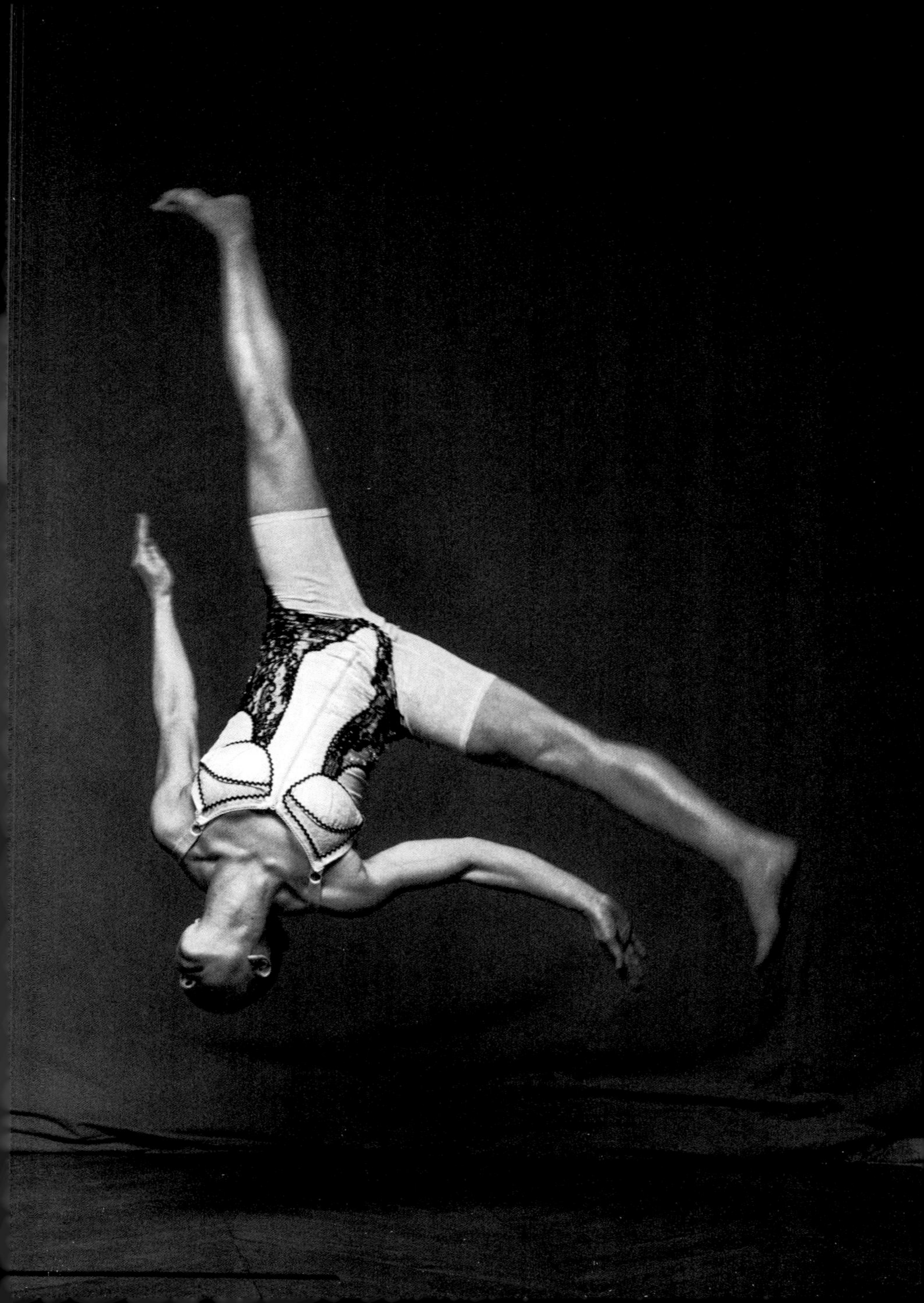

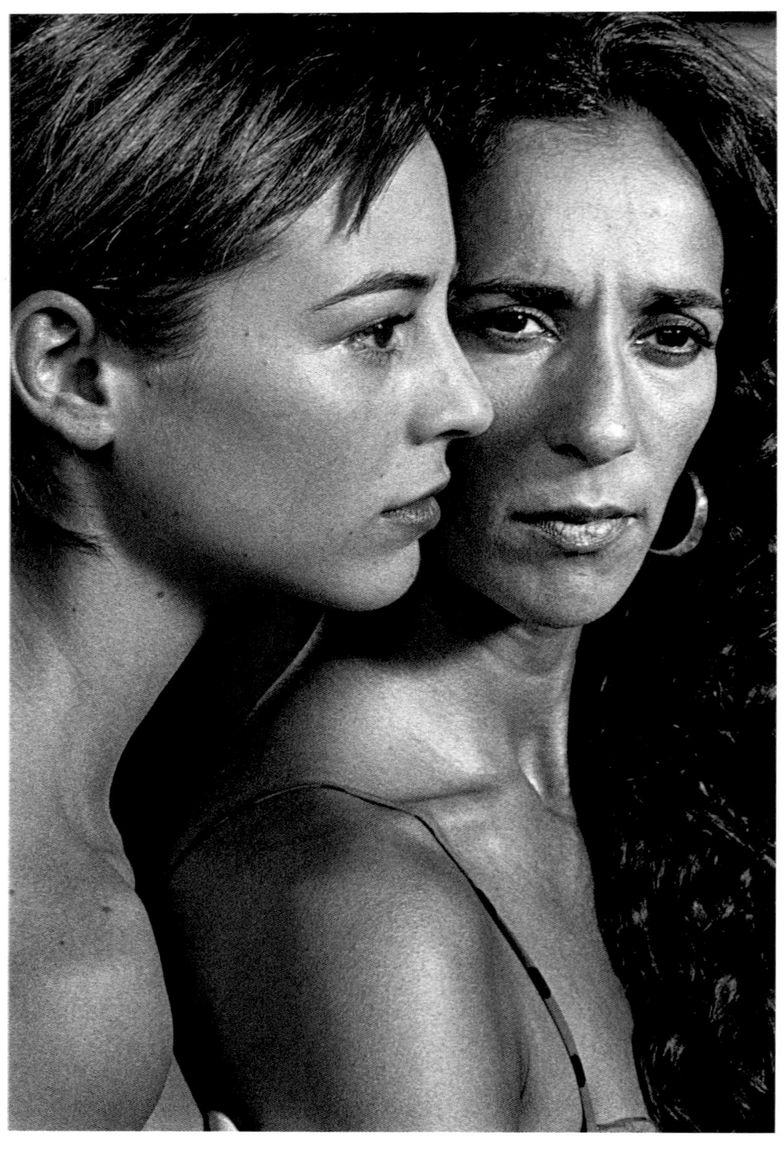

Leonor Watling & Rosario Flores
Madrid, 2001

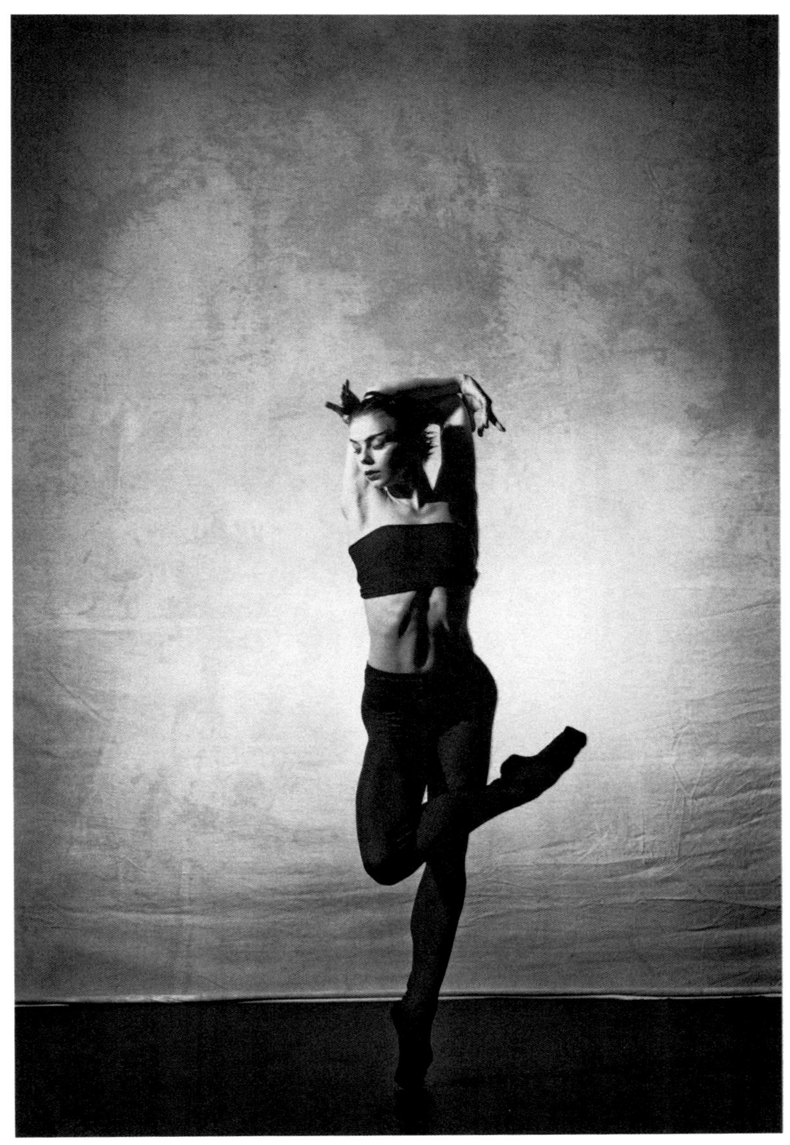

Natalia Osipova
Moscow, 2011

Georgia Frost
Los Angeles, 2006

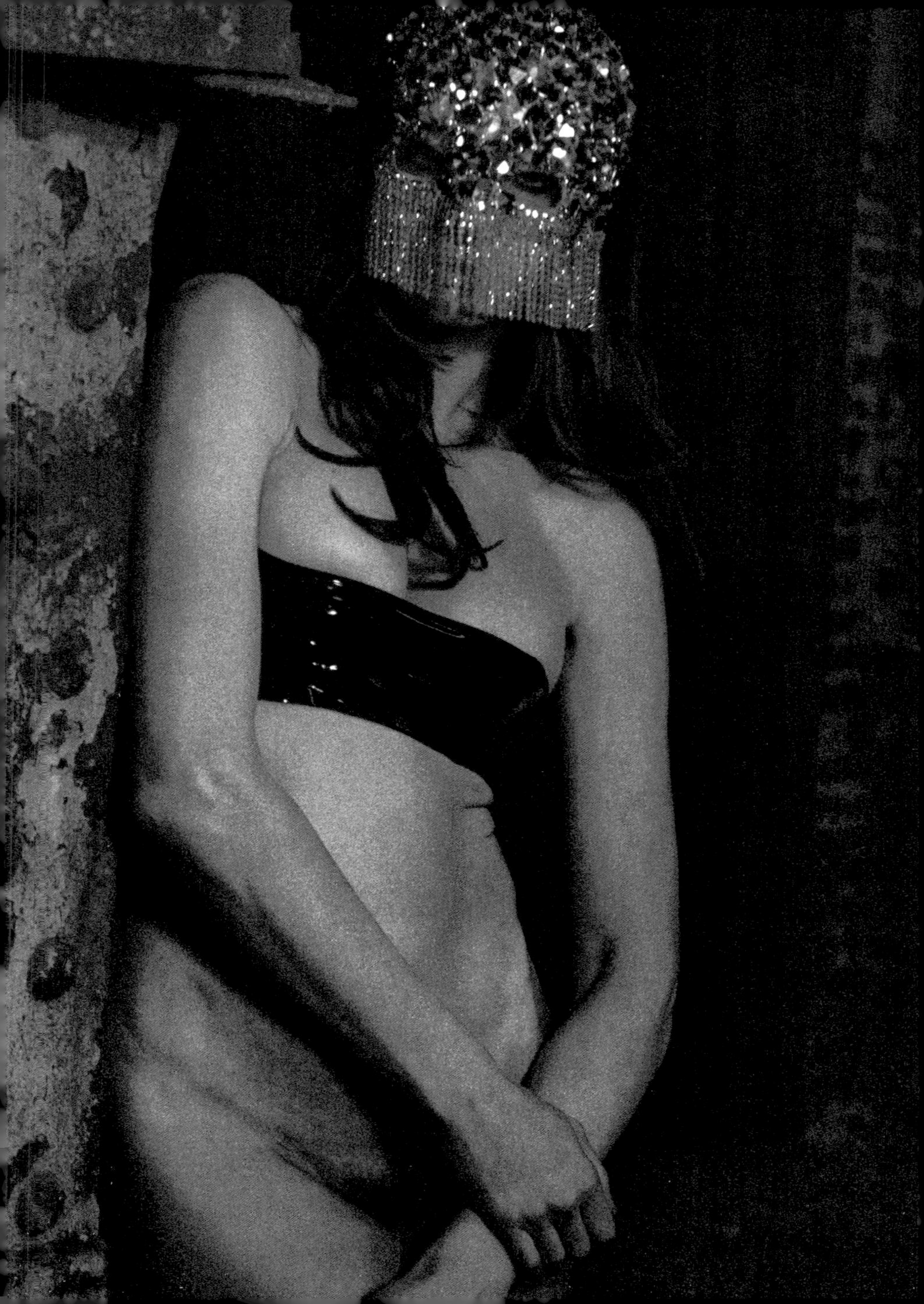

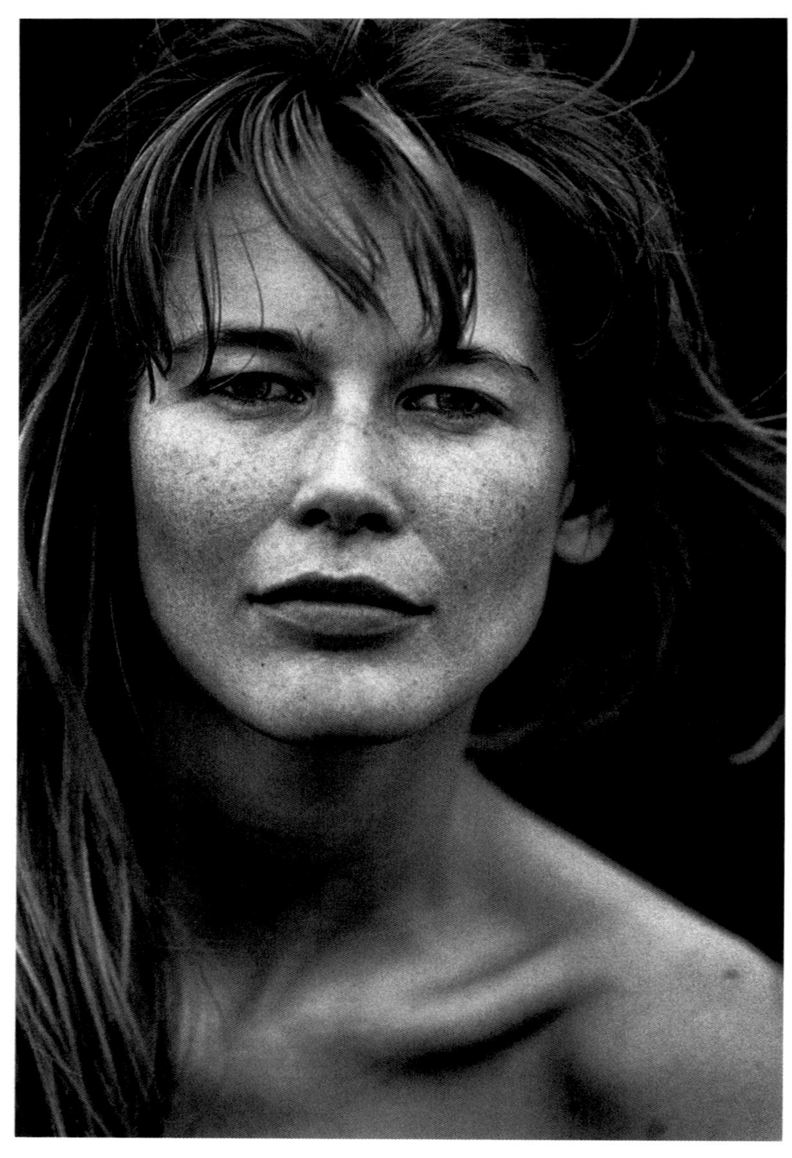

Claudia Schiffer
Santa Monica,1997

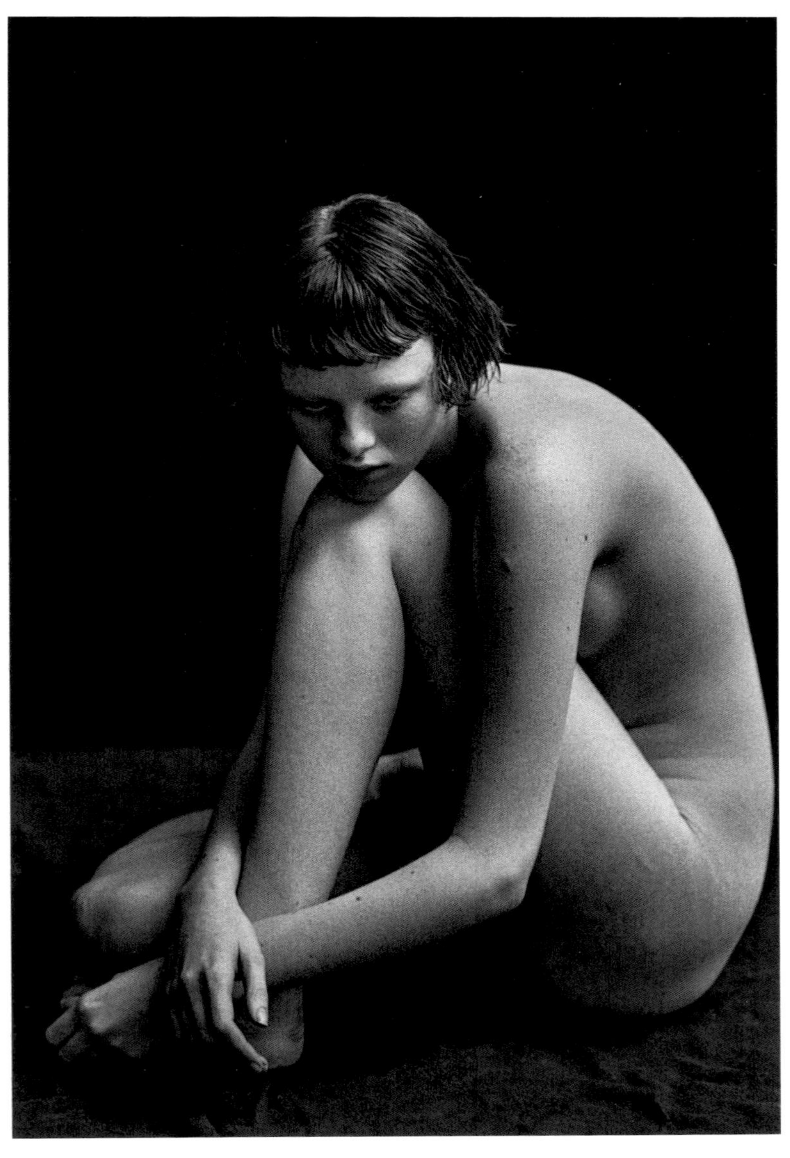

Karen Elson
Los Angeles, 1997

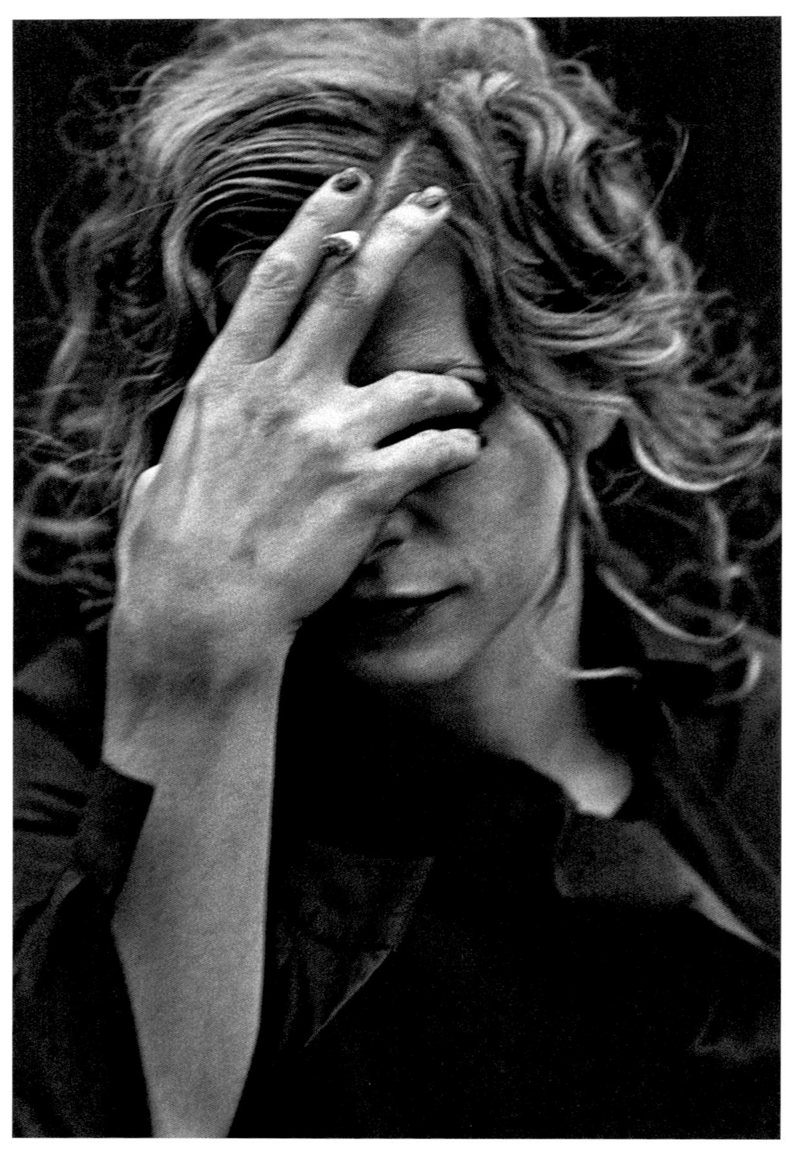

Mylène Farmer
Paris, 1999

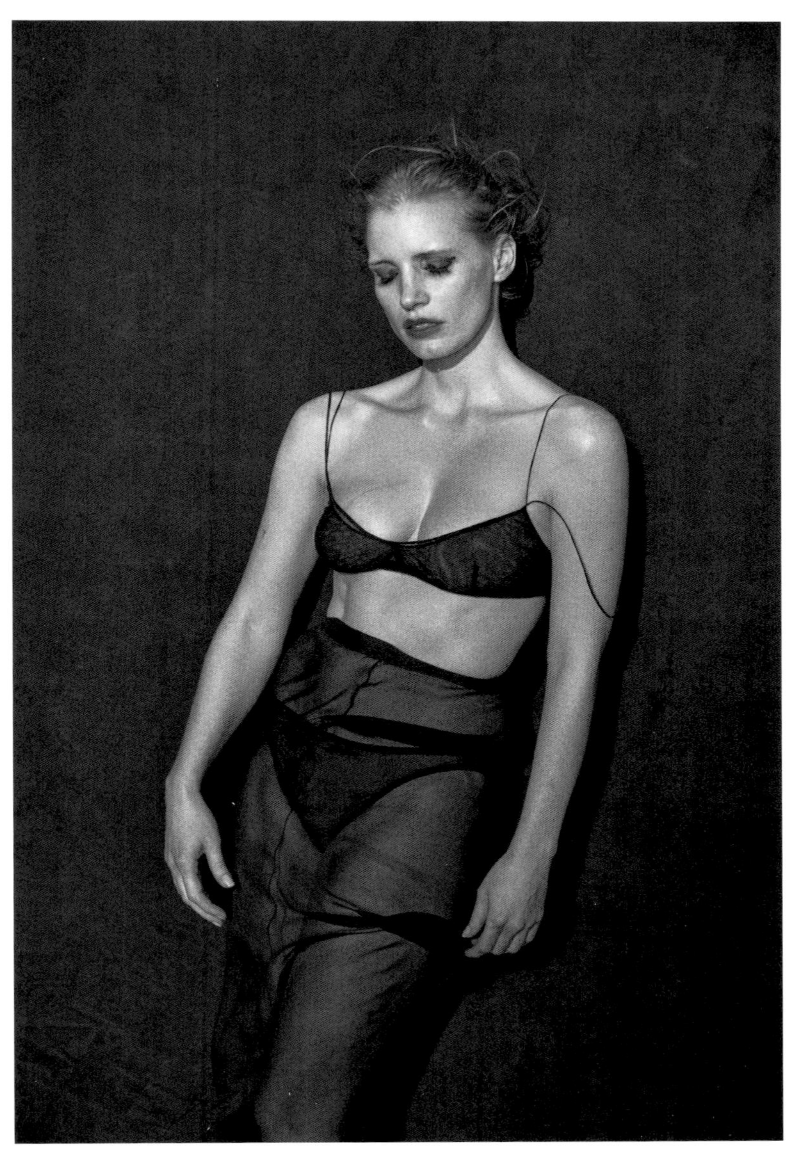

Jessica Chastain
New York, 2011

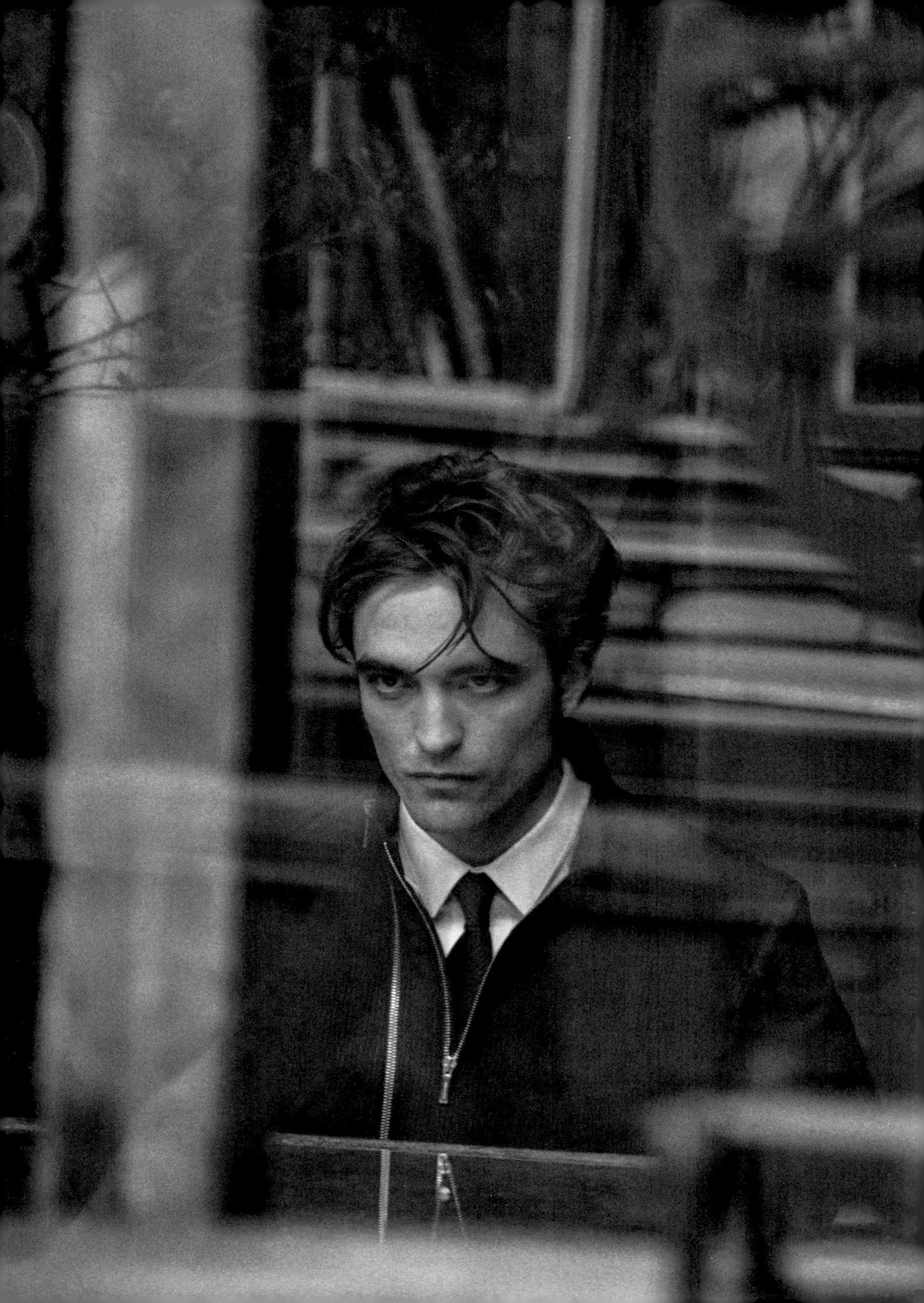

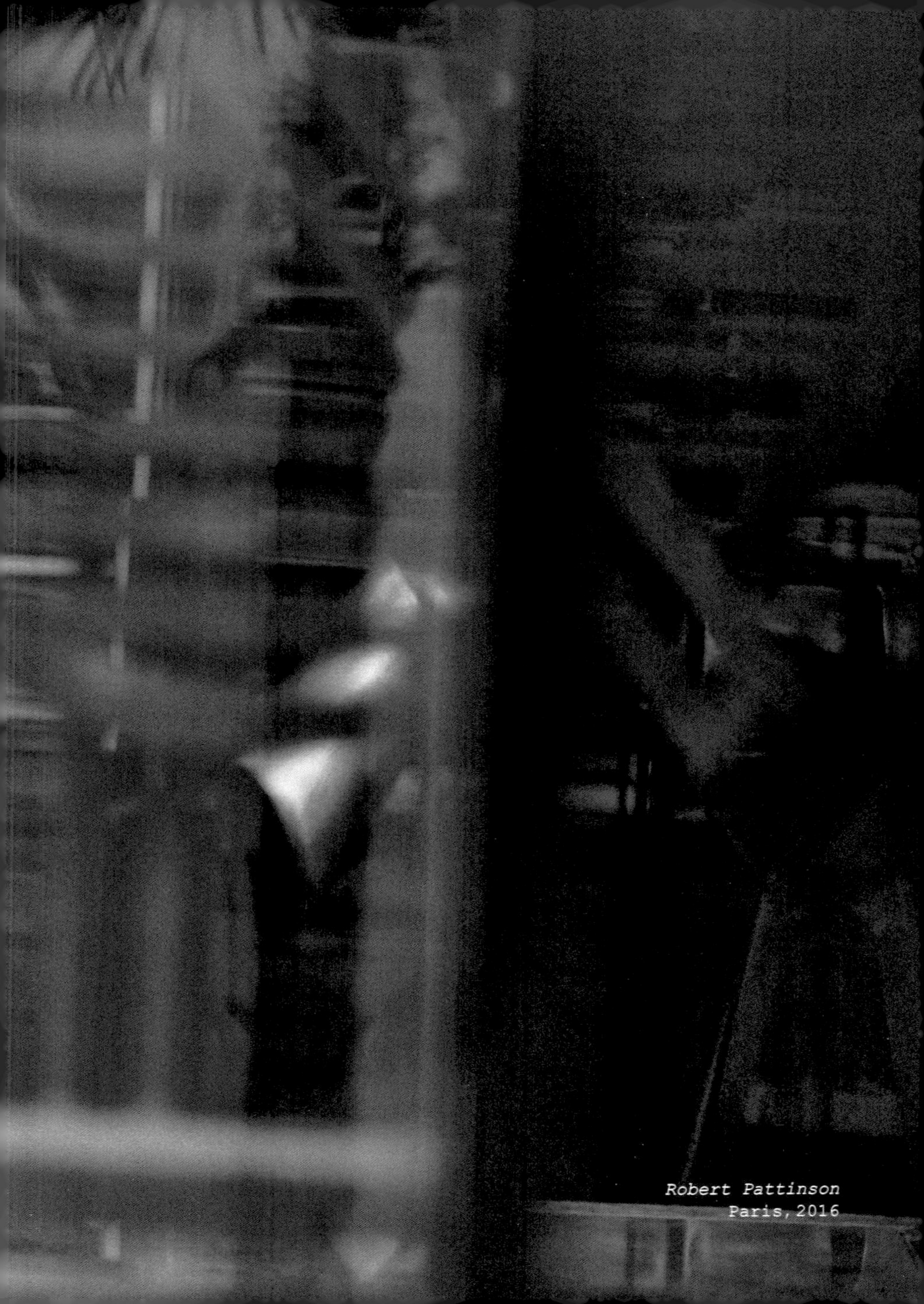
Robert Pattinson
Paris, 2016

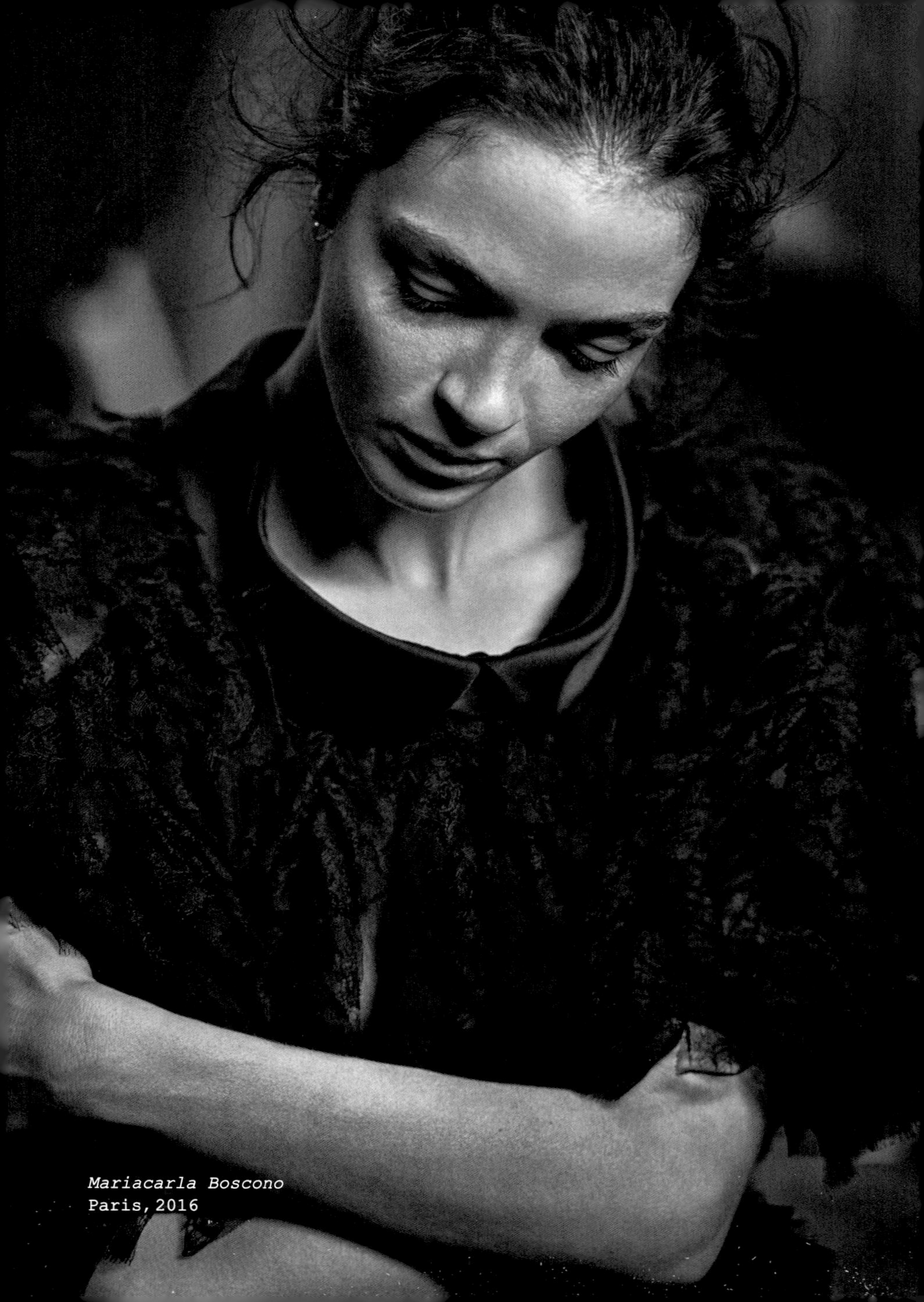

Mariacarla Boscono
Paris, 2016

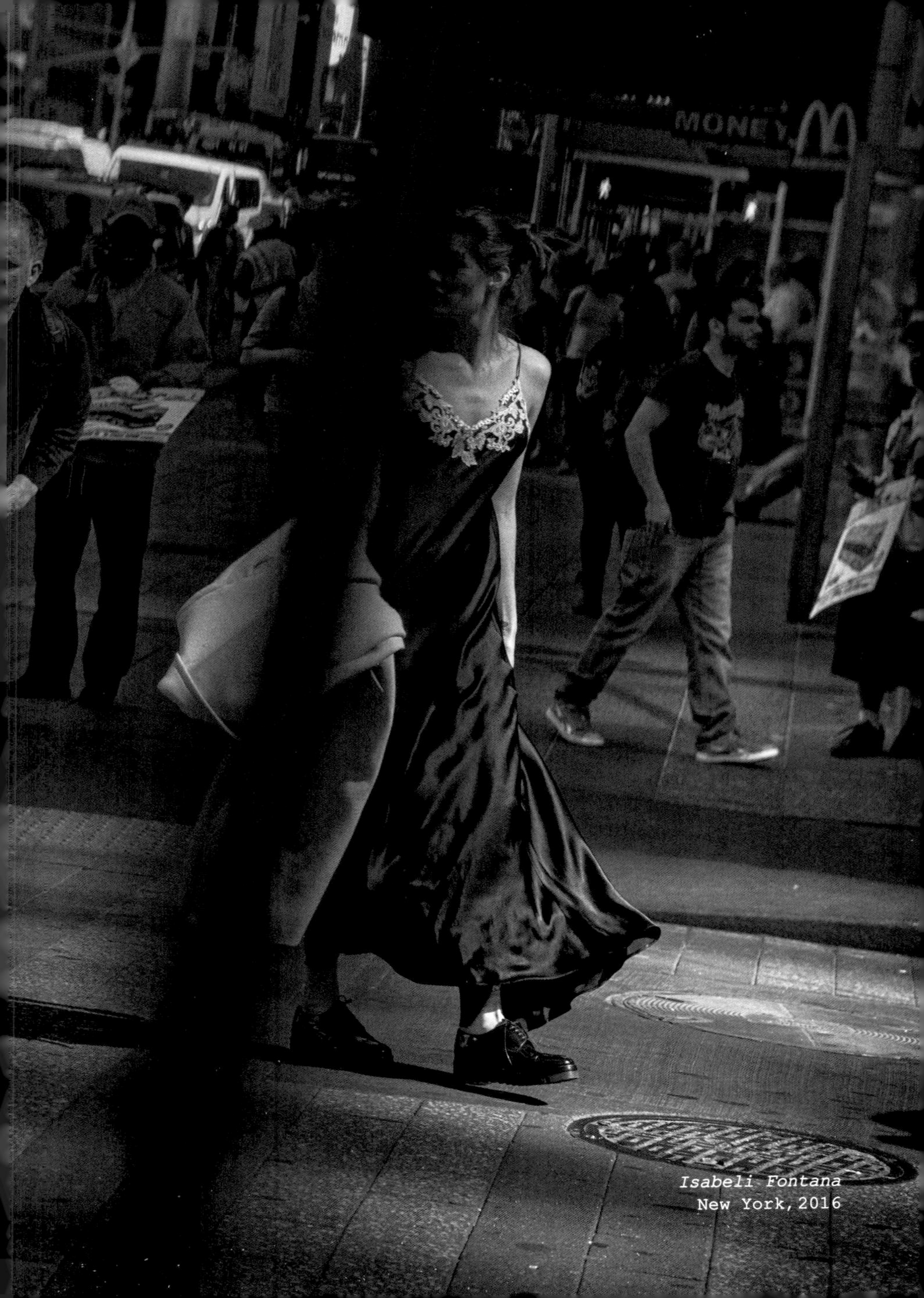

Isabeli Fontana
New York, 2016

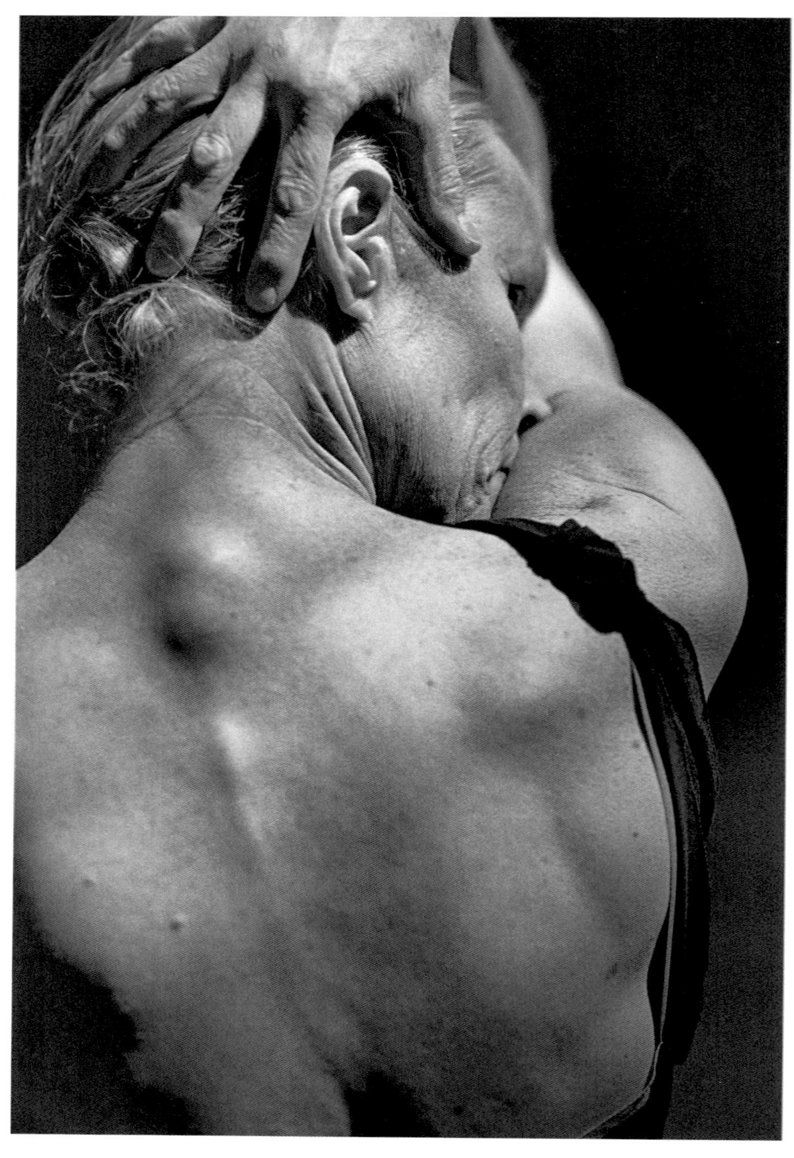

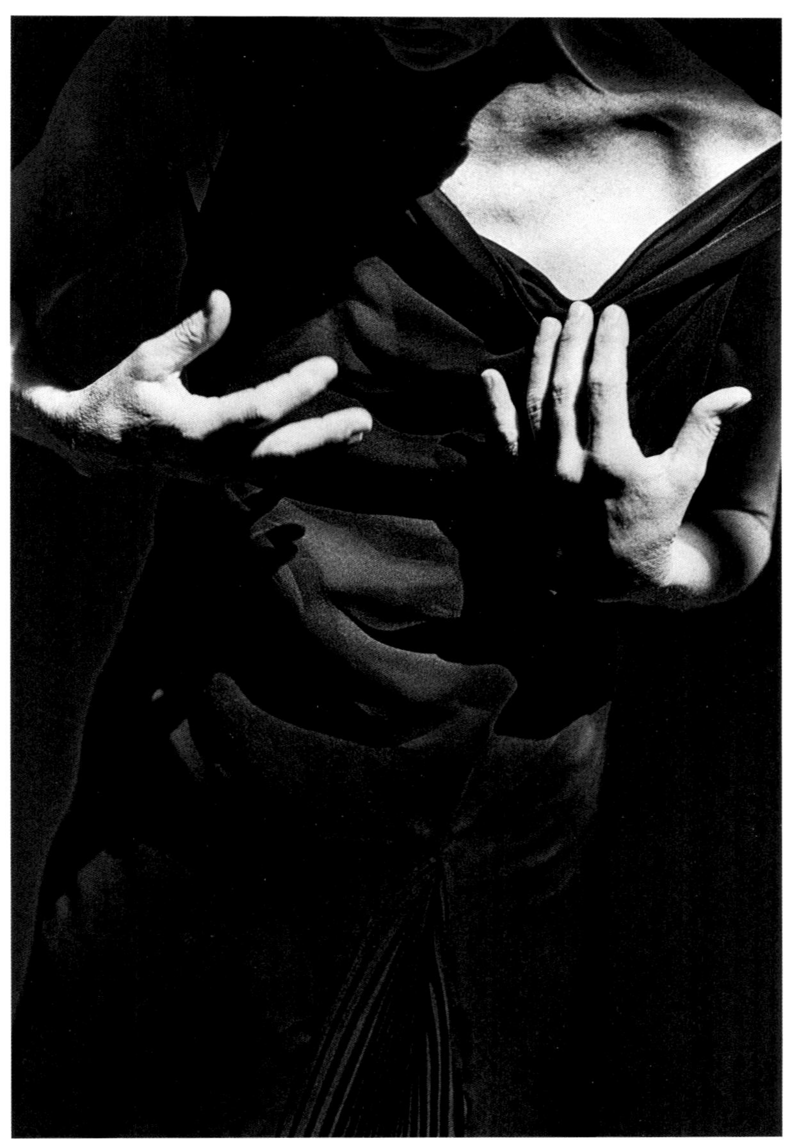

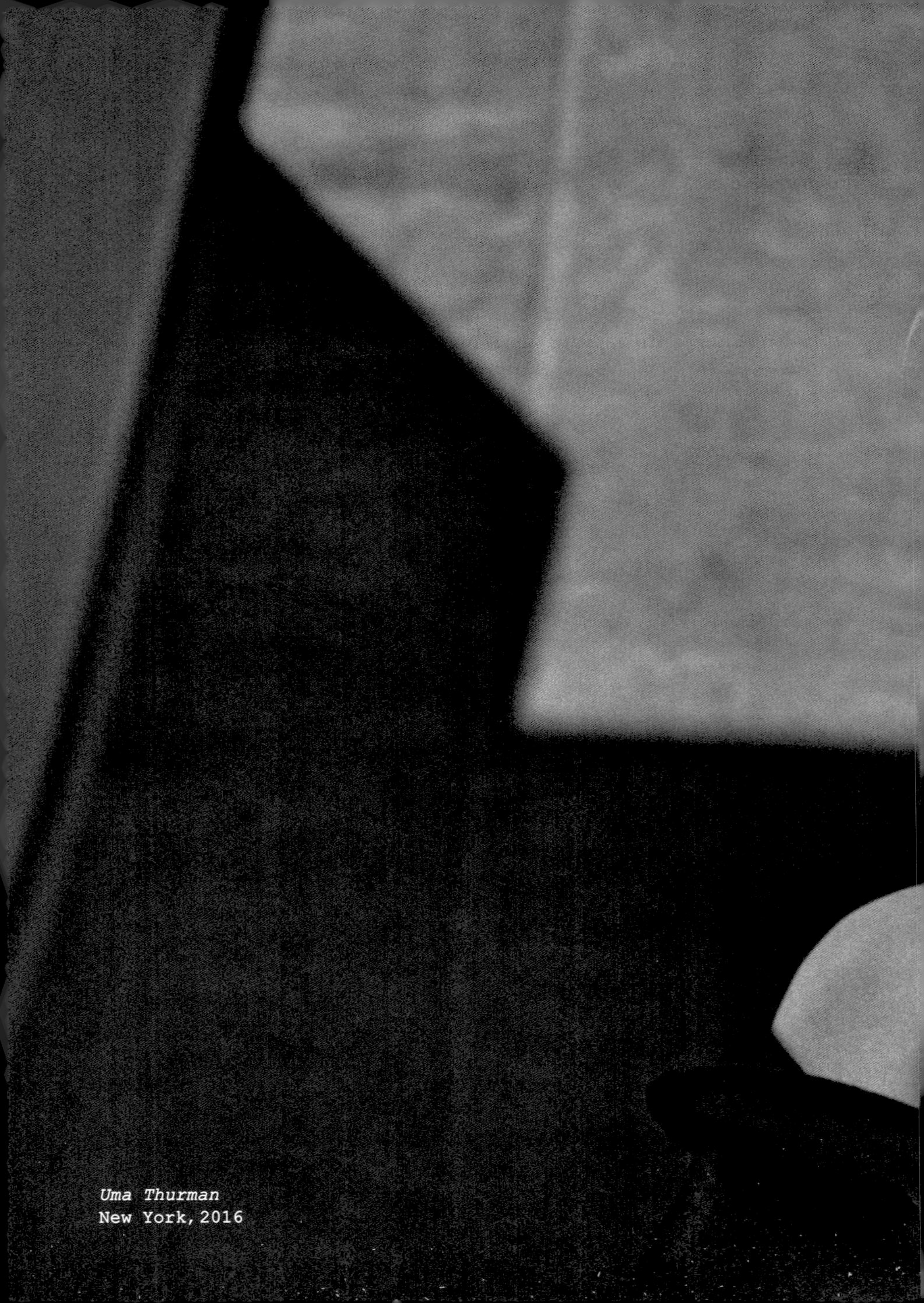

Uma Thurman
New York, 2016

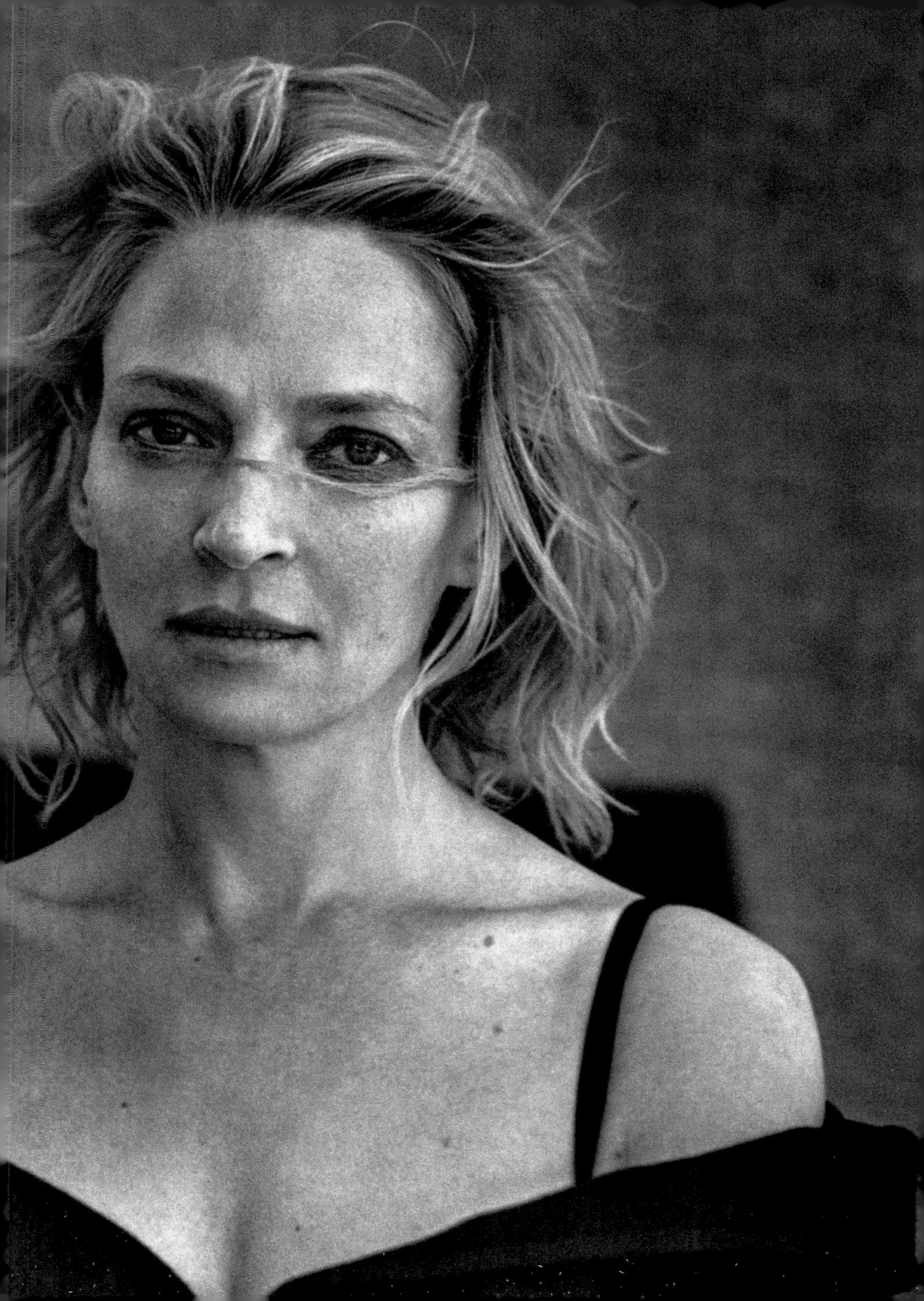

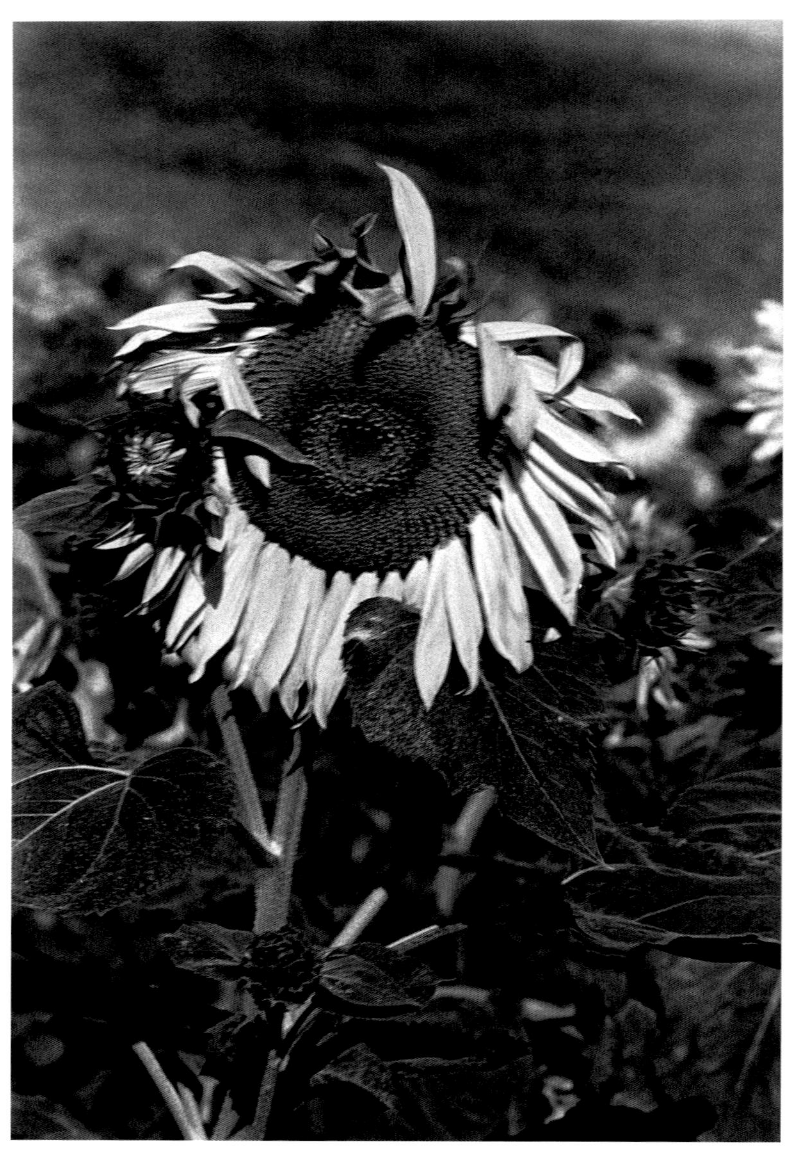

La Quinta
Sevilla, 1990

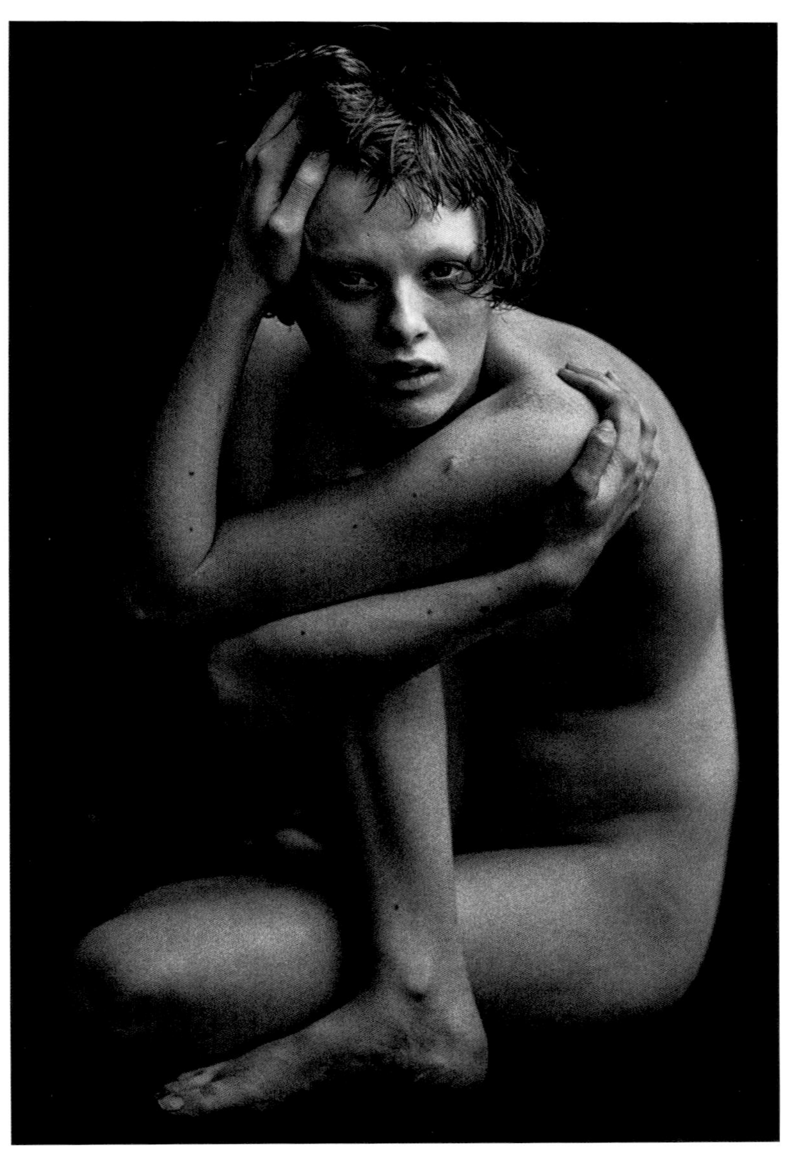

Karen Elson
Los Angeles, 1997

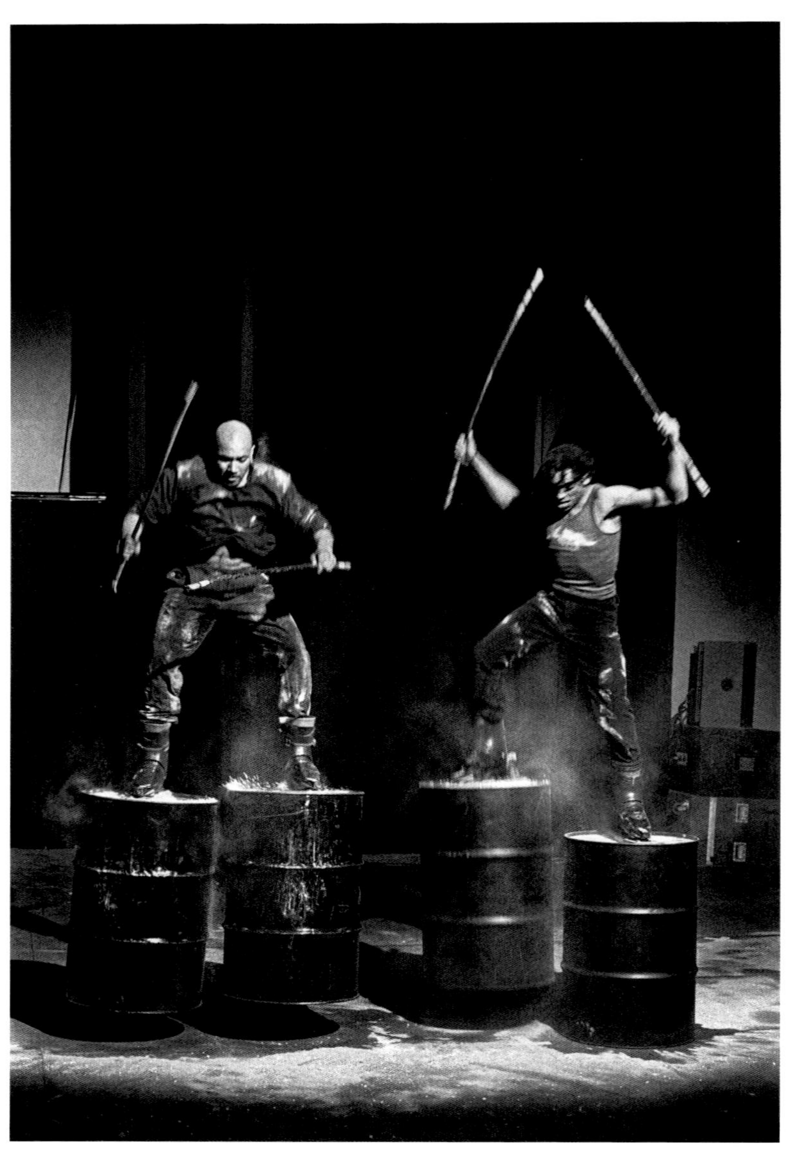

Stomp
Bologna, 1997

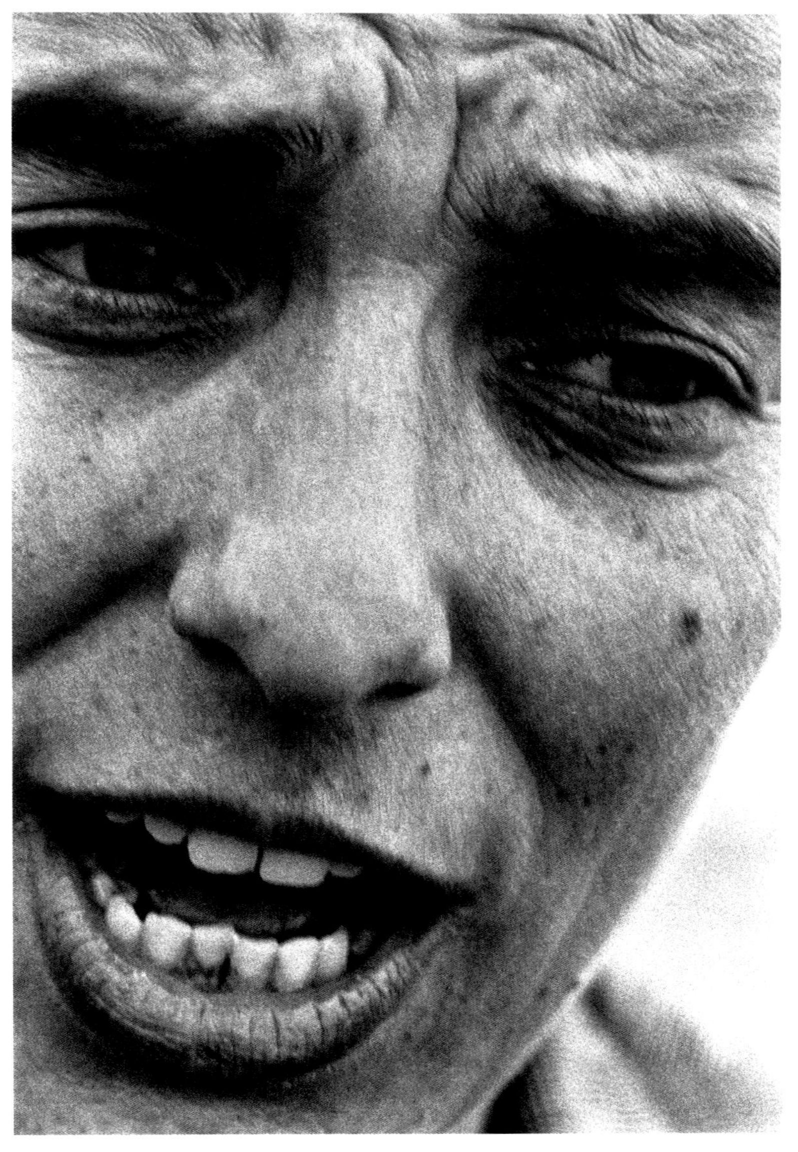

La Caita
Beauduc, 1994

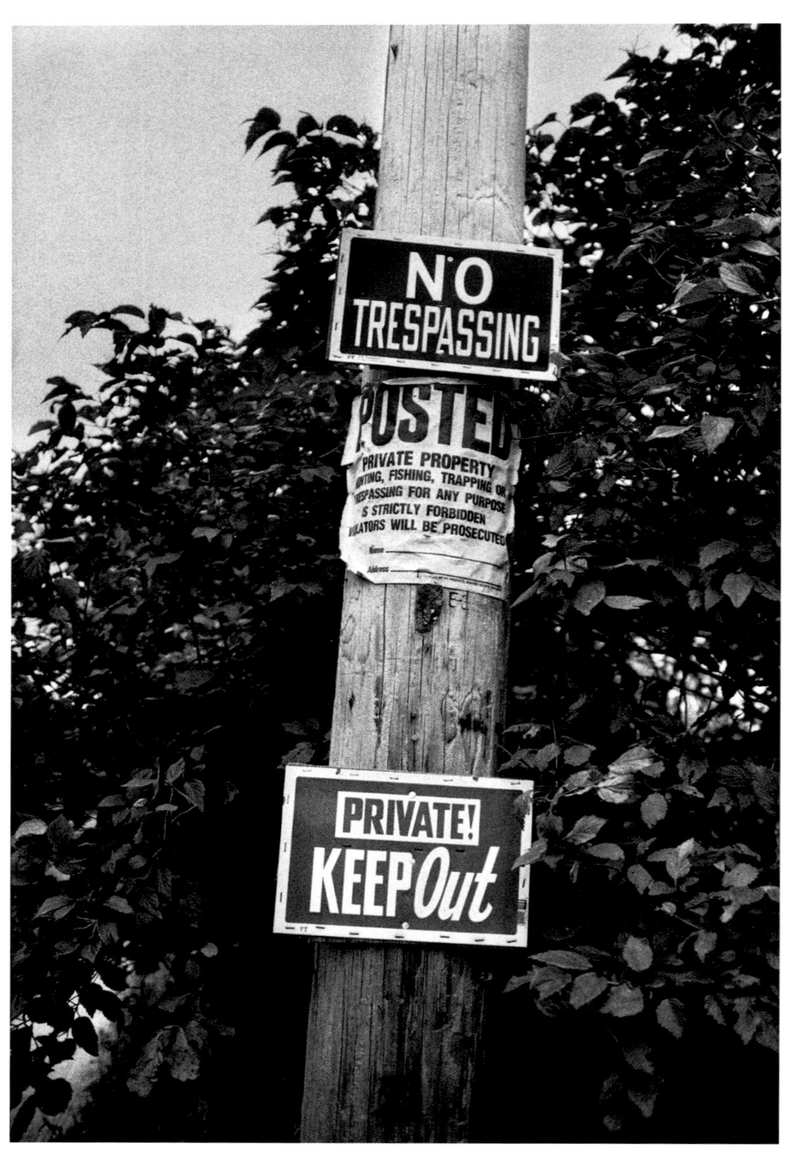

Montauk, 1997

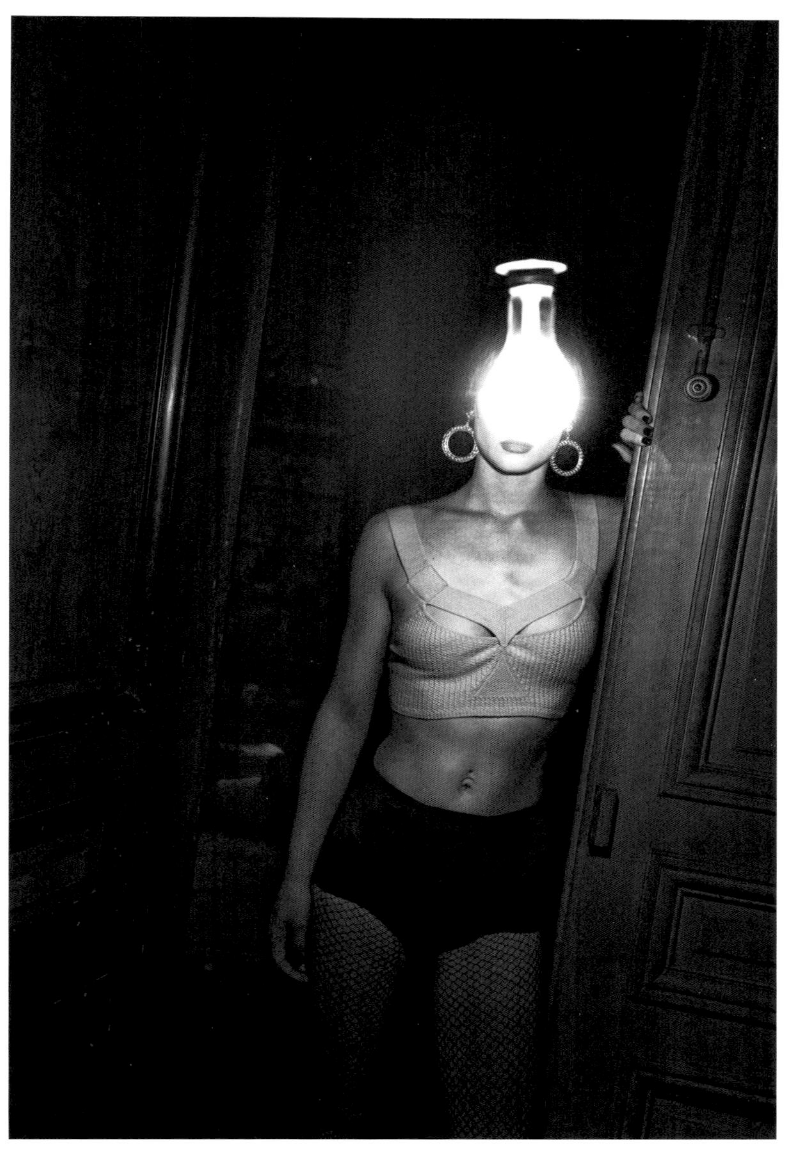

Querelle Jansen
Paris,2012

Charlotte Rampling
London, 2016

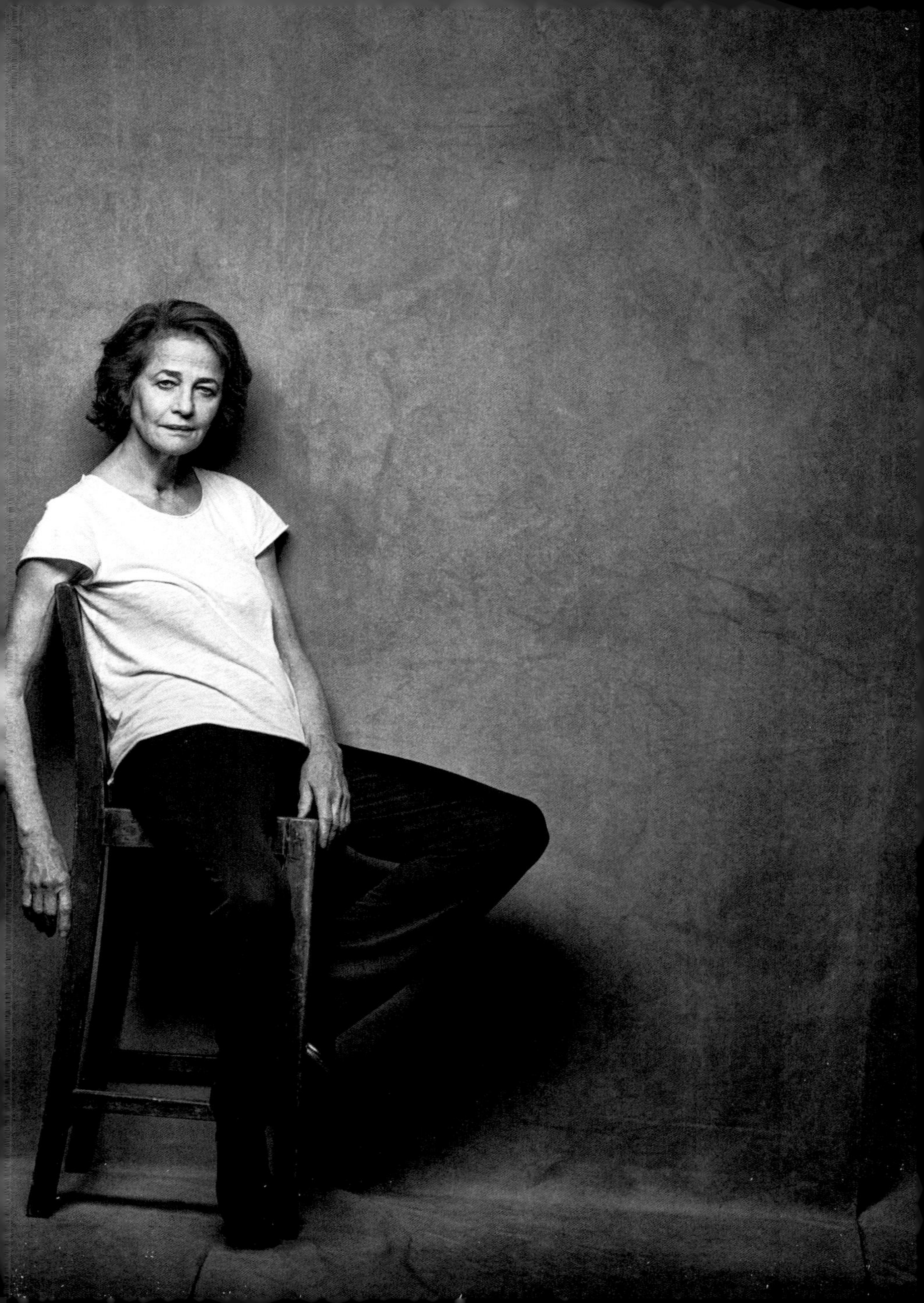

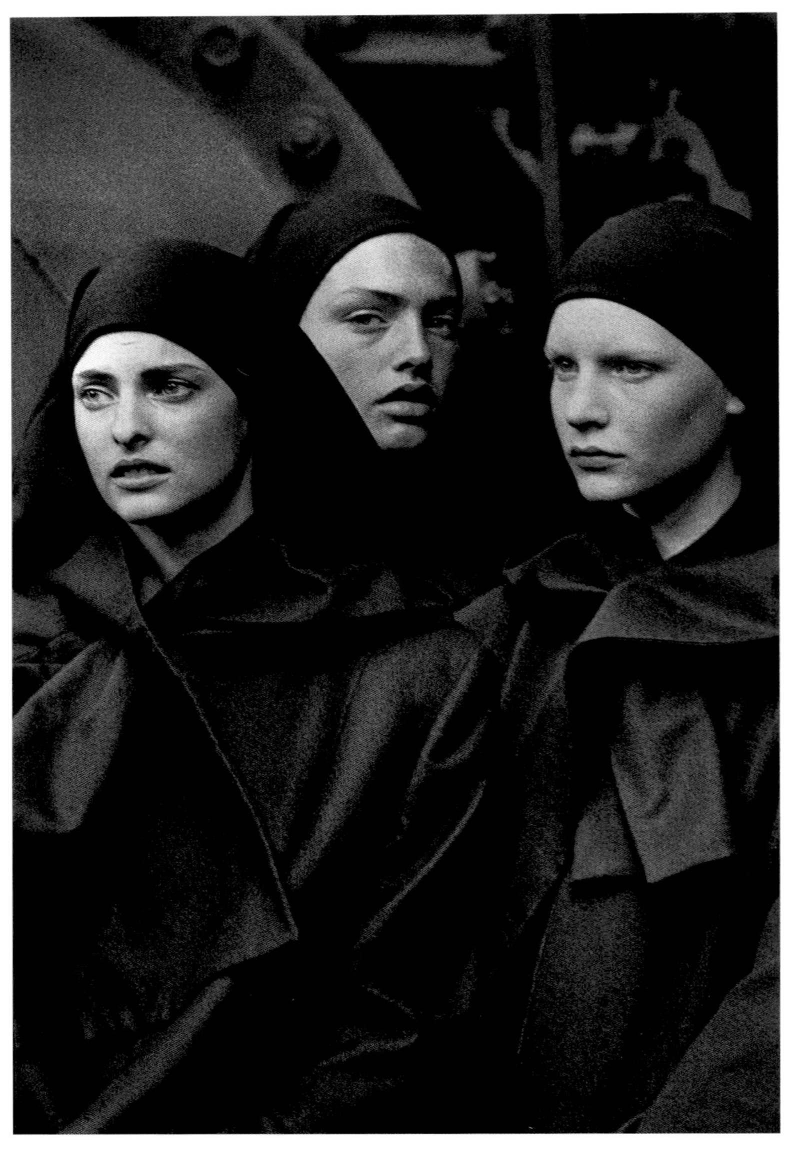

Linda Evangelista, Michaela Bercu & Kirsten Owen
Pont-à-Mousson, 1988

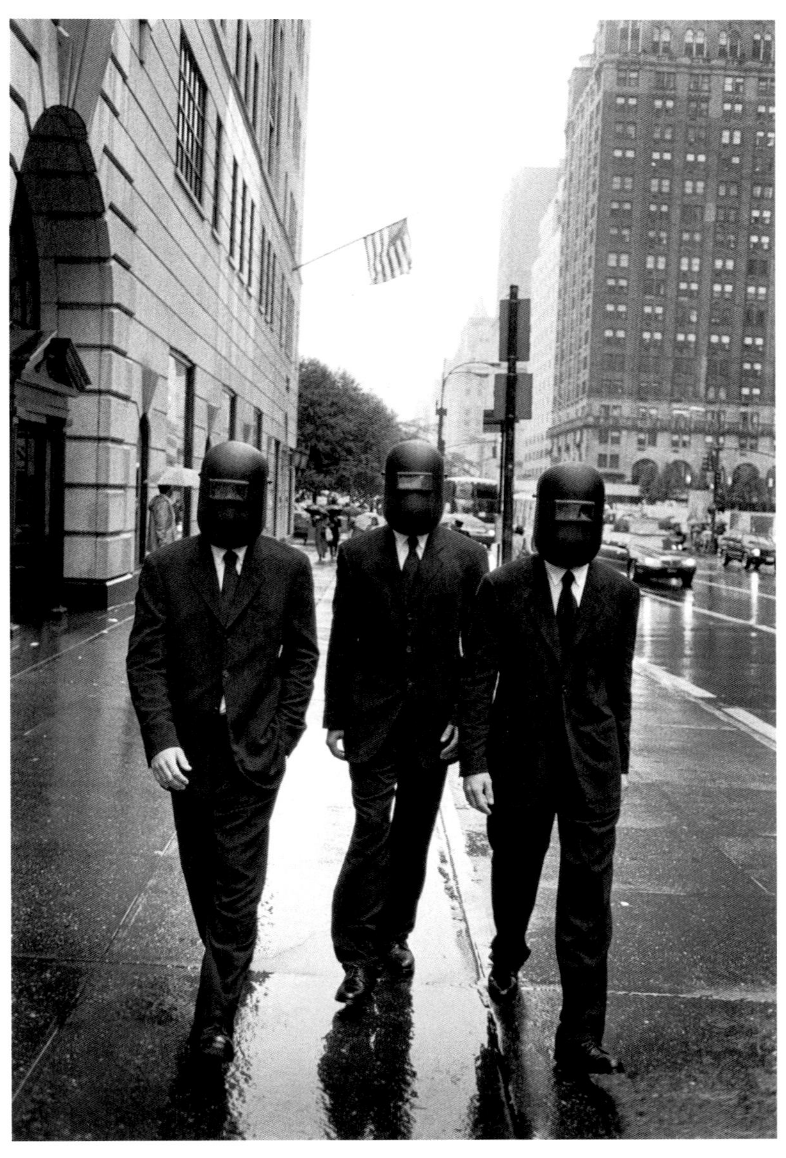

Alex Lundqvist, Norbert Michalke & Mark Vanderloo
New York, 2000

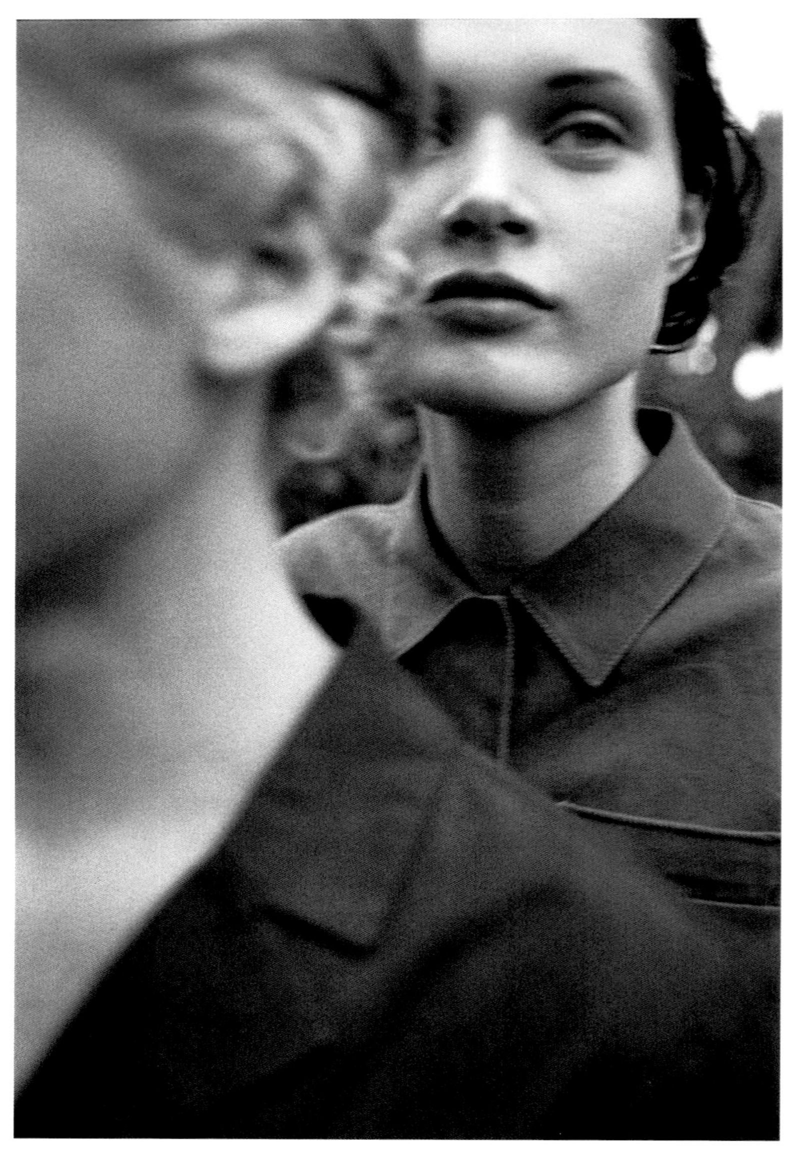

Jenny Knight & Malgosia Bela
Cap d'Antibes,1998

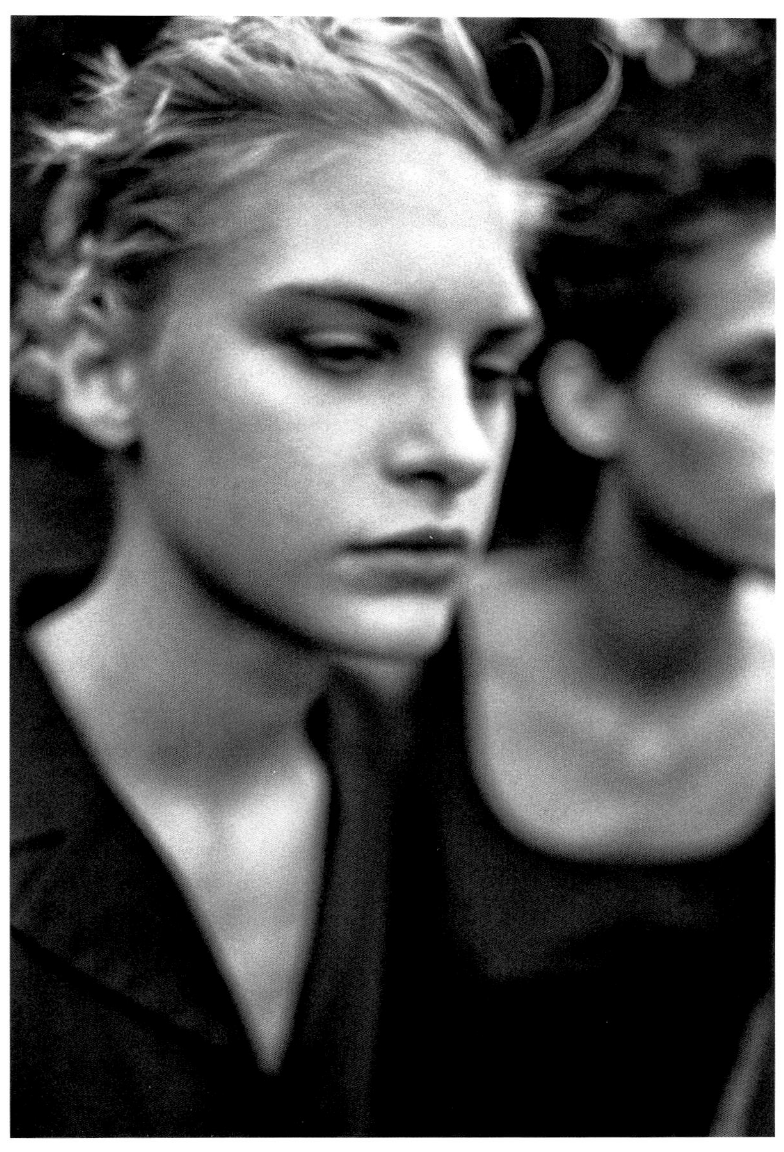

Jenny Knight & Nancy Hagen
Cap d'Antibes, 1998

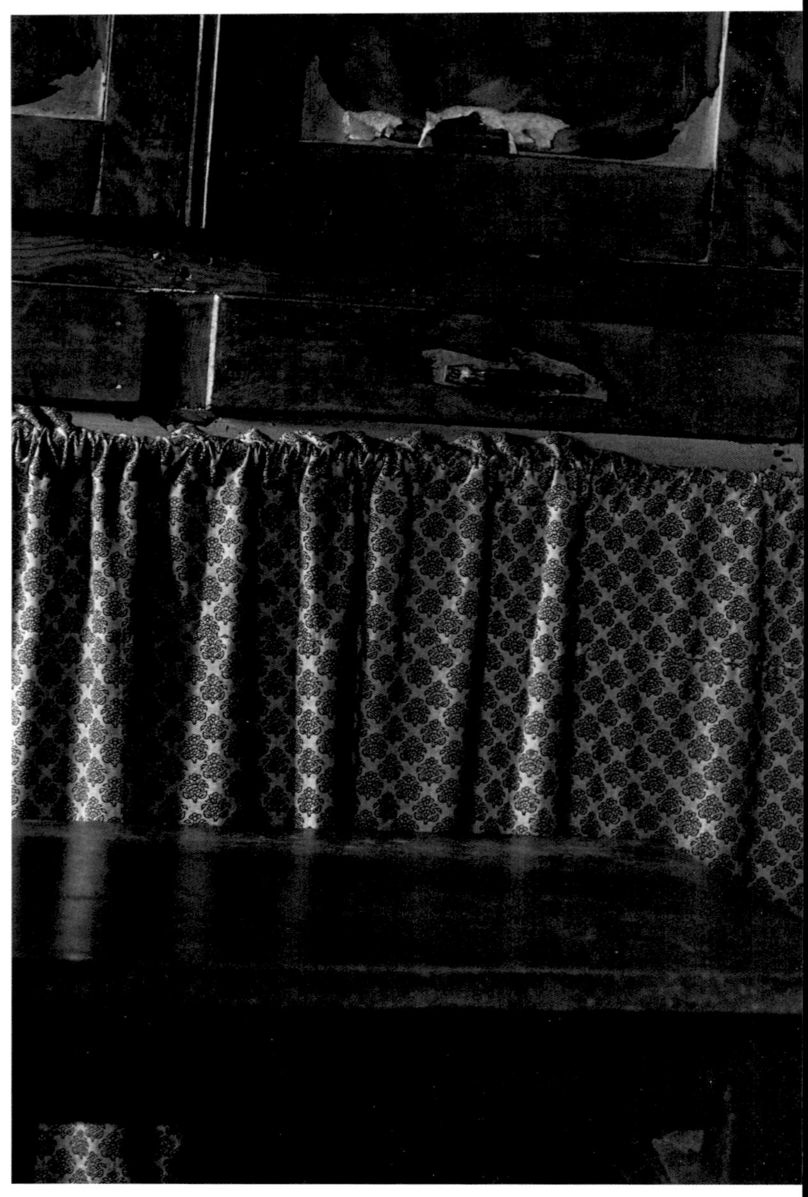

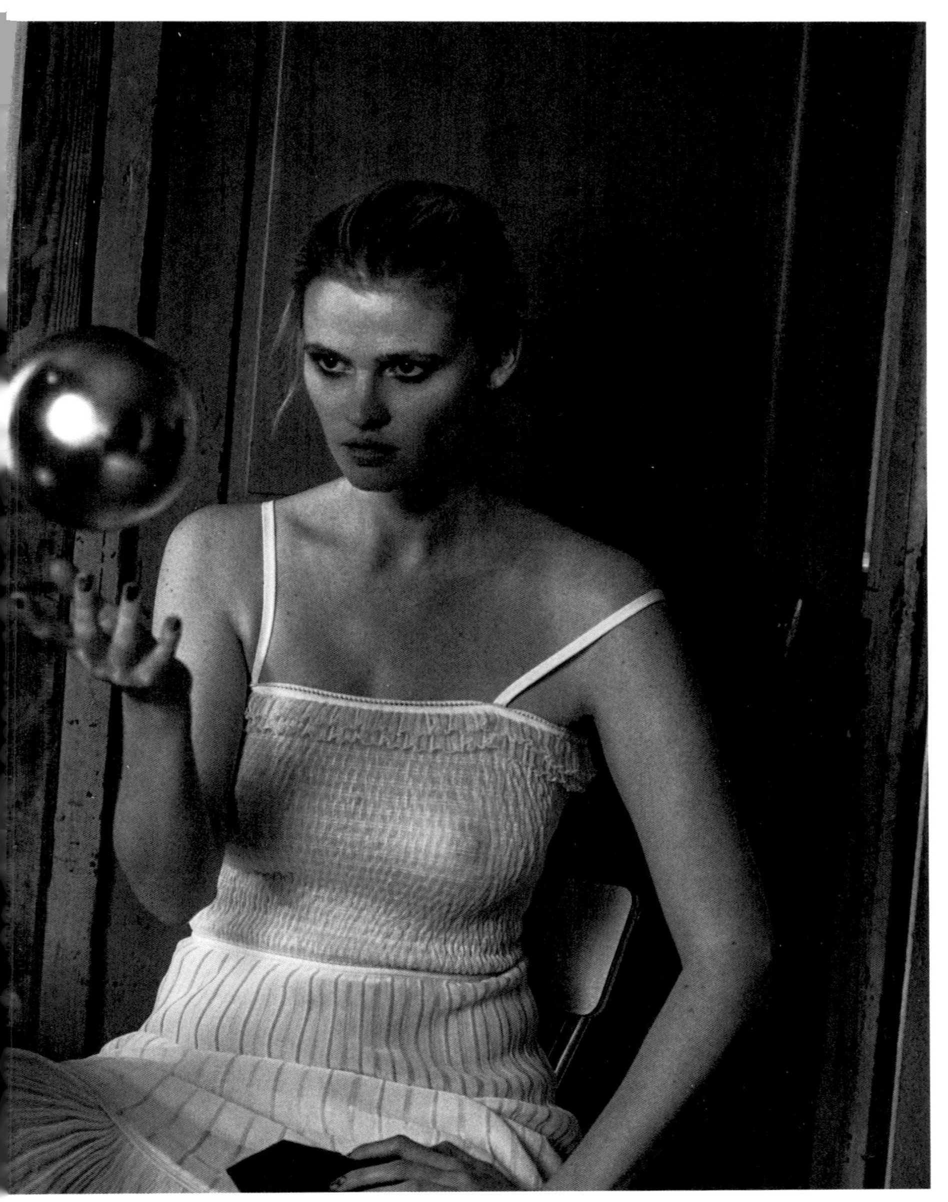

Lara Stone
Fontainebleau, 2015

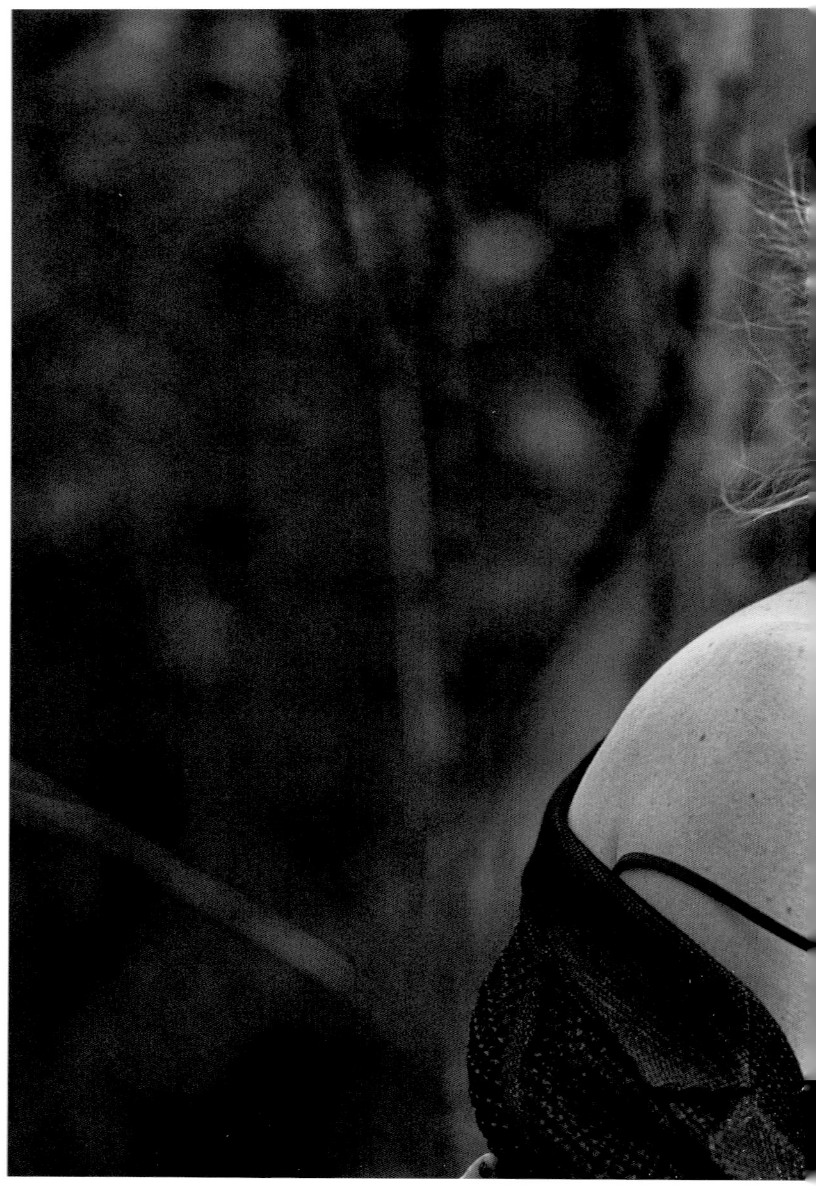

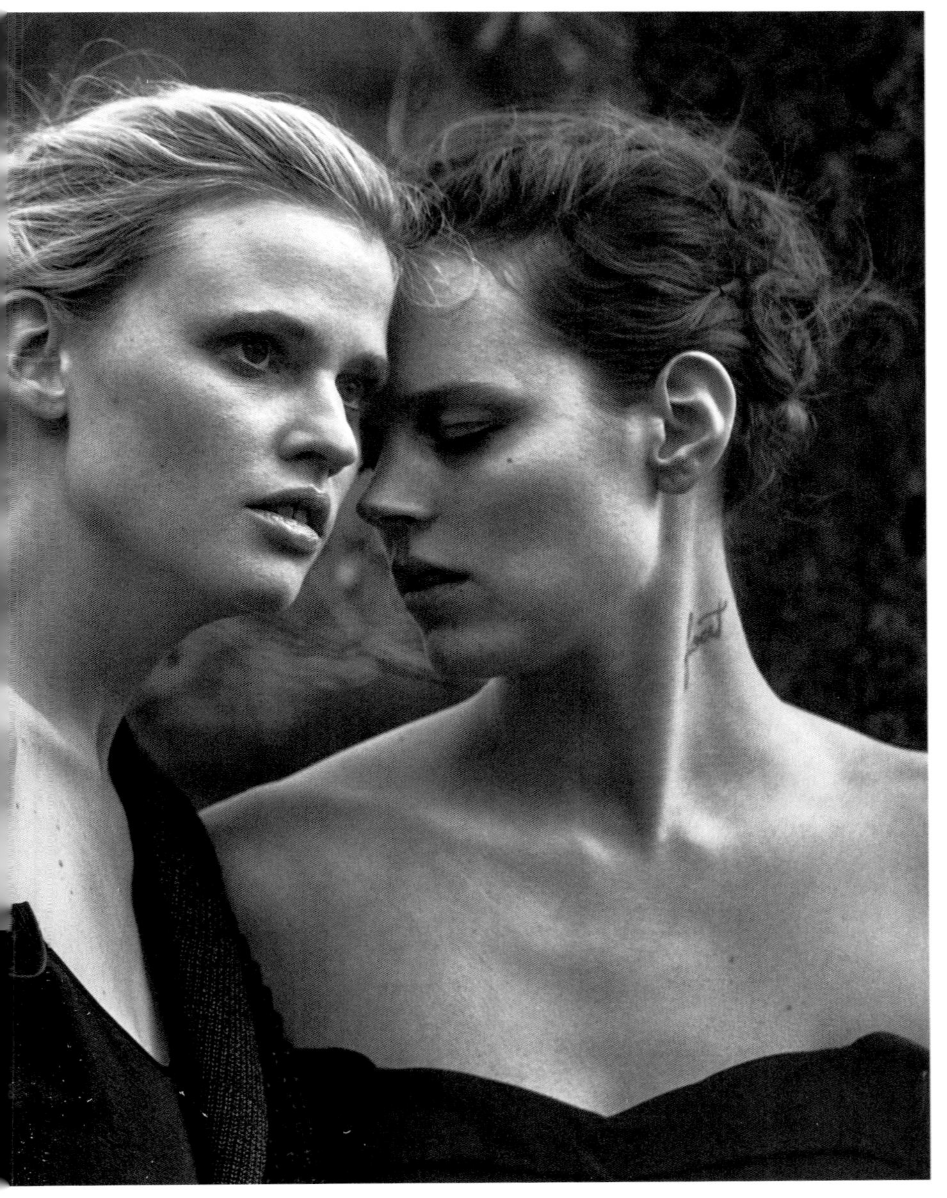

Lara Stone & Freja Beha Erichsen
Fontainebleau, 2015

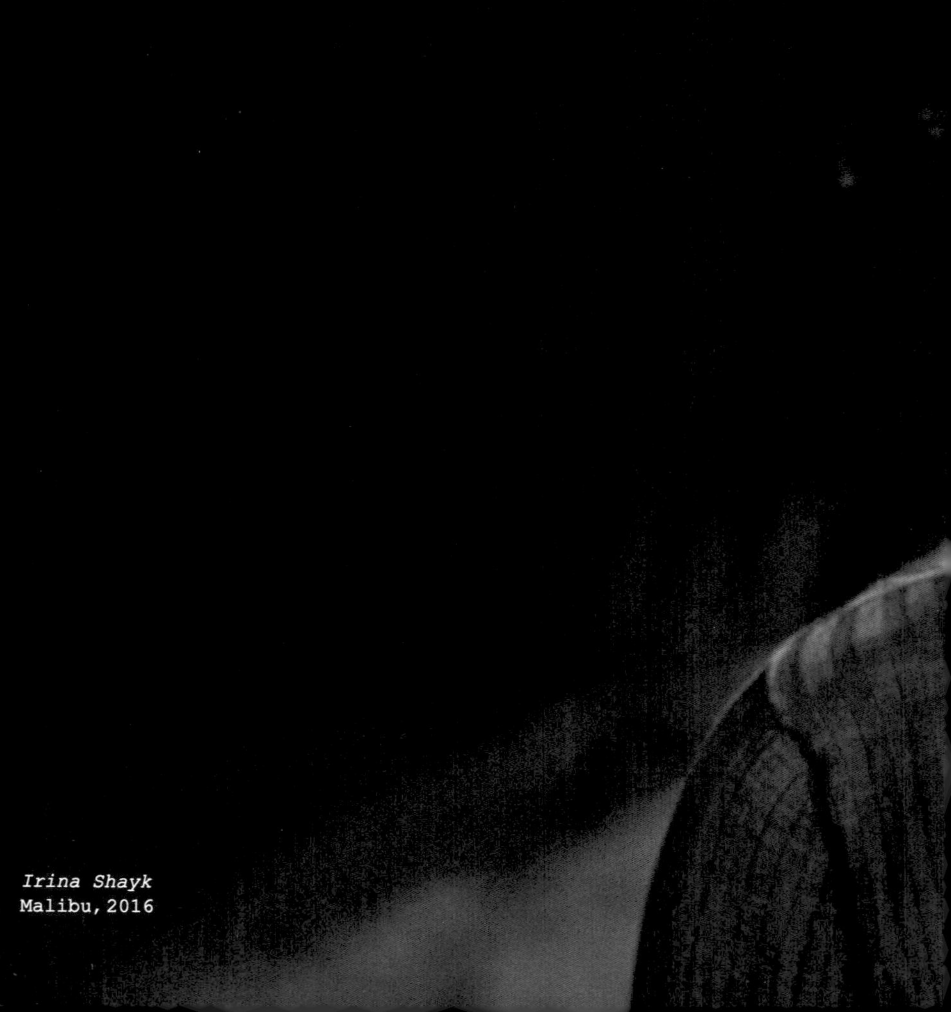

Irina Shayk
Malibu, 2016

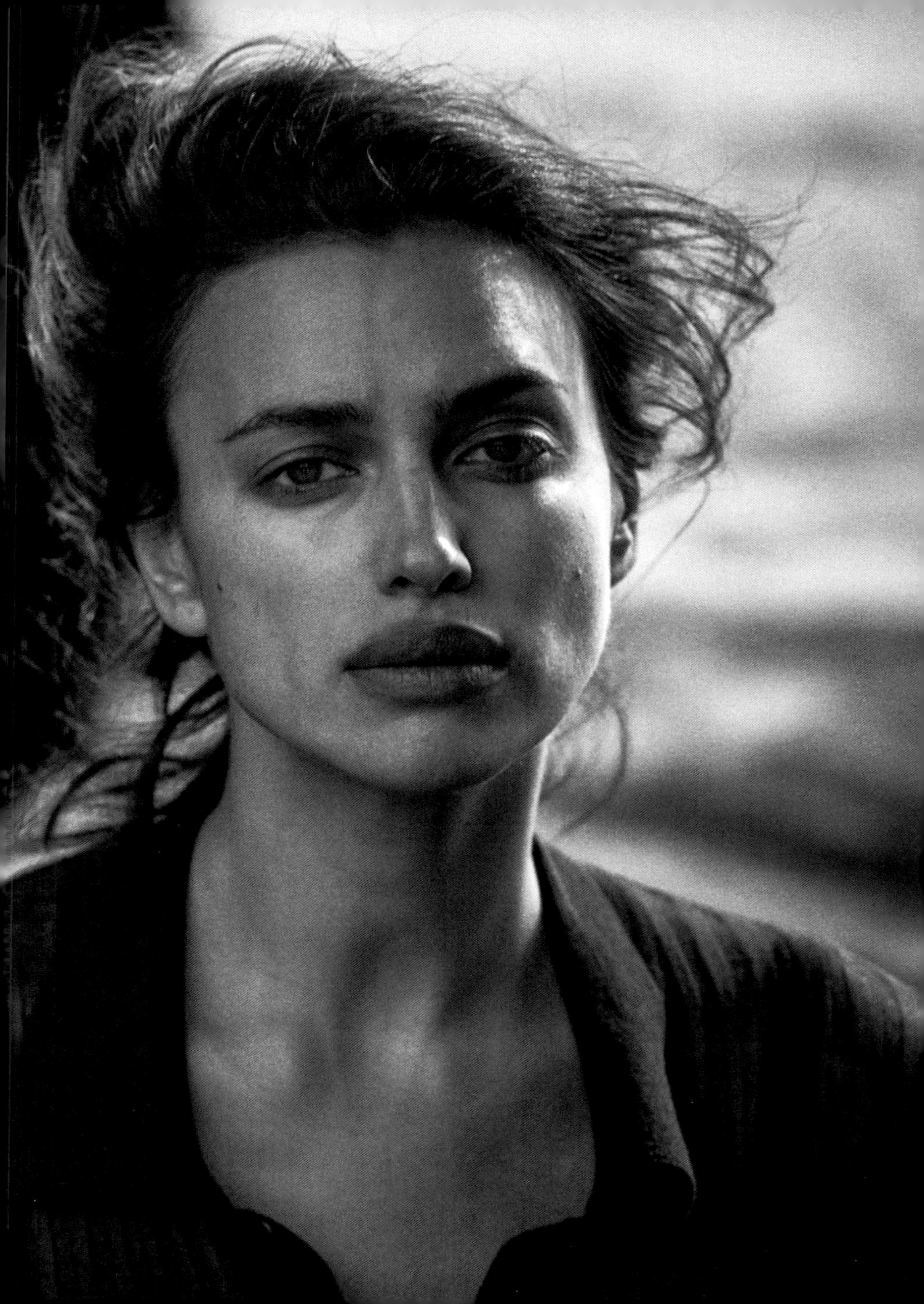

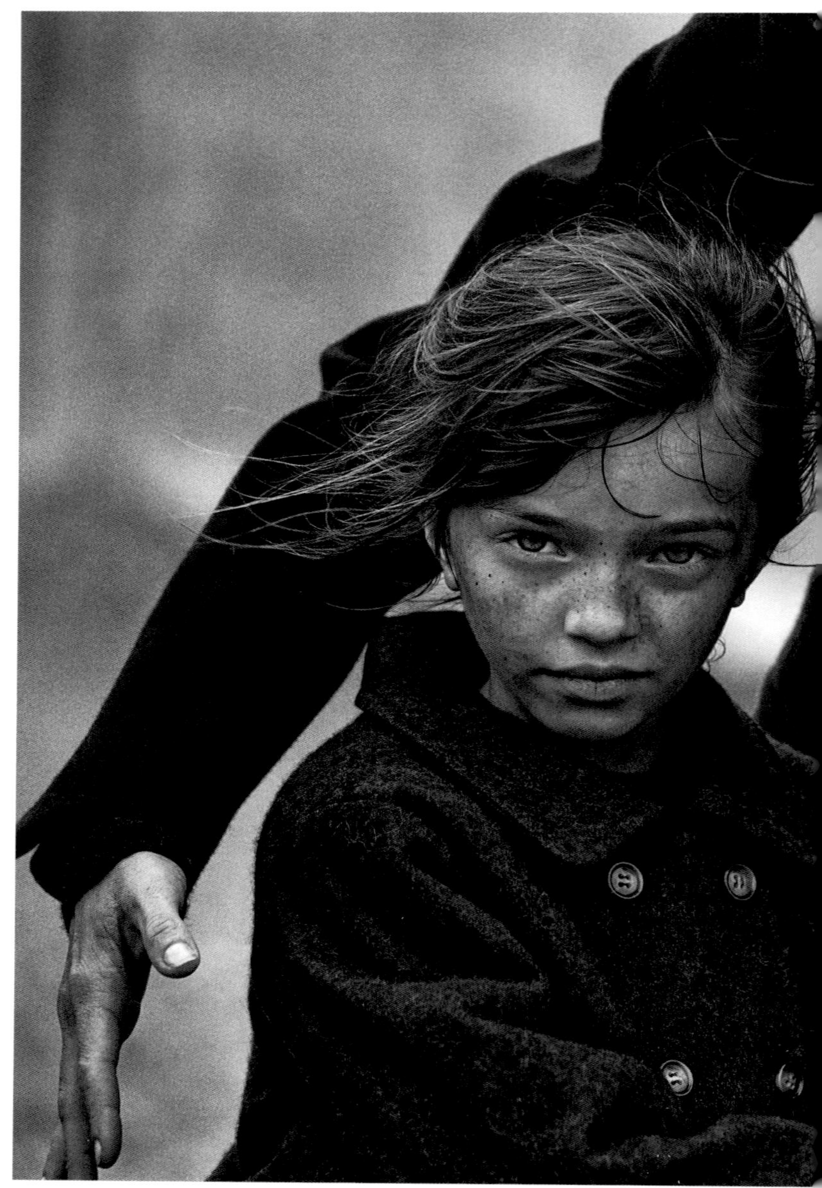

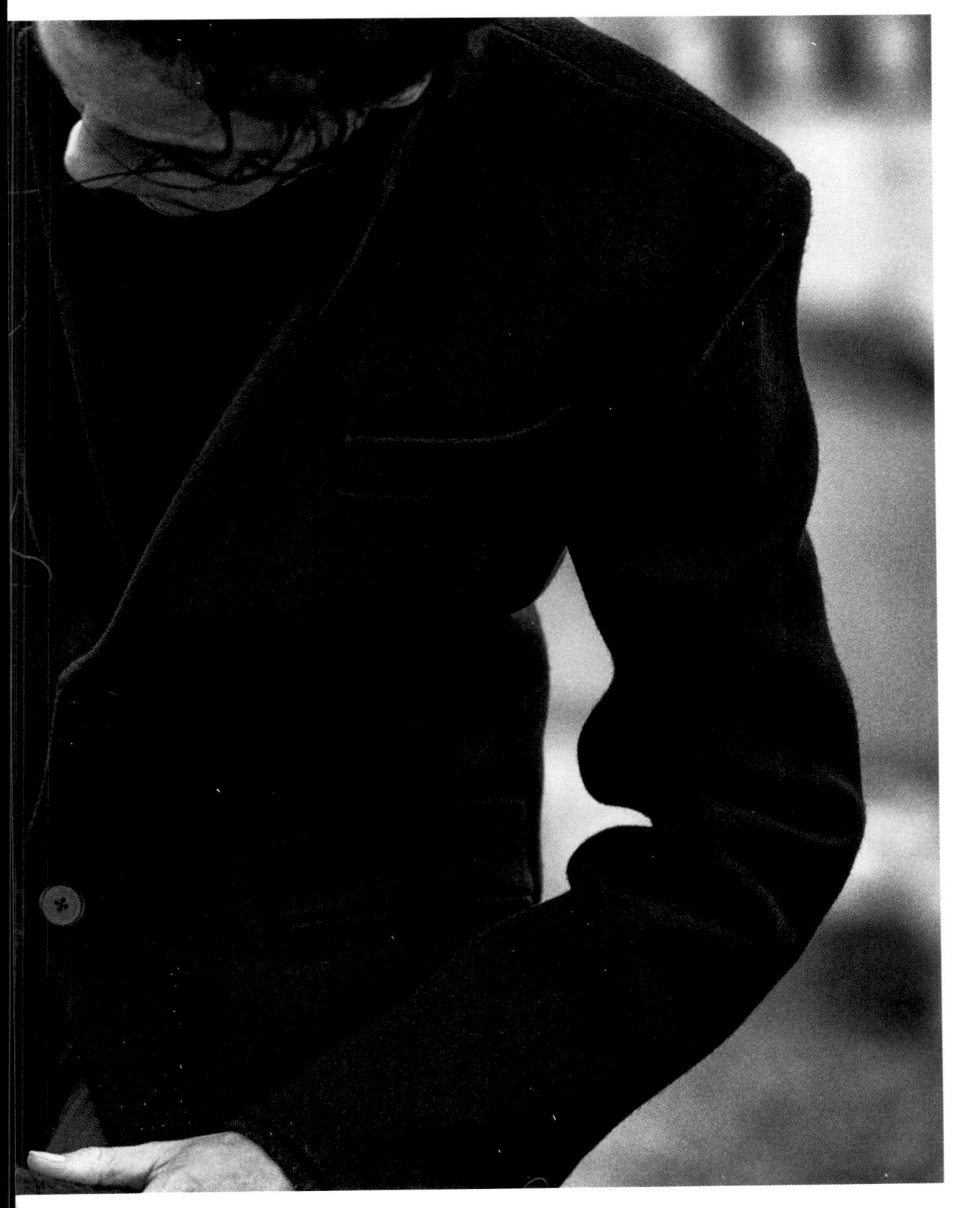

Sharon Cohendy & Mariacarla Boscono
Ault, 2014

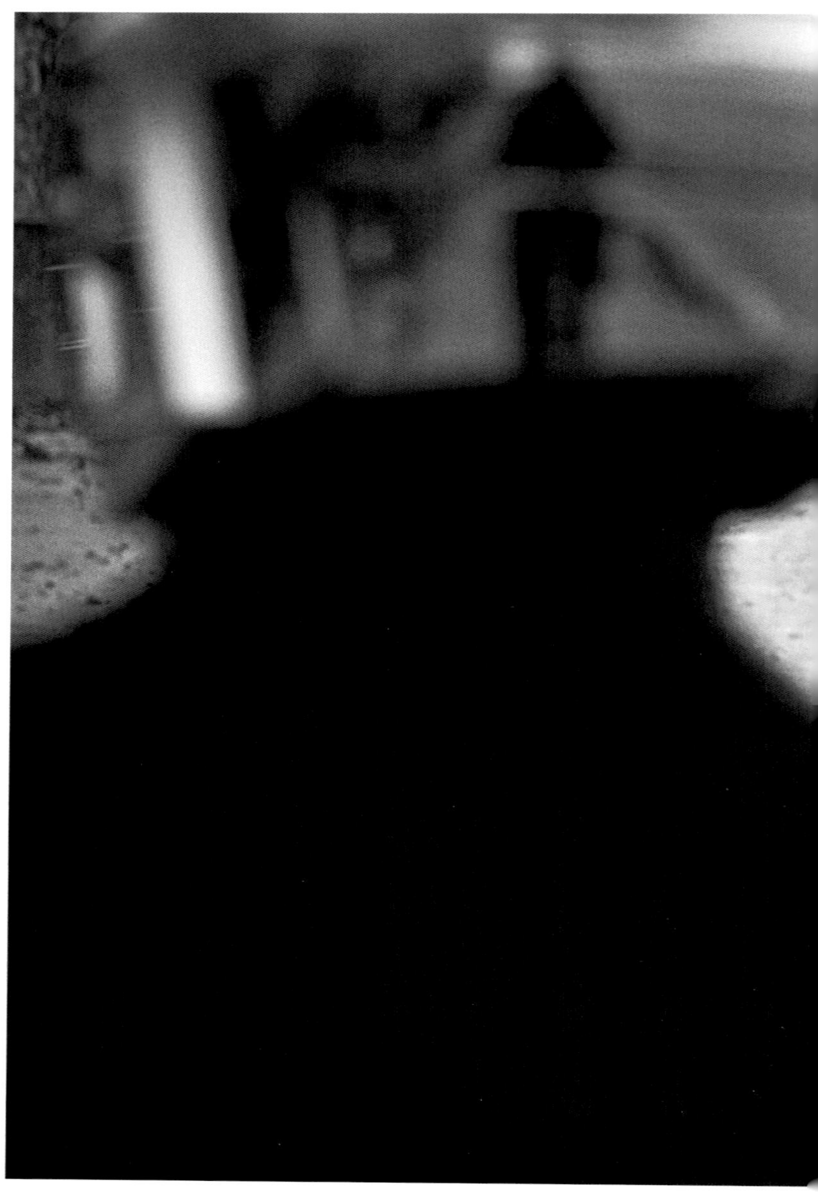

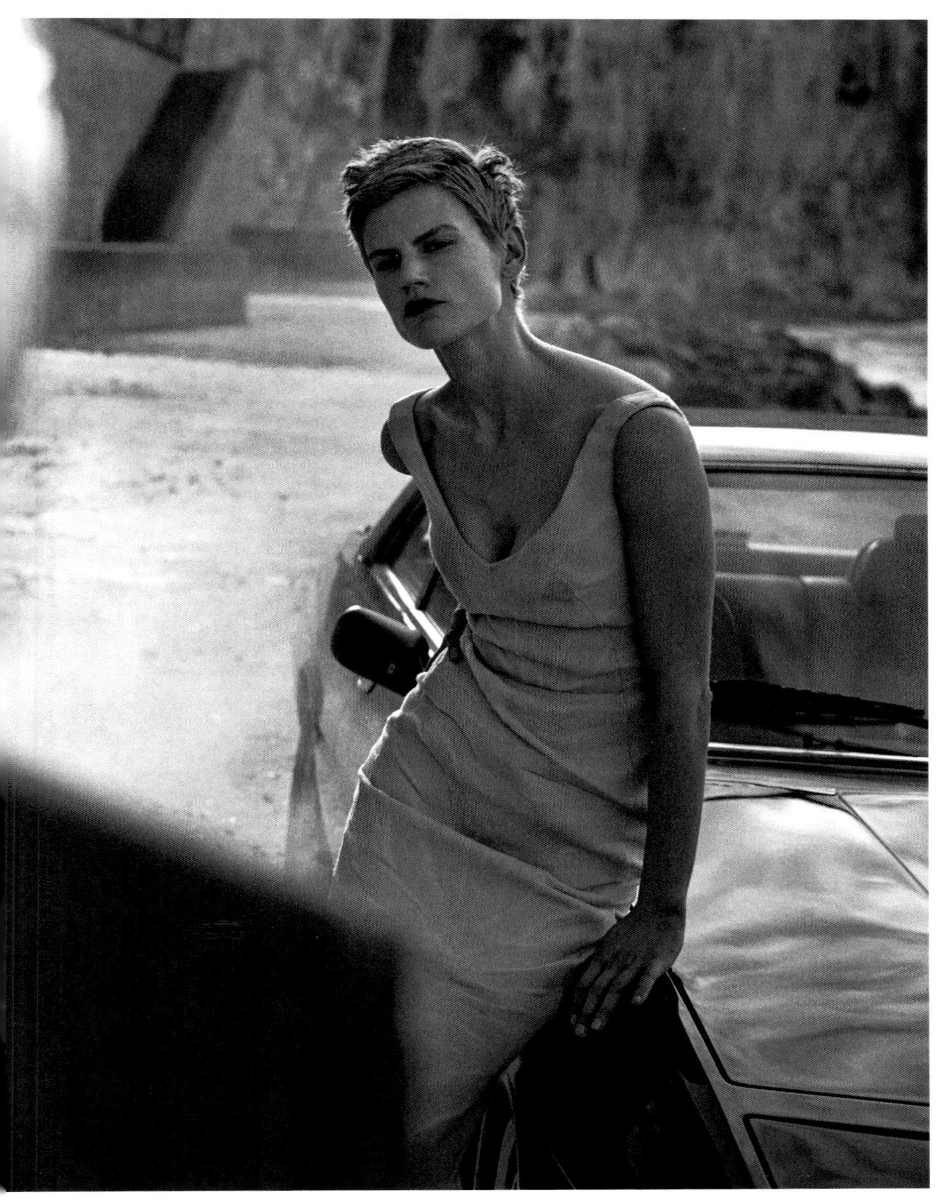

Guy-Manuel de Homem-Christo & Saskia de Brauw
Ault, 2013

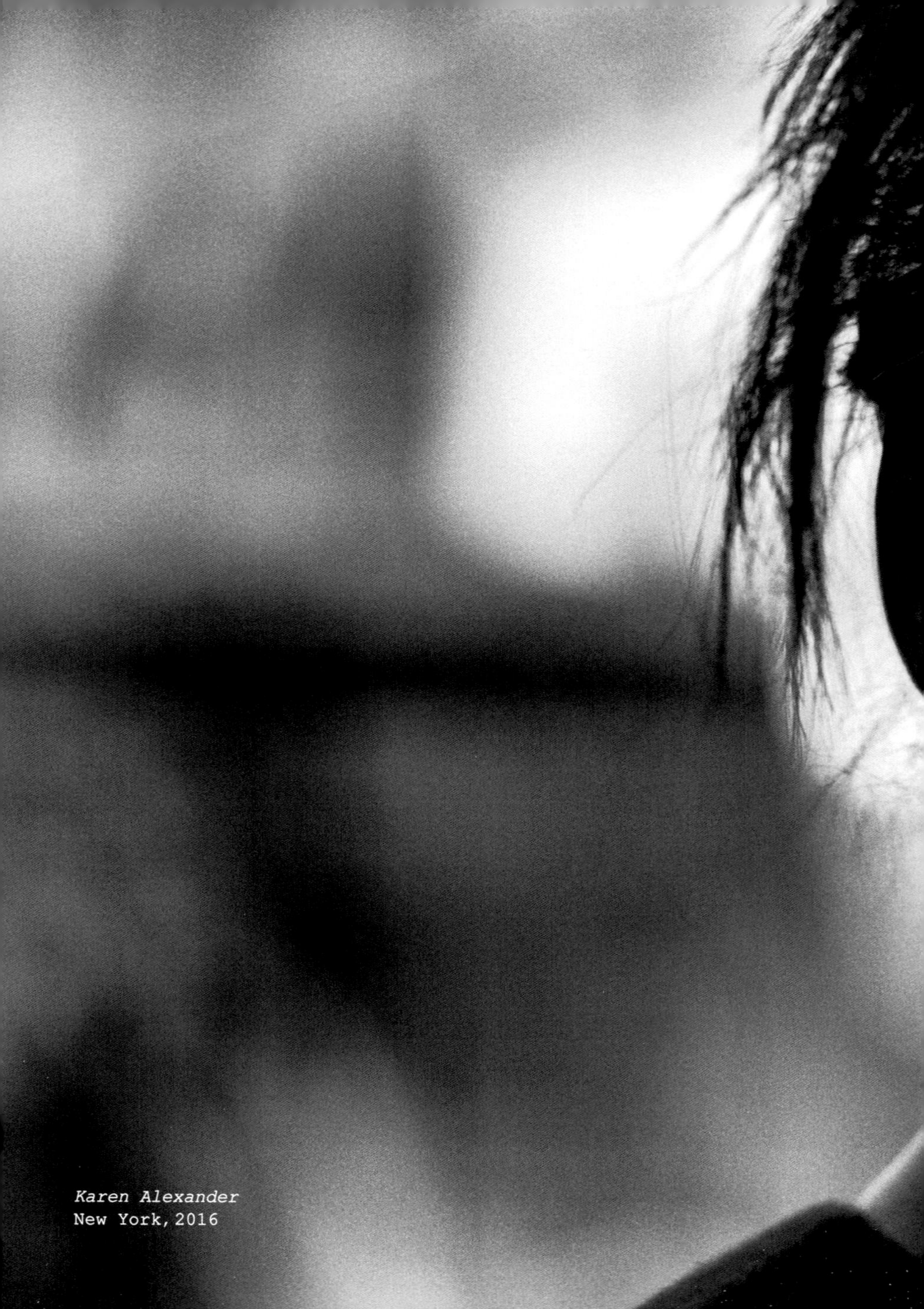
Karen Alexander
New York, 2016

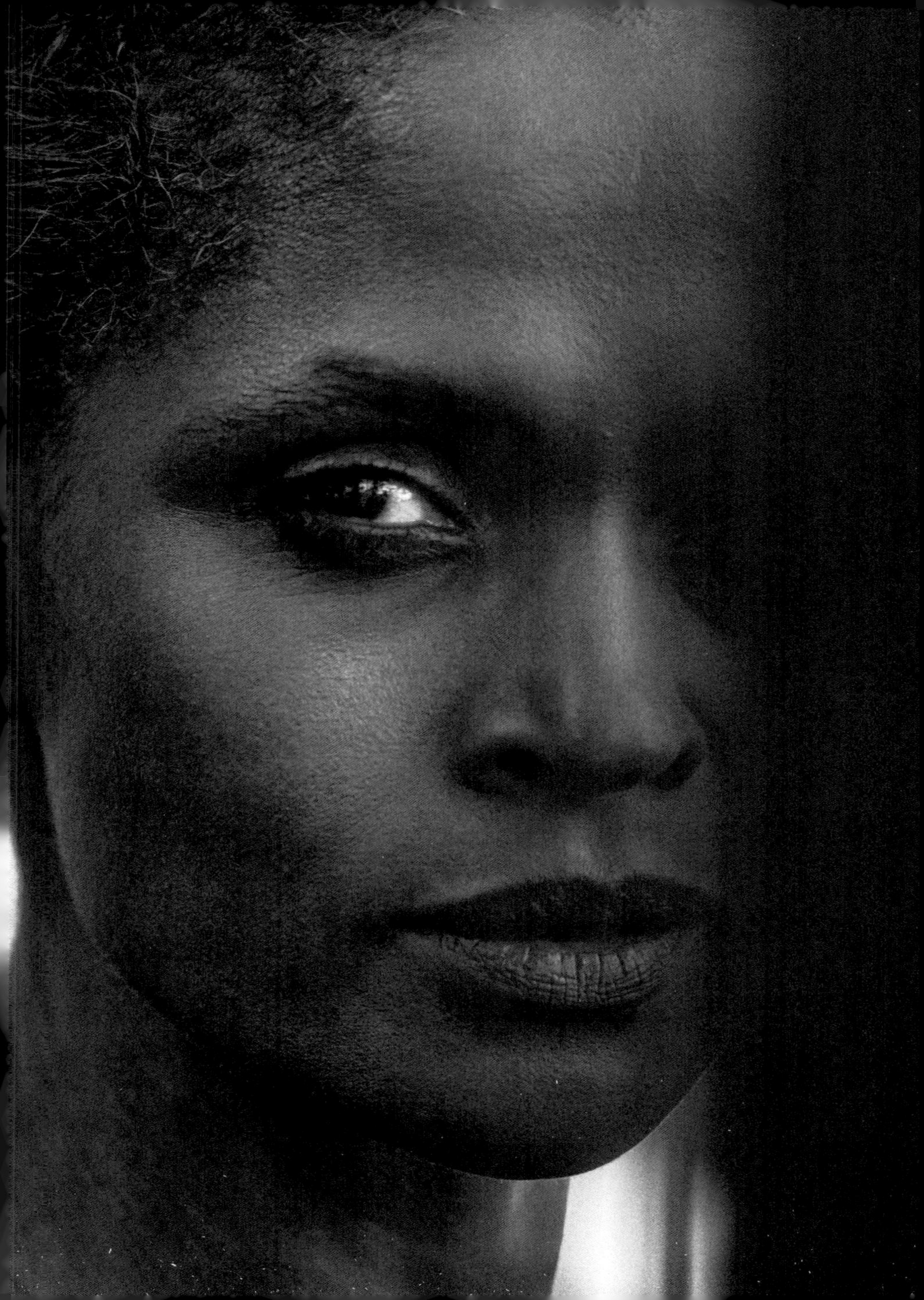

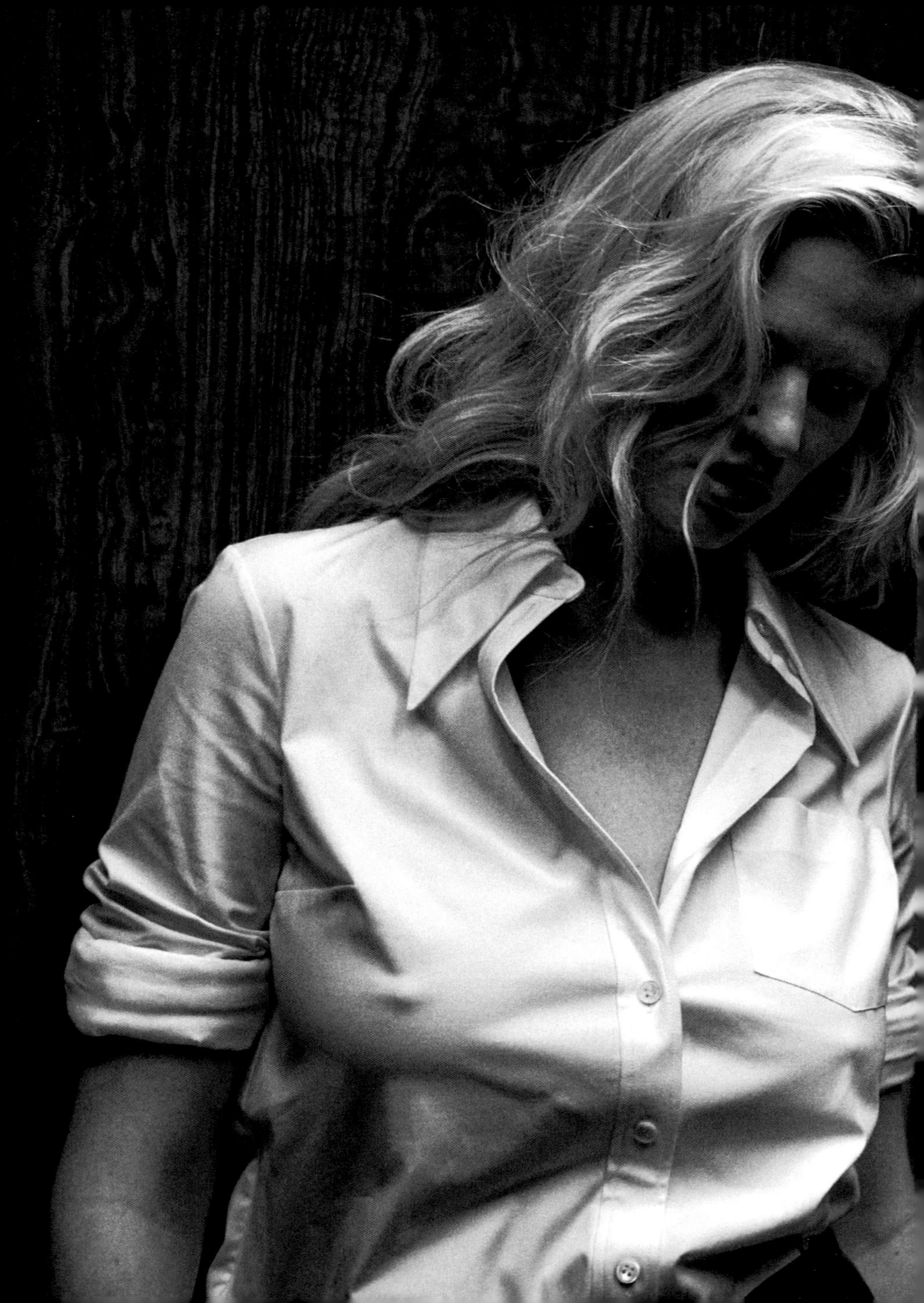

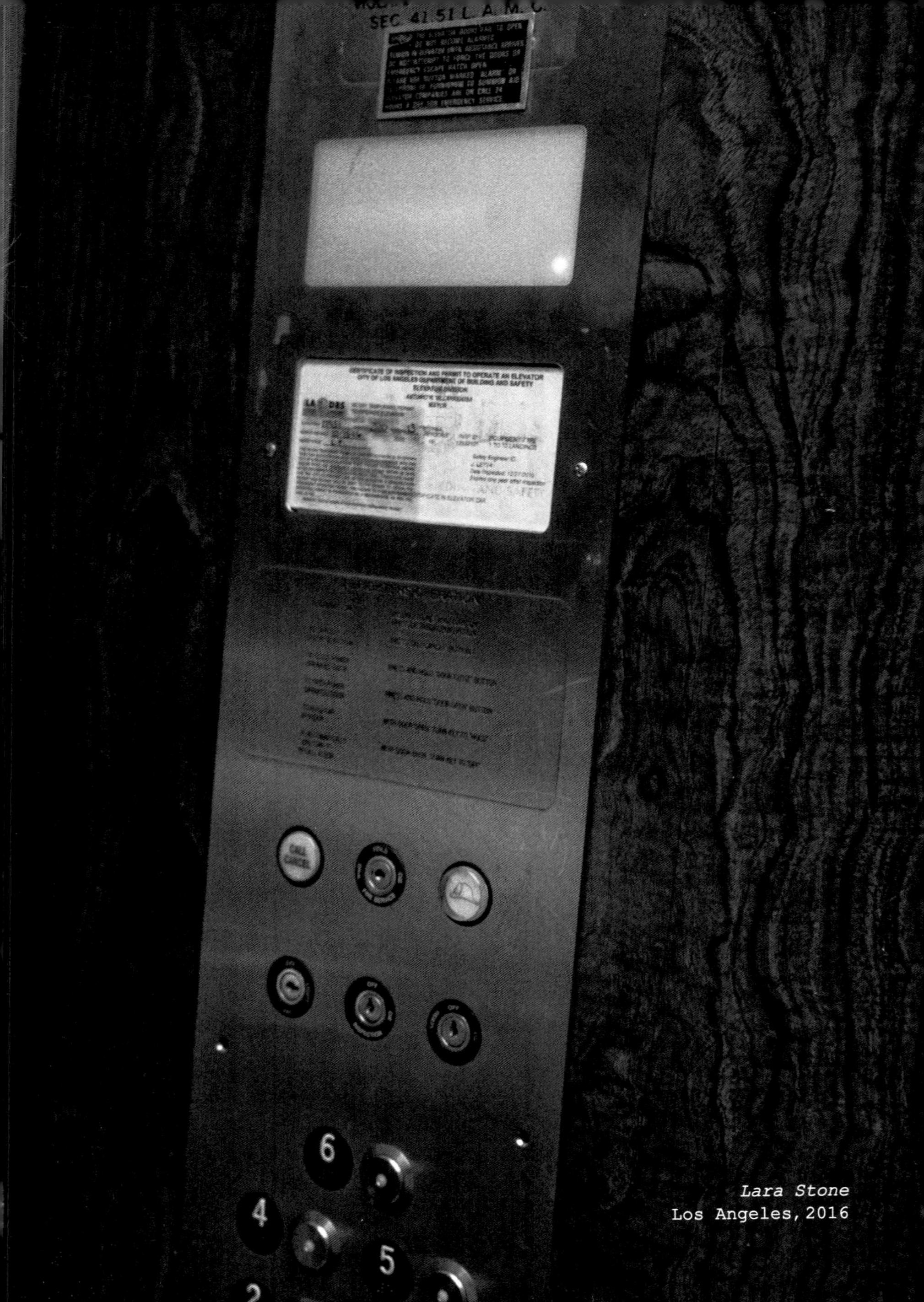

Lara Stone
Los Angeles, 2016

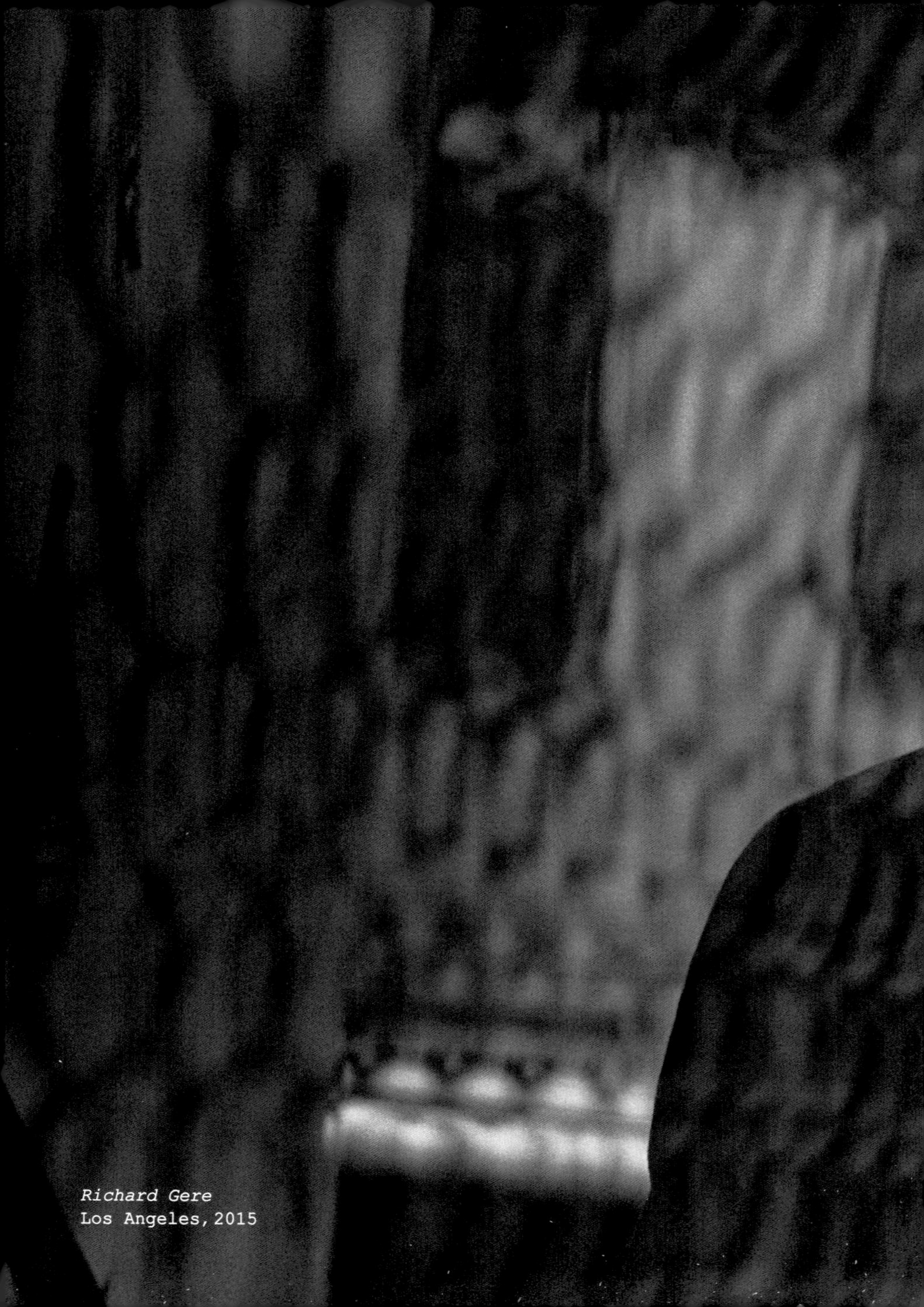

Richard Gere
Los Angeles, 2015

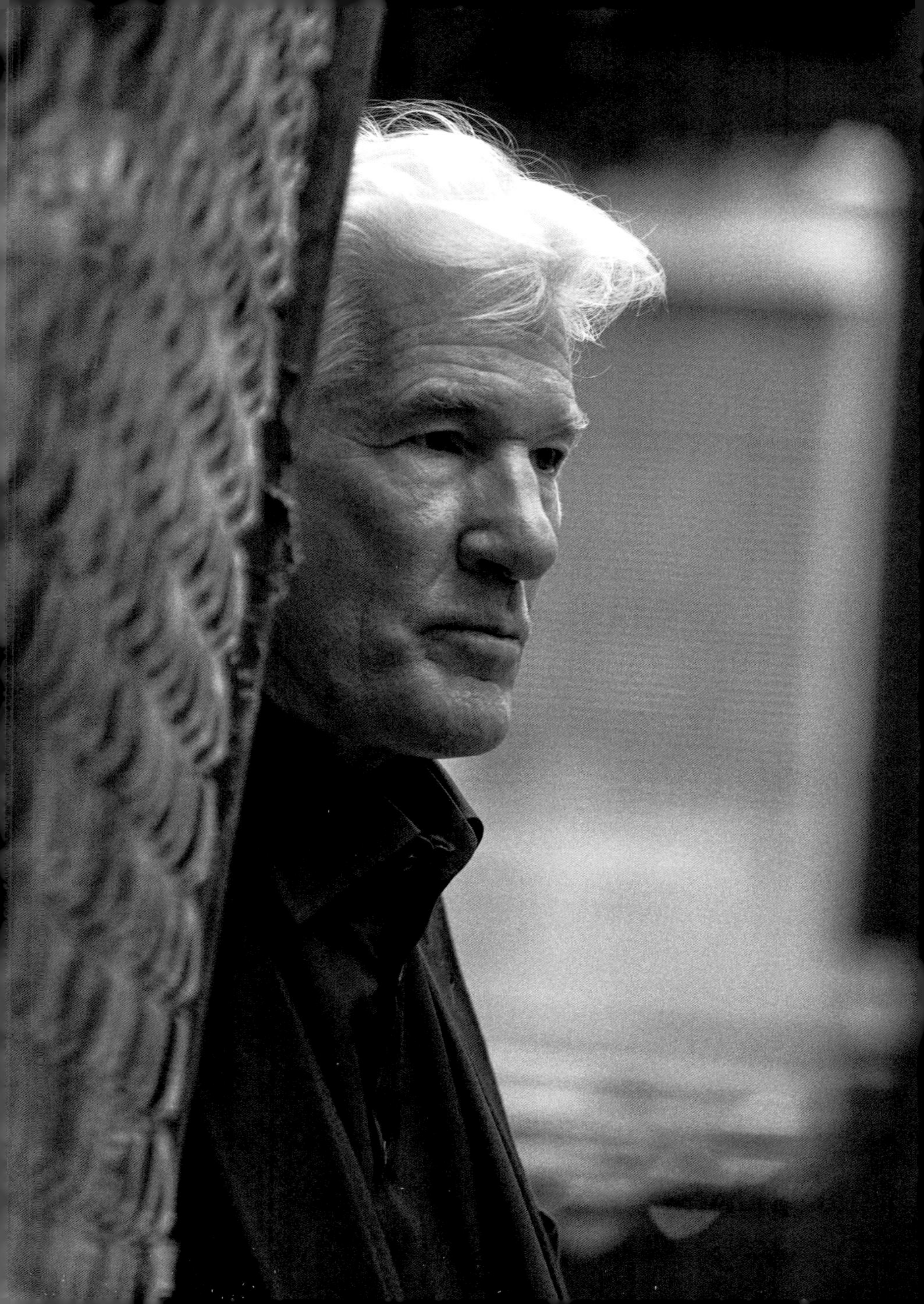

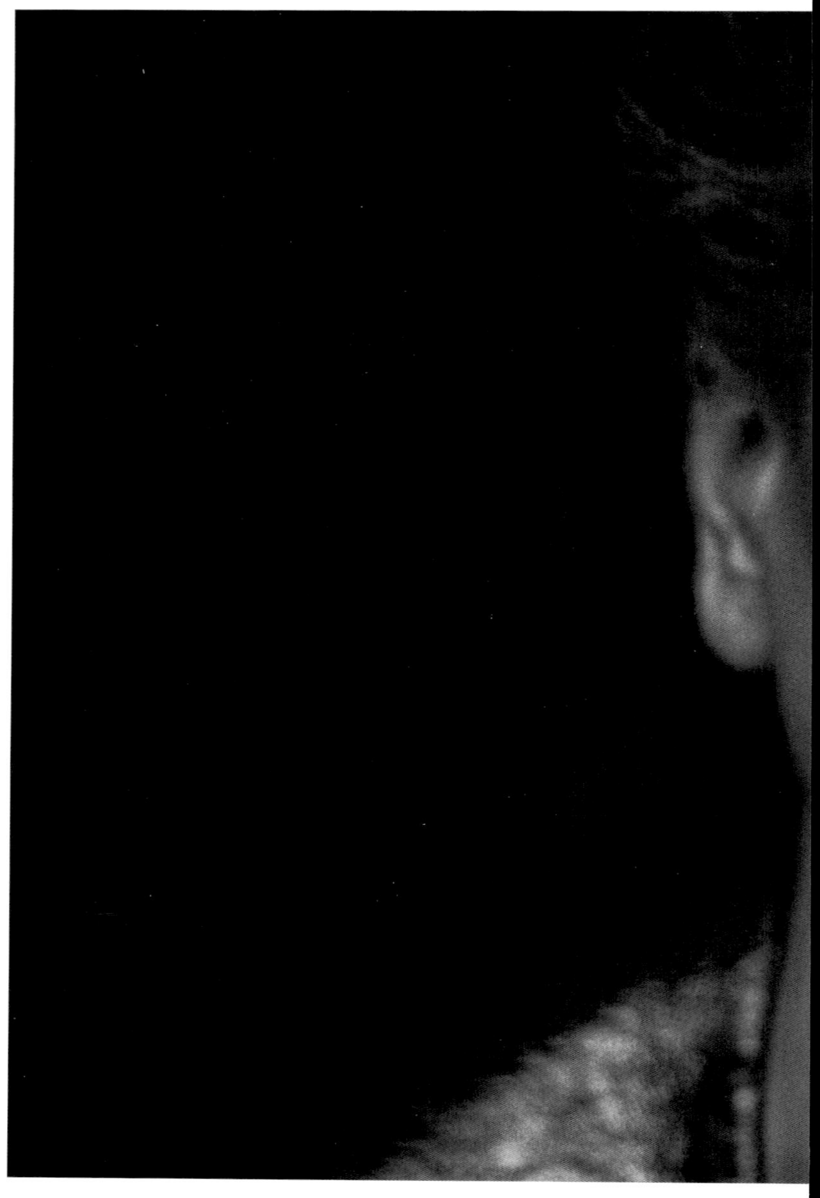

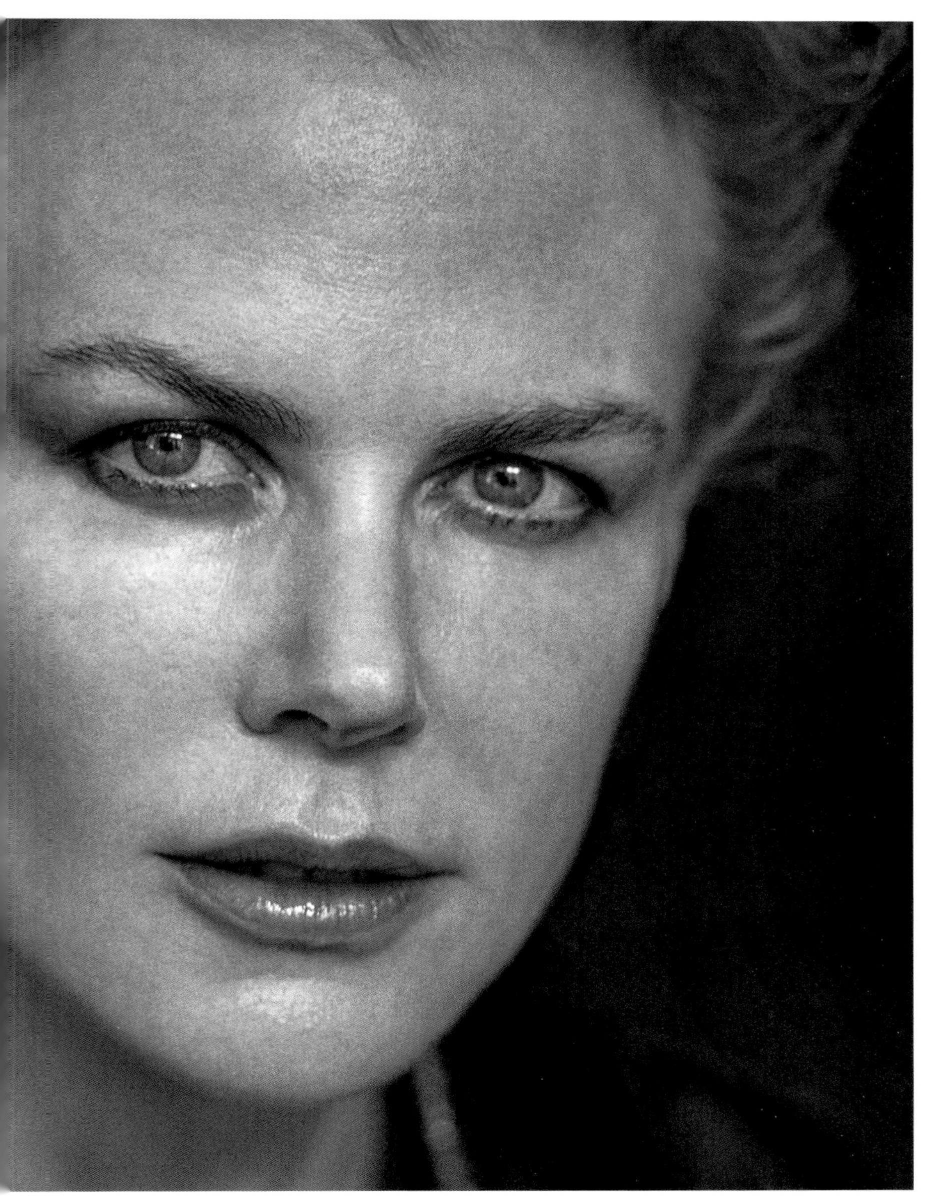

Nicole Kidman
Los Angeles, 2016

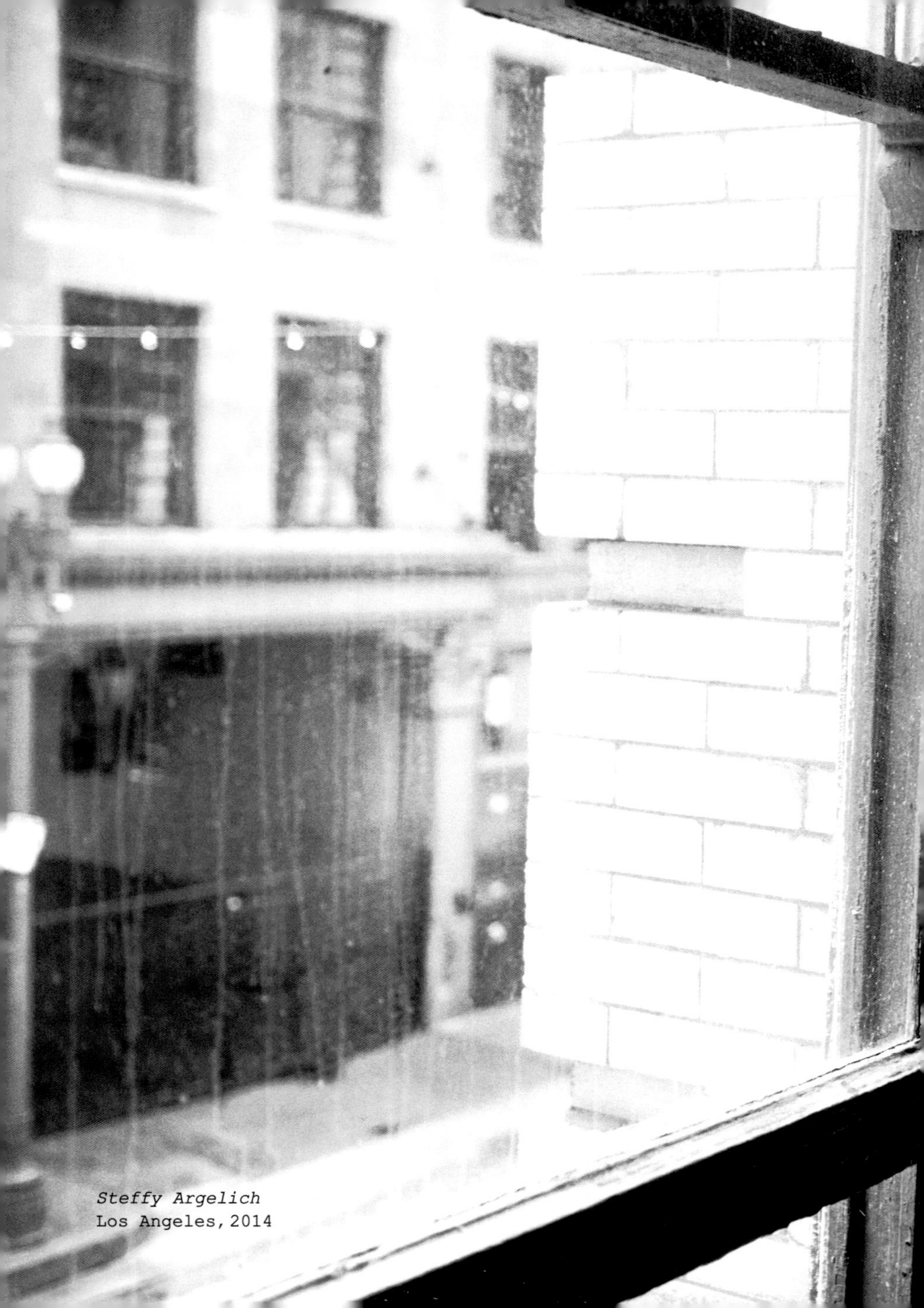

Steffy Argelich
Los Angeles, 2014

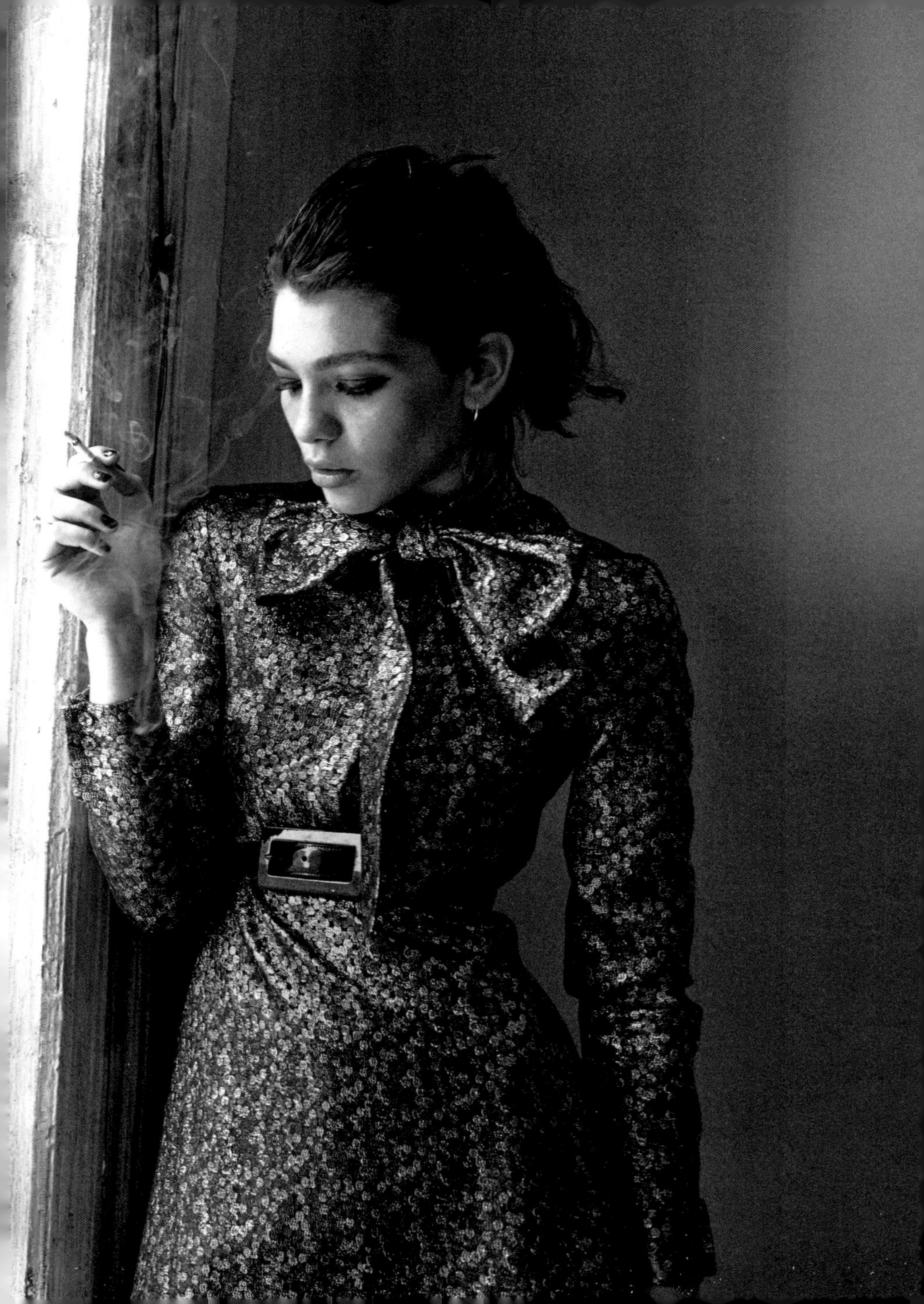

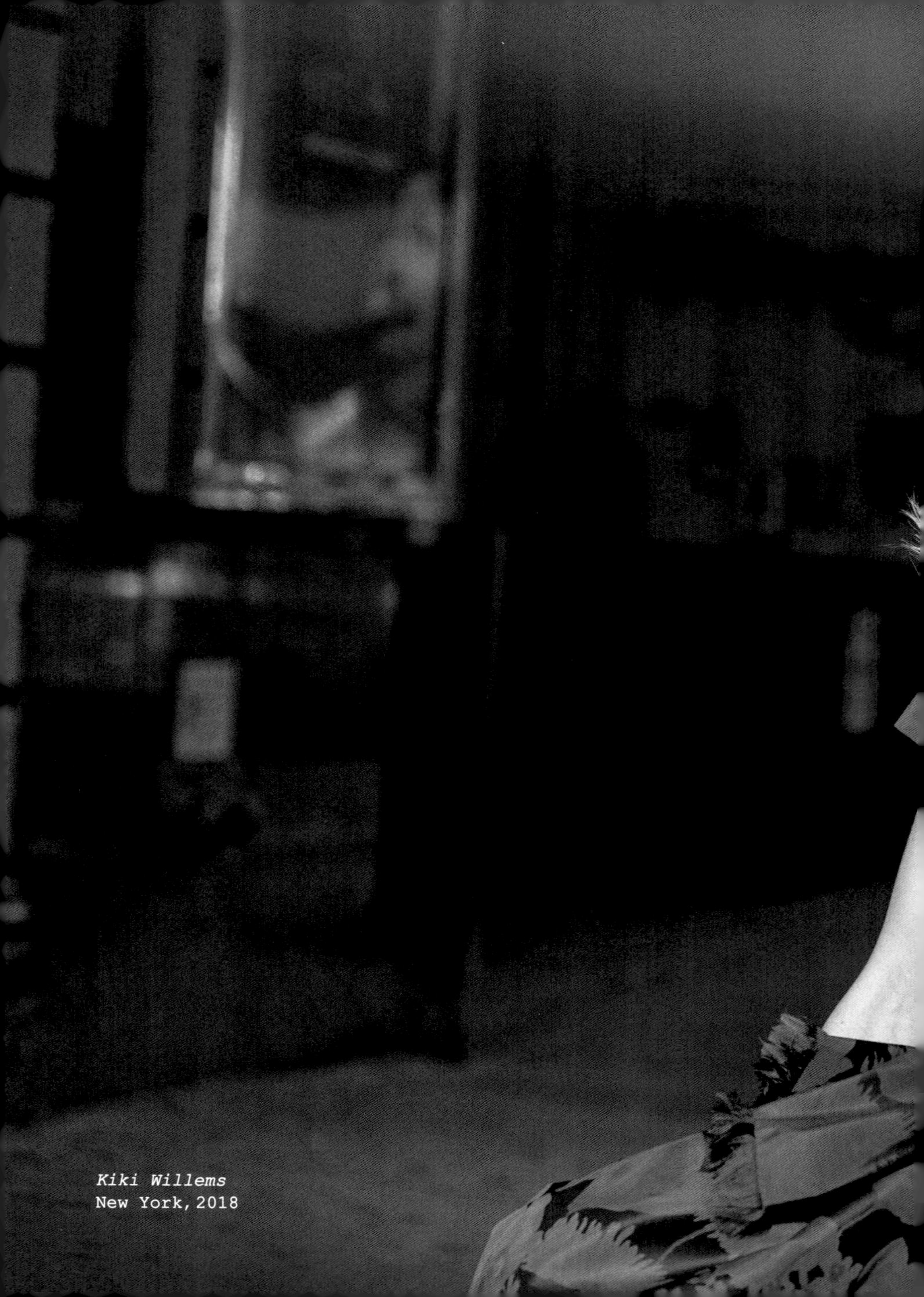
Kiki Willems
New York, 2018

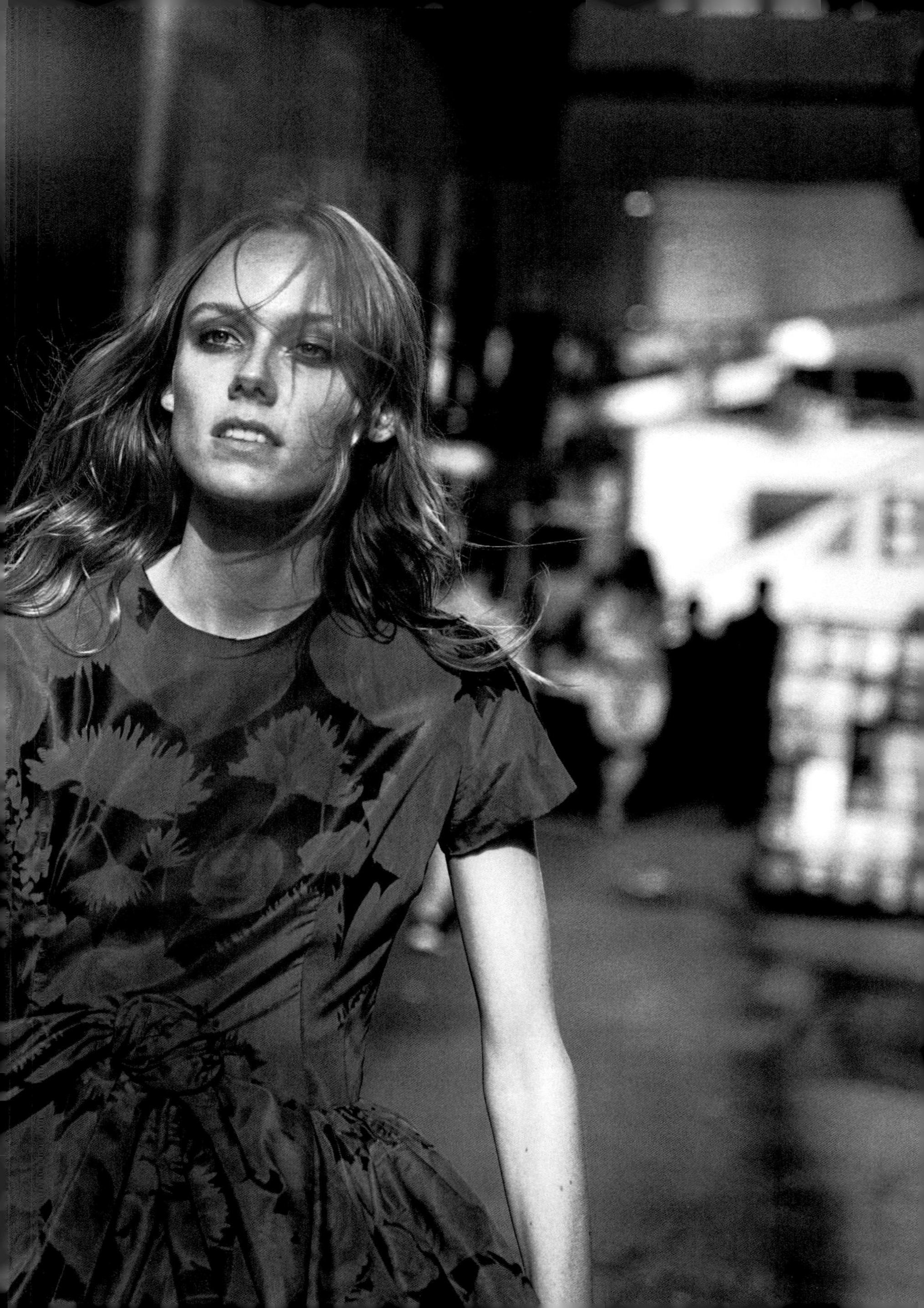

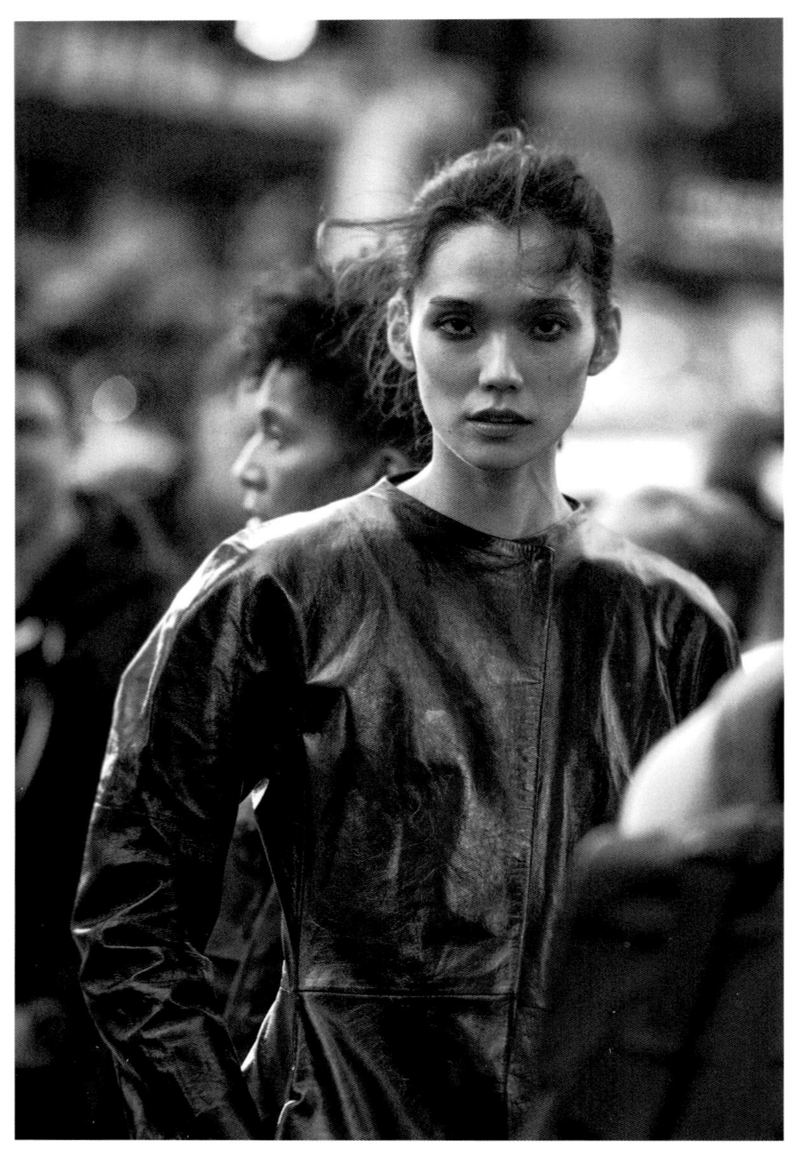

Tao Okamoto
New York, 2016

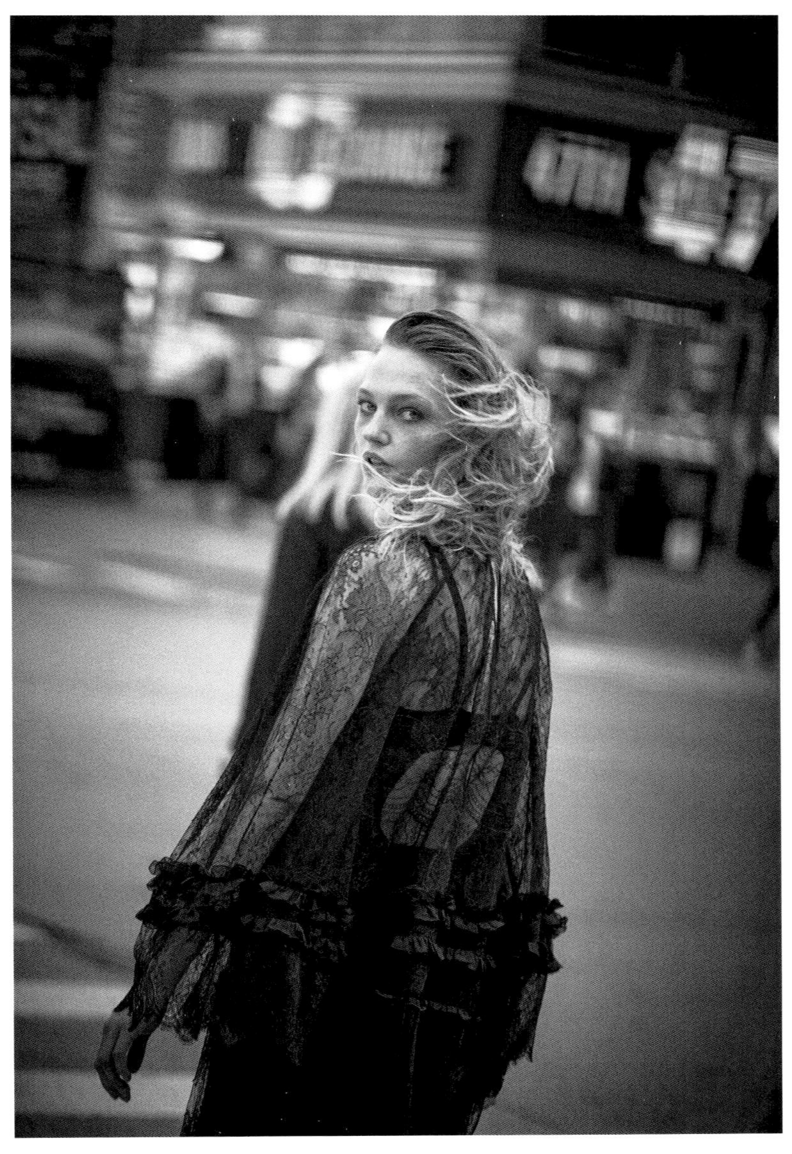

Sasha Pivovarova
New York, 2016

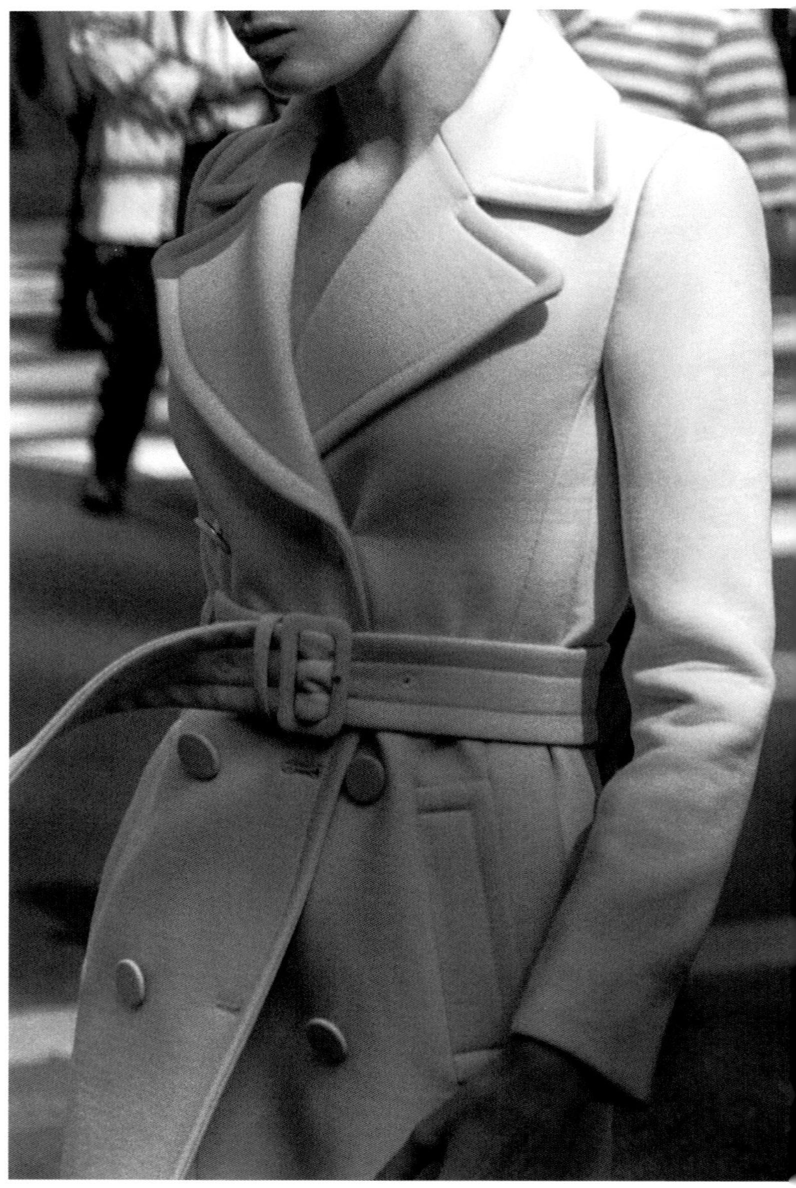

Isabeli Fontana
New York, 2016

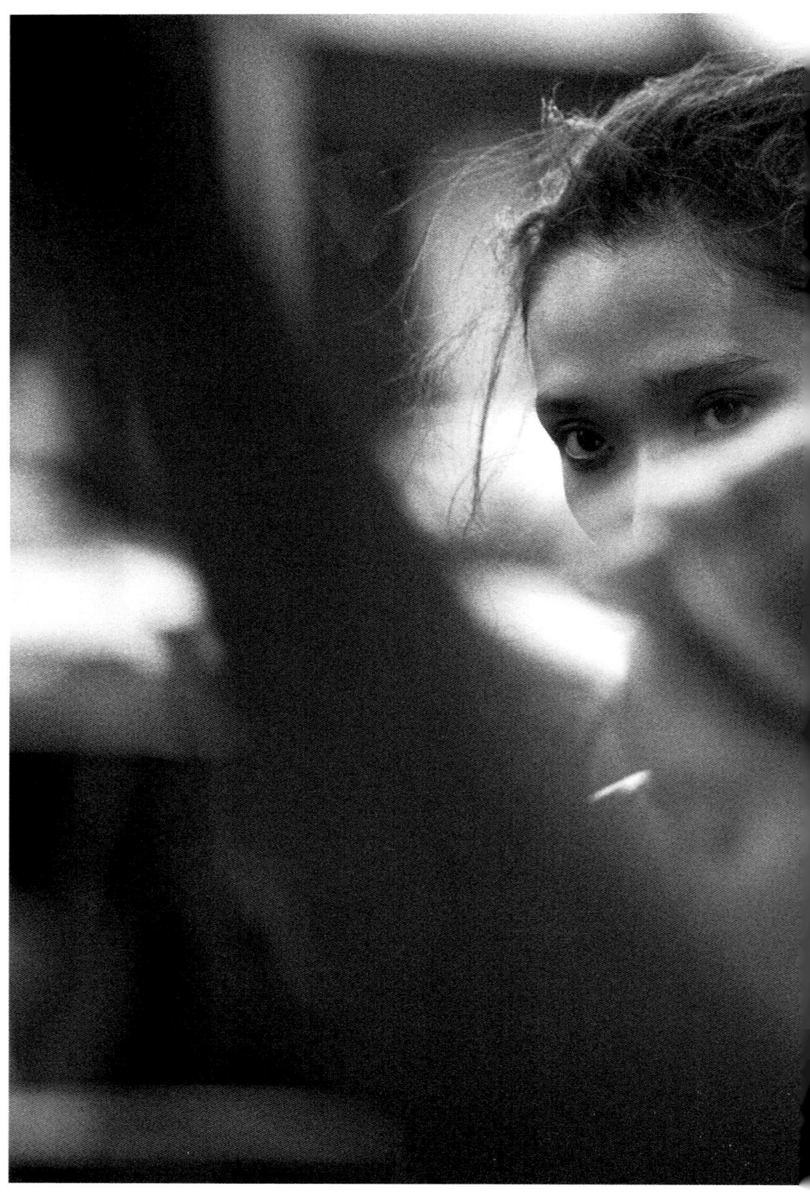

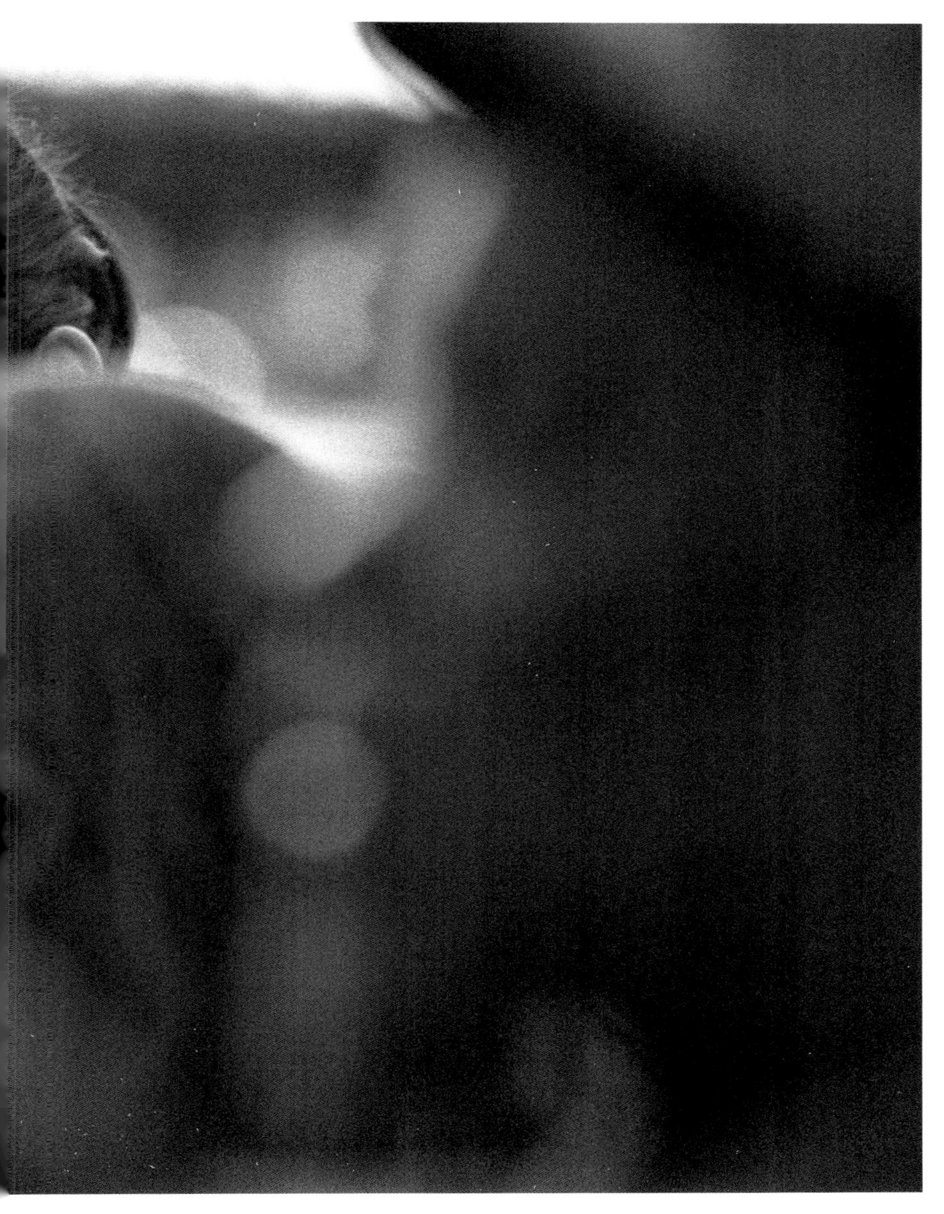

Tao Okamoto
New York, 2016

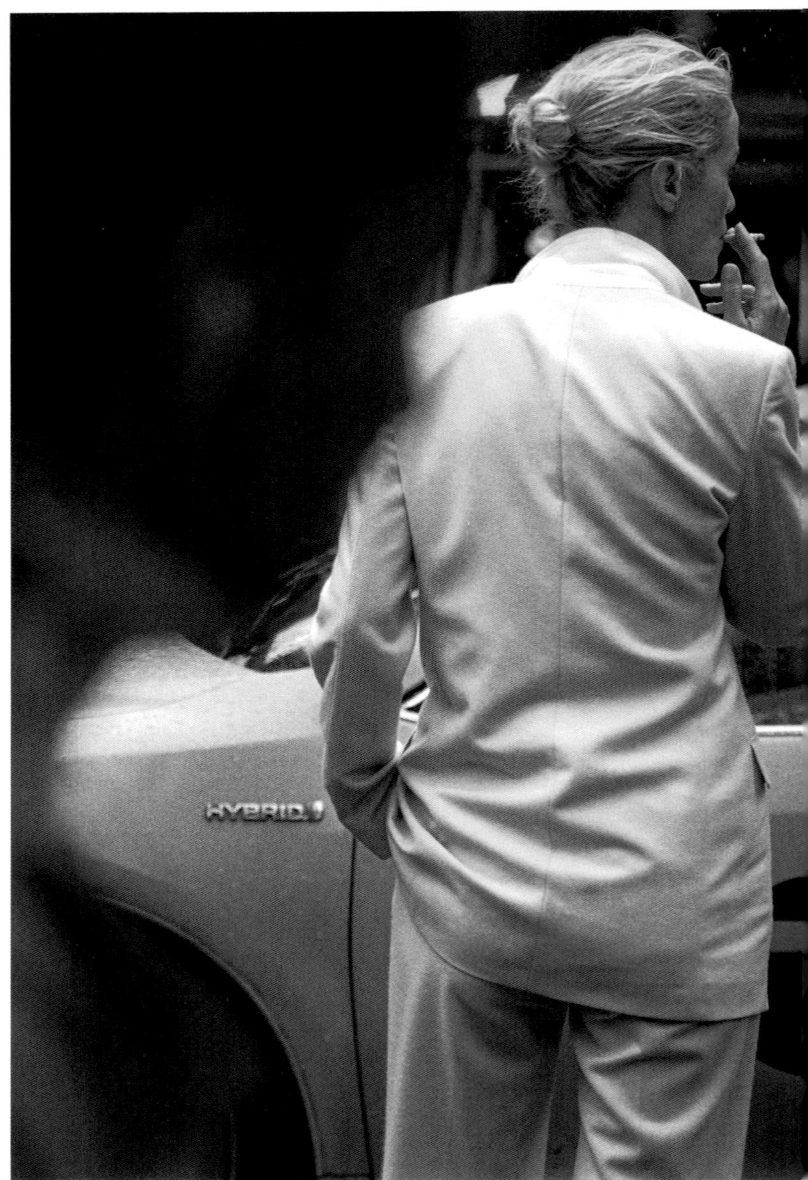
HYBRID

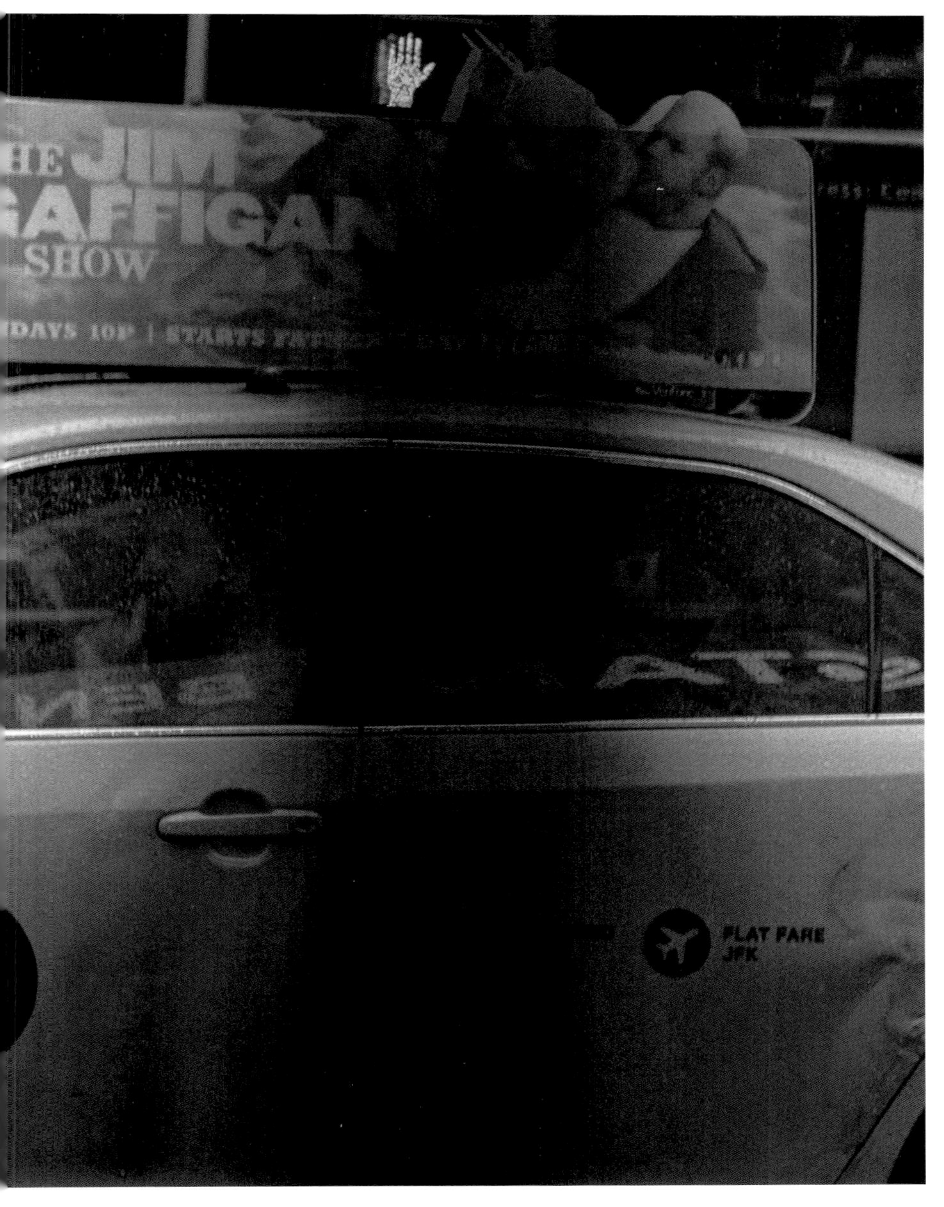

Karen Elson
New York, 2016

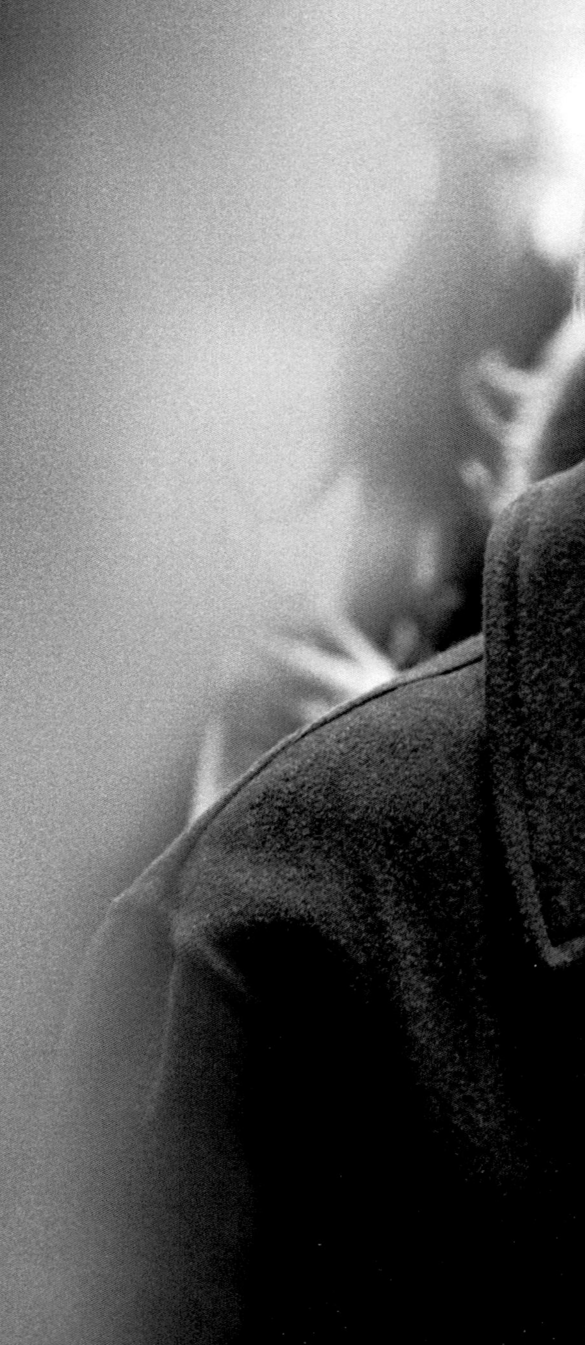

Robin Wright
New York, 2016

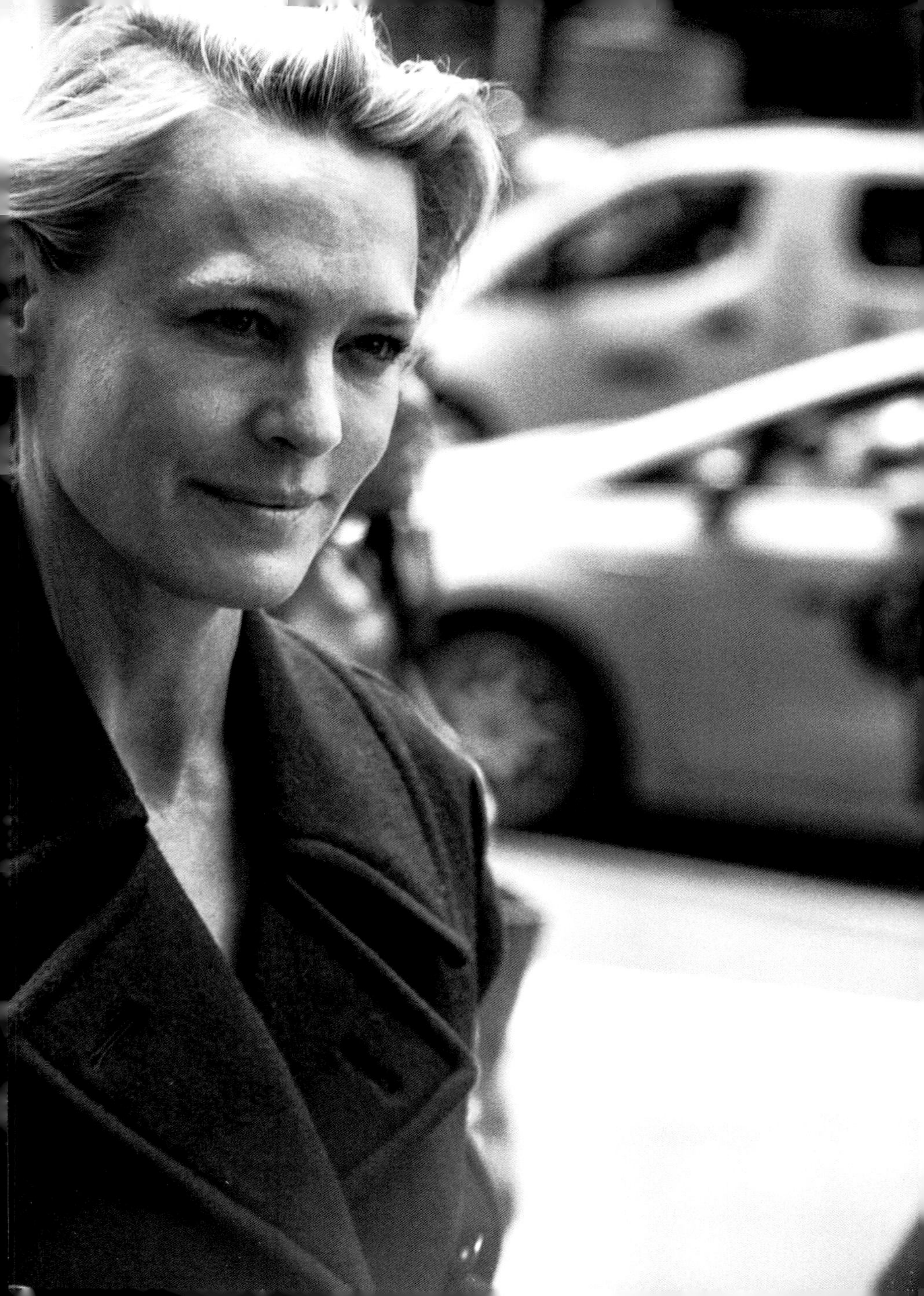

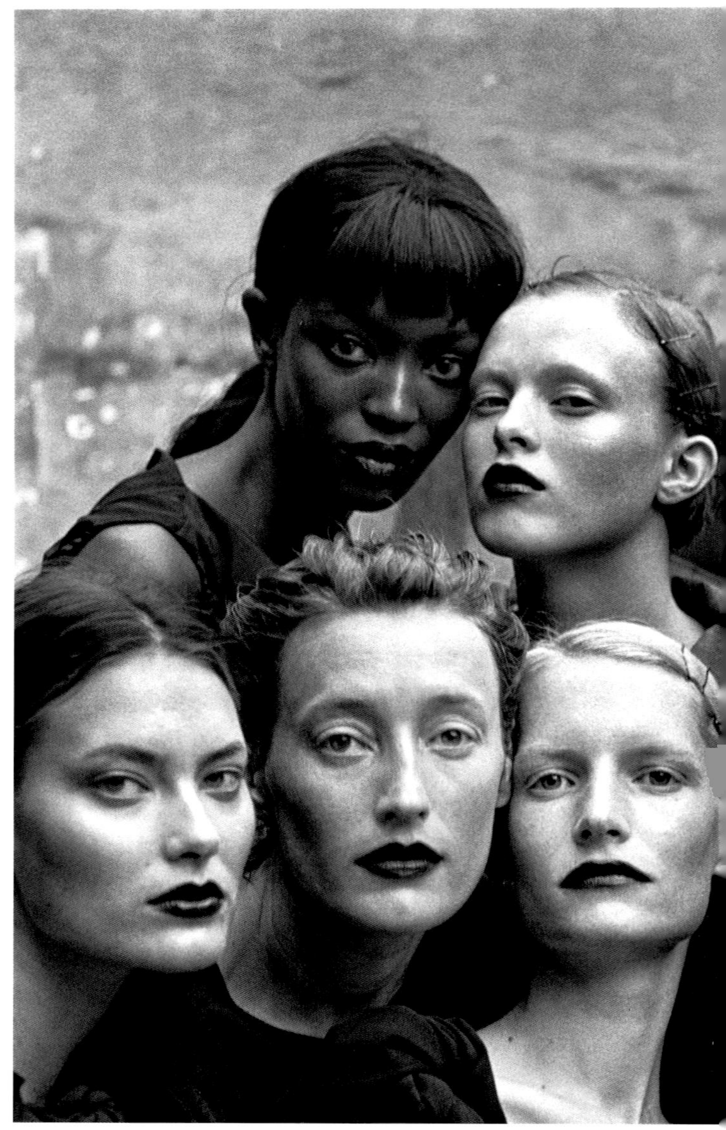

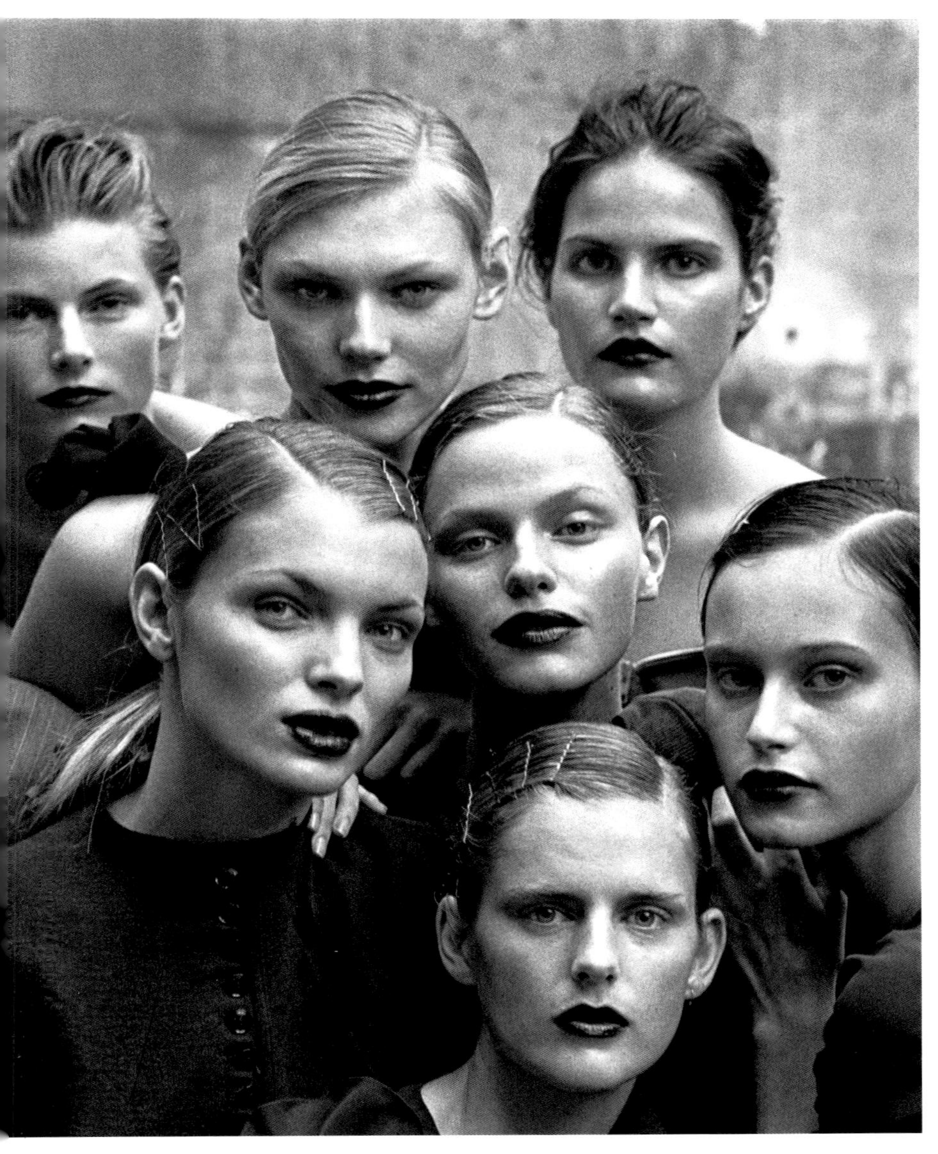

Naomi Campbell, Karen Elson, Jayne Windsor,
Shirley Mallmann, Missy Rayder, Shalom Harlow, Marie-Sophie
Wilson, Kirsten Owen, Esther Cañadas, Rachel Roberts,
Stella Tennant & Natalia Semanova, Paris, 1997

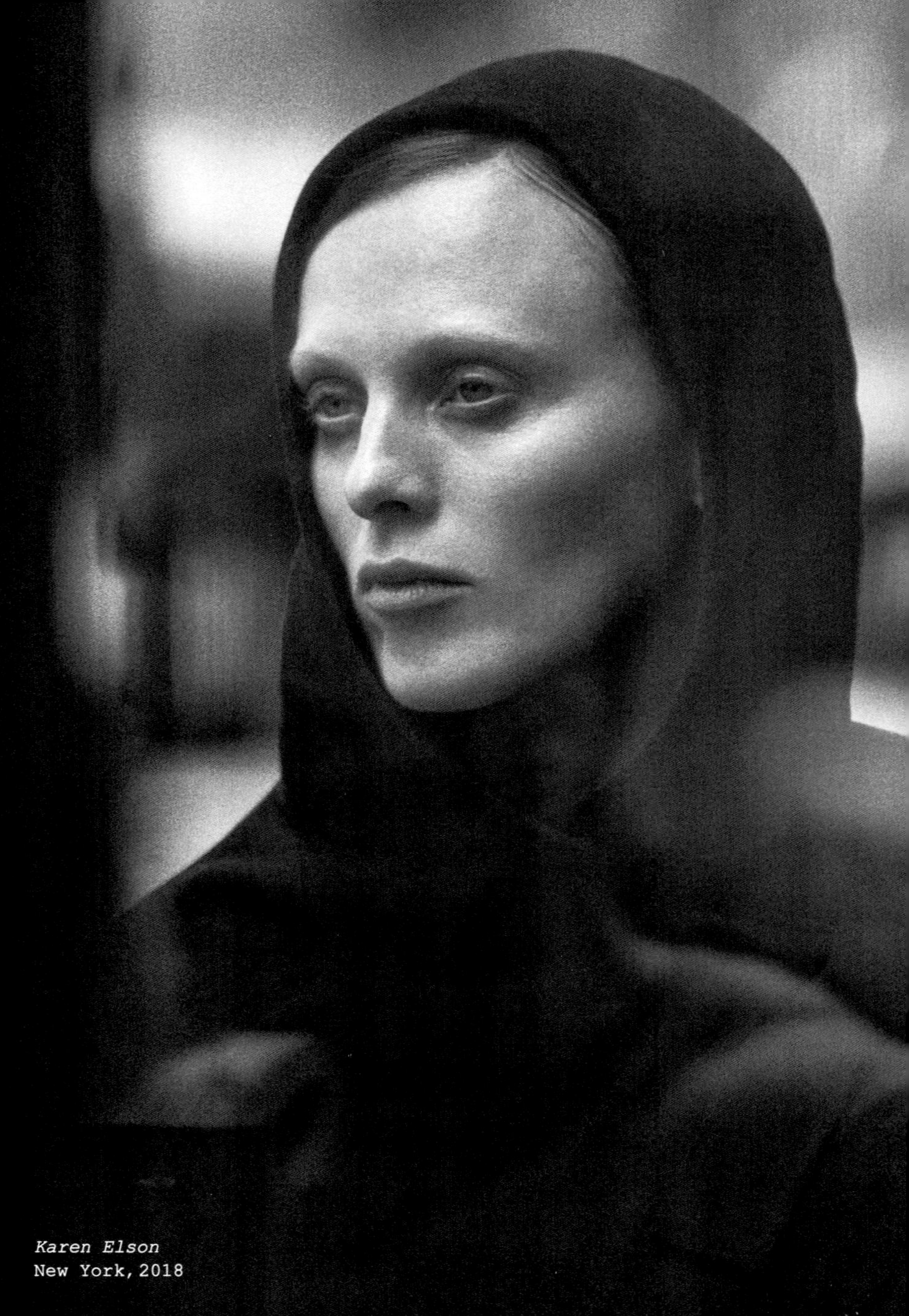

Karen Elson
New York, 2018

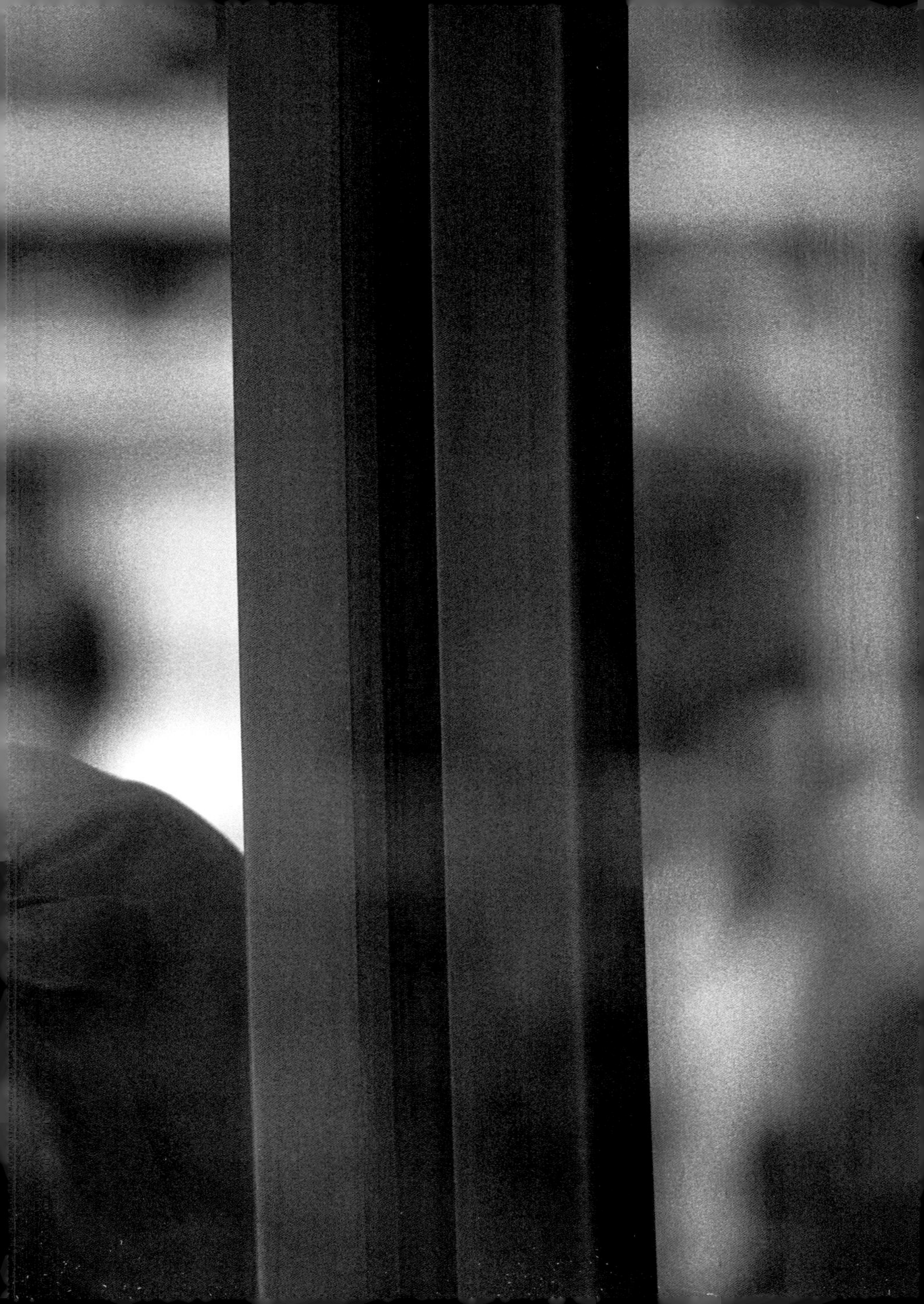

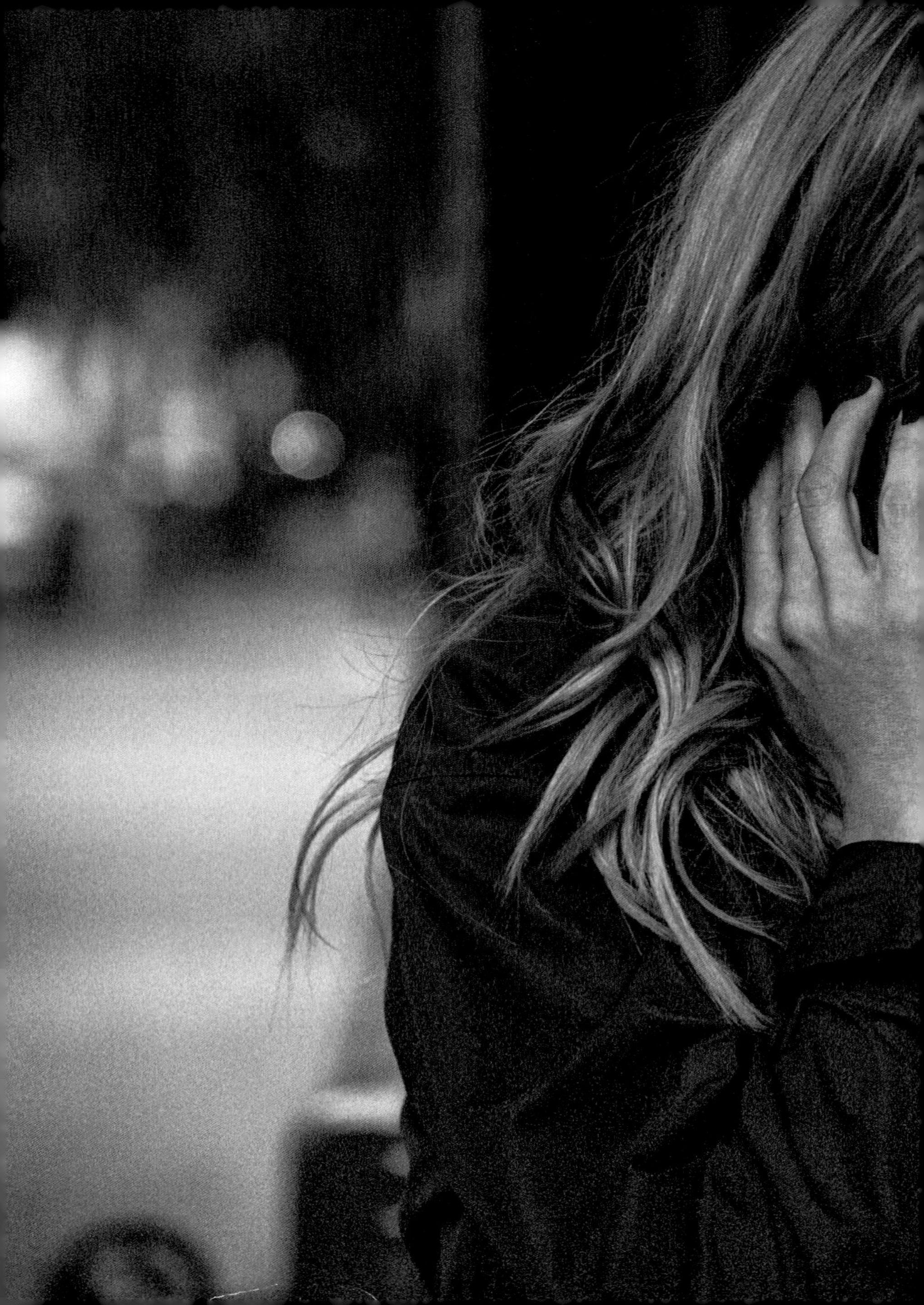

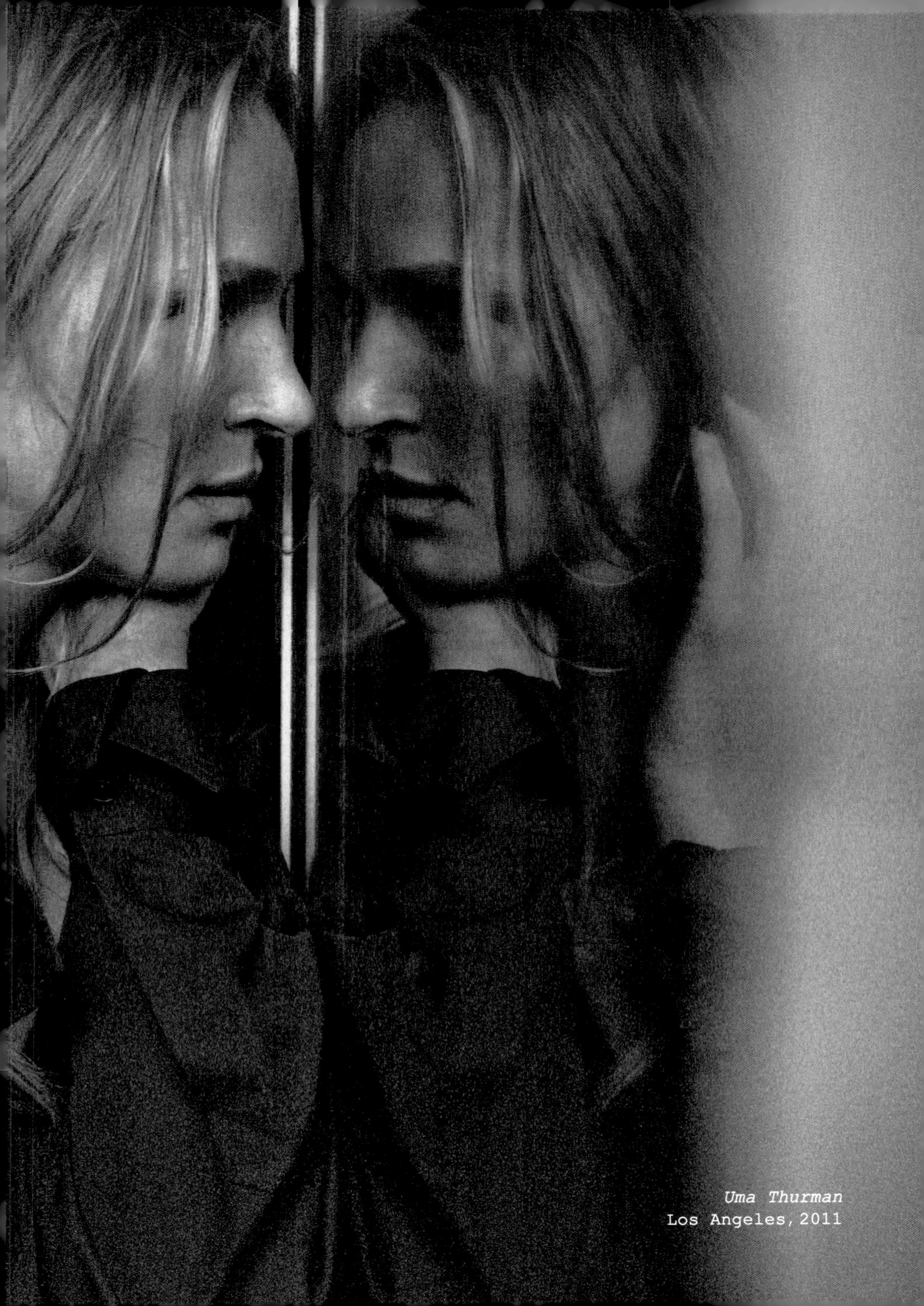

Uma Thurman
Los Angeles, 2011

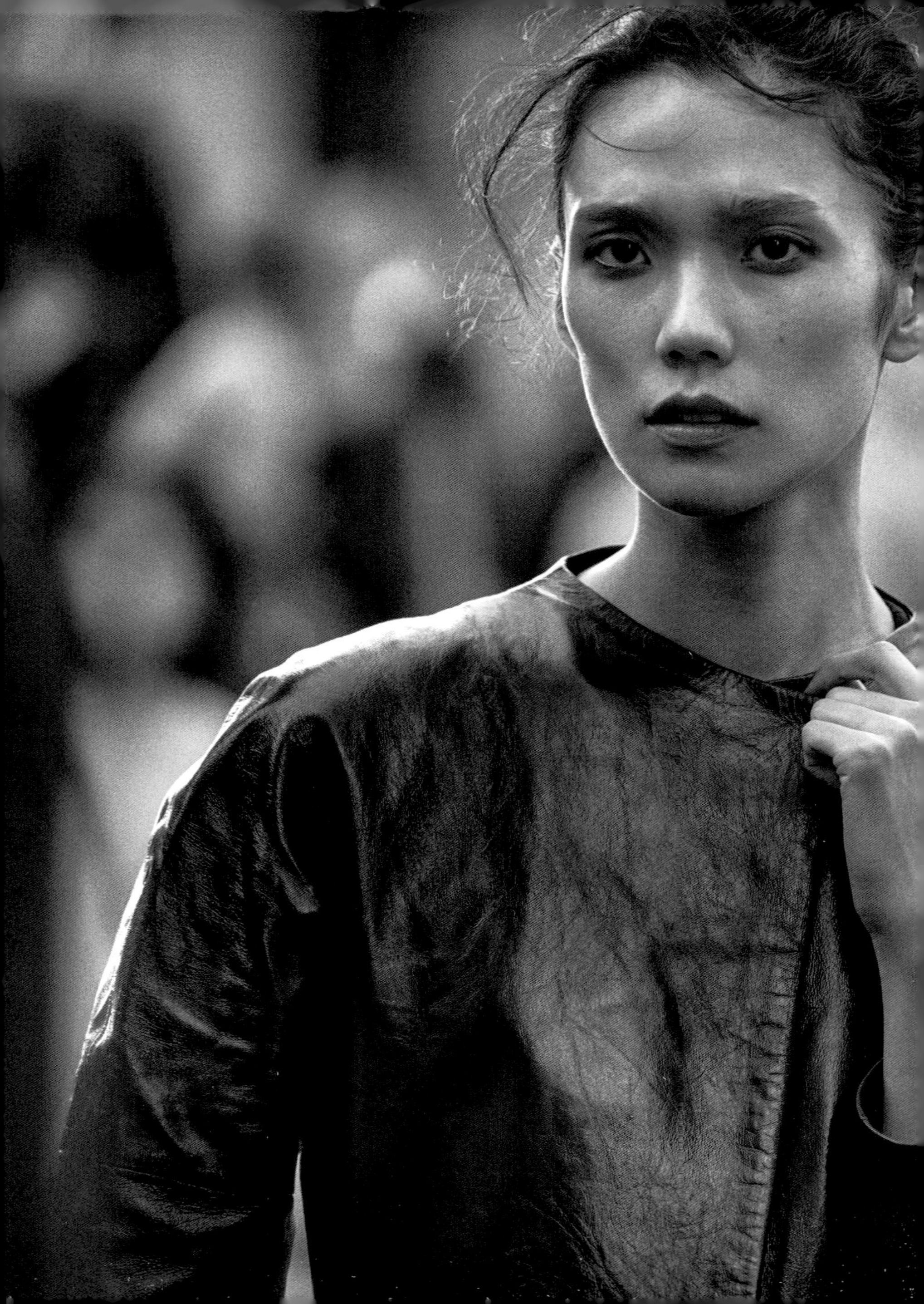

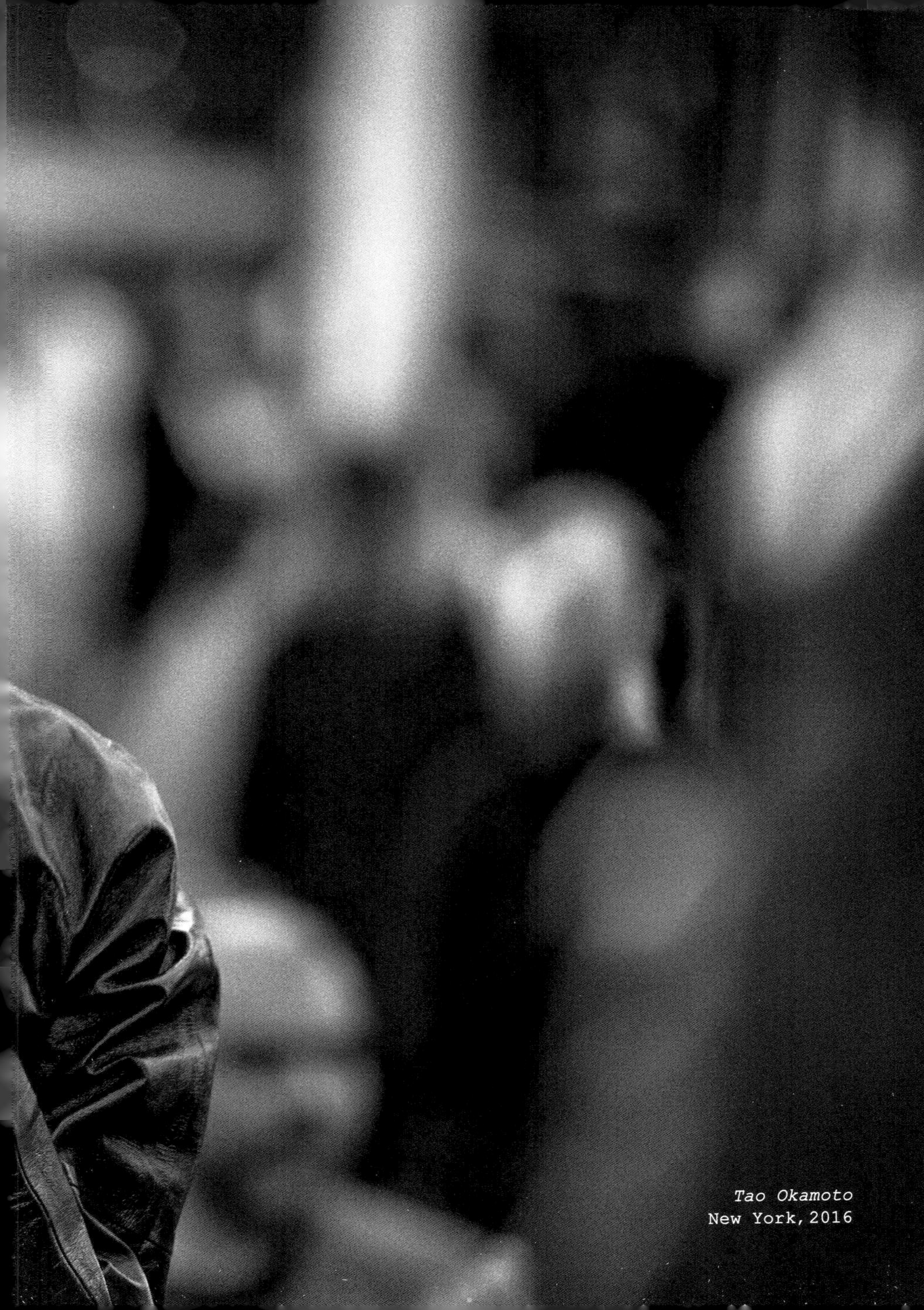

Tao Okamoto
New York, 2016

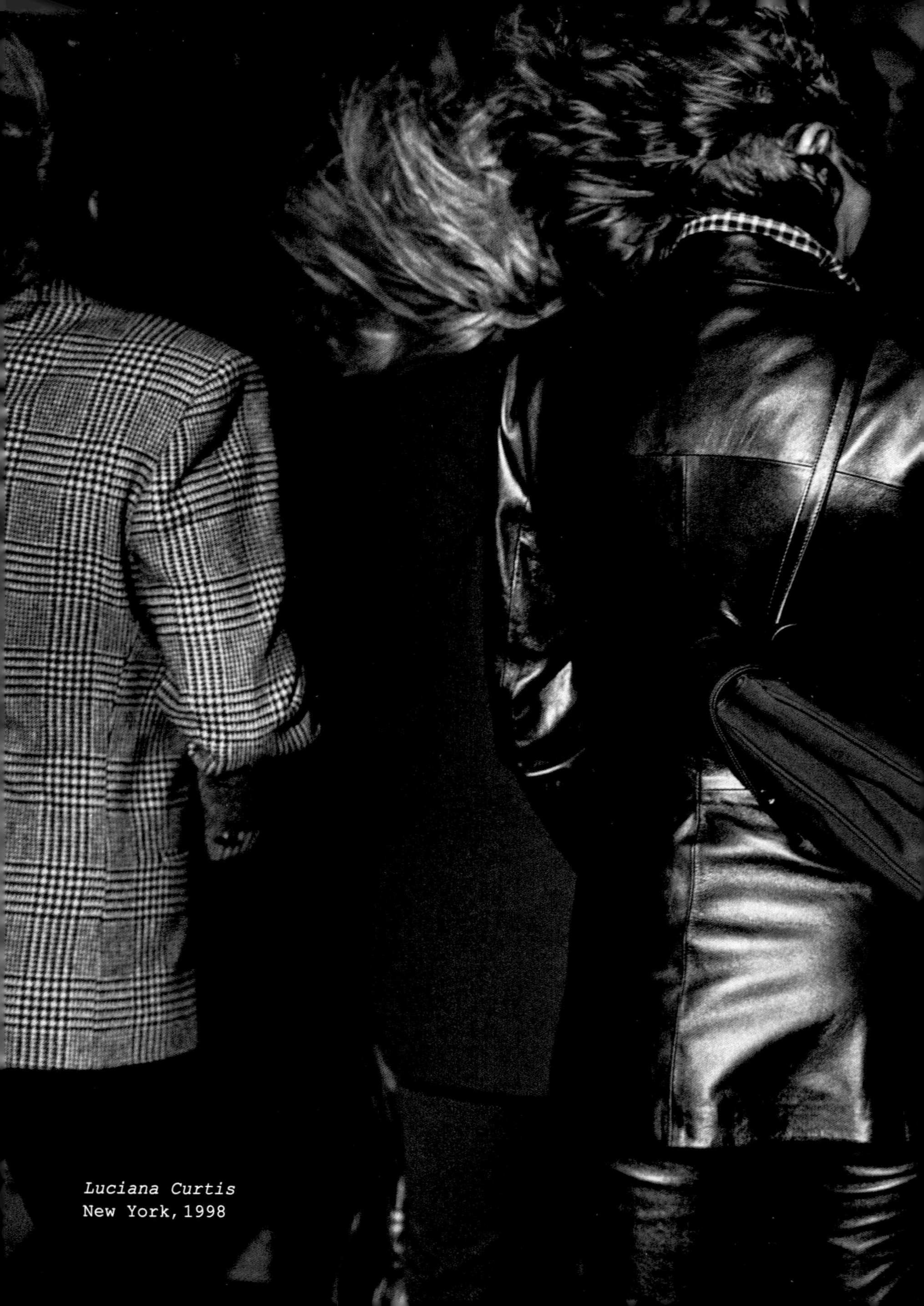

Luciana Curtis
New York, 1998

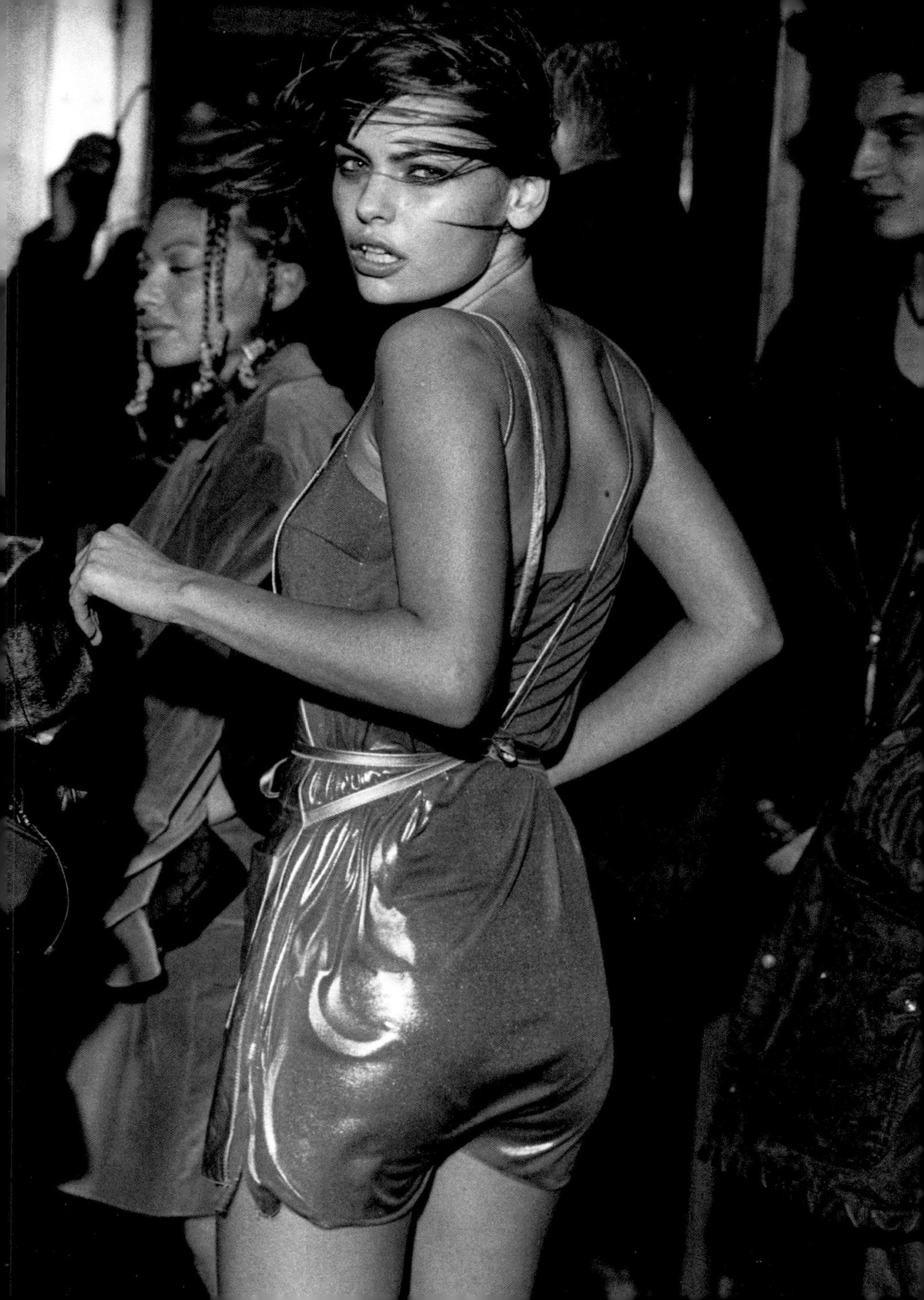

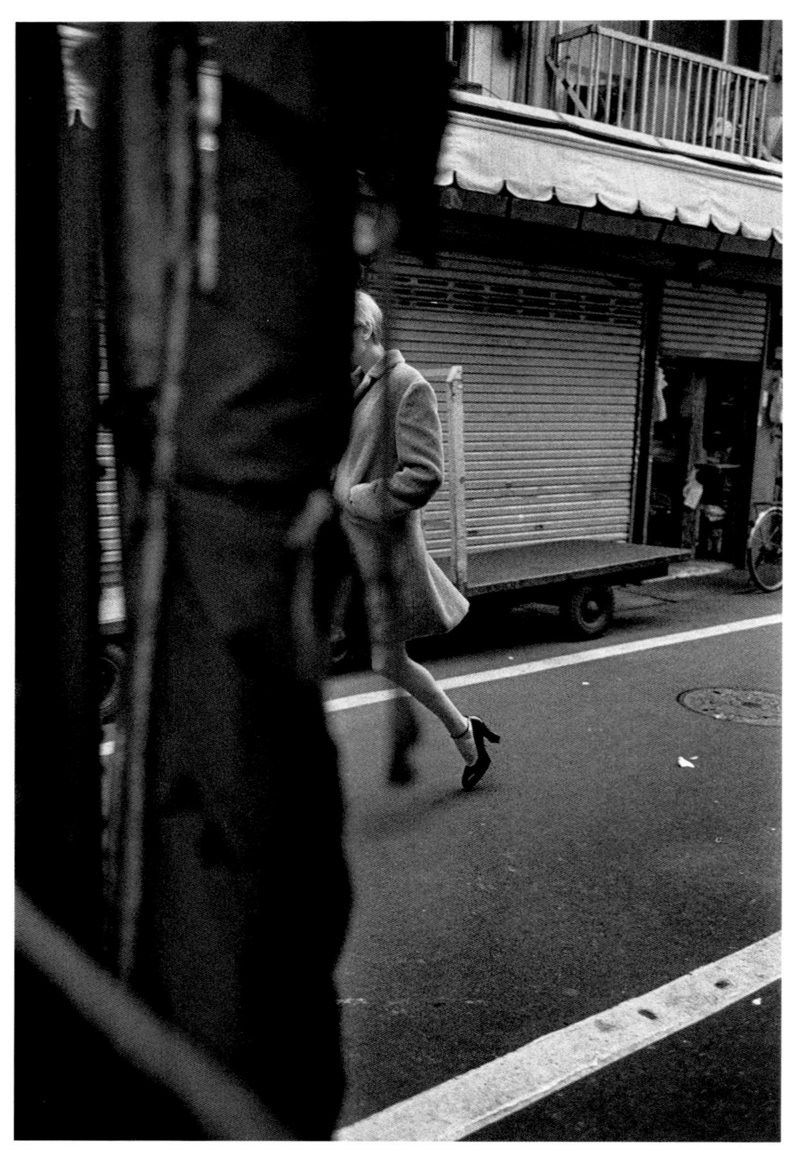

Nadja Auermann
Tokyo, 1996

We wish to thank Felix Krämer for his enthusiasm and
confidence in granting Peter absolute freedom to conceive
and mature this unprecedented installation.

His team at the Kunstpalast: Felicity Korn and Stefanie Hennig
for their valuable advice and attentive guidance
in turning Peter's "inner voice" to reality.

Wim & Donata Wenders for their enduring friendship
and inspiring words.

Special thanks to Benedikt Taschen,
Marlene and Charlotte Taschen,
Veronica Weller, Simone Philippi, and Frank Goerhardt.

We would like to thank the models,
talents, and artists present in this book
for trusting Peter to "break through the veil…"

Studio Peter Lindbergh
Benjamin Lindbergh, Thoaï Niradeth, Stefan Rappo,
Christian Tochtermann & Aurélie Adingra.

Bibliography

Alberto Giacometti/
Peter Lindbergh.
Saisir l'invisible,
ex.cat. Giacometti
Institute,
Paris 2019.

Peter Lindbergh:
Shadows on the Wall,
TASCHEN,
Cologne 2017.

Lindbergh/Winogrand.
Women, ed. by
Ralph Goertz, ex.cat.
NRW Forum, Düsseldorf,
Verlag der Buchhandlung
Walther König,
Cologne 2017.

Peter Lindbergh:
A Different Vision on
Fashion Photography, ed.
by Thierry-Maxime Loriot,
TASCHEN,
Cologne 2016.

Peter Lindbergh:
Images of Women 2,
Schirmer/Mosel,
Munich 2014.

Peter Lindbergh:
The Unknown,
Schirmer/Mosel,
Munich 2011.

Peter Lindbergh:
Untitled 116,
Schirmer/Mosel,
Munich 2006.

Peter Lindbergh:
Stories,
Arena Editions,
Santa Fe, NM, 2002.

Peter Lindbergh:
Images of Women,
Schirmer/Mosel,
Munich 1997.

Peter Lindbergh:
Ten Women,
Schirmer/Mosel,
Munich 1996.

Peter Lindbergh was born in 1944 as Peter Brodbeck in what is now Leszno, Poland, a town which at the time was part of the German Wartheland. Shortly after his birth, the family moved to Duisburg, where he spent his childhood and youth. Following a short career as a window dresser in Berlin, he attended the art academy in 1962, where he studied painting. Brodbeck continued his artistic training at the Werkkunstschule in Krefeld where, in 1969, his first exhibition was held at the Galerie Denise René-Hans Mayer. It was only then that he decided to switch to photography. Initially, he trained with the commercial photographer Hans Lux in Düsseldorf, and then went on to establish his own photography studio in 1973, which he soon ran under the professional name of Lindbergh. Together with photographers Helmut Newton, Guy Bourdin, and Hans Feurer, he joined the publishing group of the magazine *Stern*. In 1978, a commission took him to Paris, where he made his breakthrough.

Towards the end of the 1980s, his natural, approachable photographs of young women garnered international attention, establishing the era of the supermodel. Throughout a career spanning more than 40 years, Peter Lindbergh's photographs appeared in magazines such as *Vogue*, *Harper's Bazaar*, *The New Yorker*, *Interview*, *Rolling Stone*, *W Magazine*, and the *Wall Street Journal*. His work is seen in museum collections all around the world, including those of the Victoria and Albert Museum, London; the Centre Pompidou, Paris; the Metropolitan Museum of Art, New York; as well as the Kunstpalast, Düsseldorf. Peter Lindbergh lived and worked in Paris until his death in September 2019.

This book is published on the occasion of the exhibition

PETER LINDBERGH: UNTOLD STORIES

Curator
PETER LINDBERGH

Studio Peter Lindbergh
BENJAMIN LINDBERGH,
THOAÏ NIRADETH

Kunstpalast, Düsseldorf
February 5 to
June 1, 2020

Board of Directors
FELIX KRÄMER,
HARRY SCHMITZ

Advisor to the
Director General
FELICITY KORN

Project Coordinator
STEFANIE HENNIG

Registrar
DOROTHEA NUTT

Press
MARINA SCHUSTER,
CHRISTINA BOLIUS

Marketing
and Digital
CHRISTIAN HUPERTZ,
CHRISTINE BÖHM,
VERENA CROLLA

Education
BIRGIT VAN DE WATER,
FRIEDERIKE VAN DELDEN,
MIRIAM VON GEHREN

Infrastructure and
Exhibition Technicians
ANDREAS NABROTZKY,
BASTIAN ERHARD

Sponsoring
DOROTHEE VON DEUTSCH,
KATHARINA NEUMANN

Museum Shop
MARCELLA VON
UTHMANN-GILLESSEN,
KARINA KULLMANN

Conservation
RESTAURIERUNGSZENTRUM
DER LANDESHAUPTSTADT
DÜSSELDORF,
SCHENKUNG HENKEL

The exhibition is
sponsored by

Principal Sponsor
PORSCHE

LUMA FOUNDATION
DIOR
PINSENT MASONS

Education Partner
SIPGATE

SÜDDEUTSCHE ZEITUNG
WDR 3

Additional venues

Museum für Kunst und Gewerbe Hamburg
June 20 to
November 1, 2020

Director
TULGA BEYERLE

Managing Director
UDO GOERKE

Assistant to the
Director
FRIEDERIKE PALM

Project Coordinator
DENNIS CONRAD

Research Associate
SVEN SCHUMACHER

Infographics
FONS HICKMANN M23

Art Handling
ANNIKA POHL-OZAWA

Public Relations
MICHAELA HILLE,
LENA DROBIG

Marketing
SILKE OLDENBURG,
ULRIKE BLAUTH

Education
MANUELA VAN ROSSEM,
FRIEDERIKE FANKHÄNEL

Technical Manager
THOMAS FREY

Exhibition Management
FRANK HILDEBRANDT

Technical
Exhibition Team
EGON BUSCH,
DAMIAN KOWALCZYK,
MIKE MARTENS,
GRIGORI MEDVEDEV

The exhibition
is sponsored by
ANNEGRET AND
CLAUS-G. BUDELMANN

**Hessisches
Landesmuseum,
Darmstadt**
December 4, 2020 to
March 7, 2021

Director
MARTIN FAASS

Project Coordinator
MECHTHILD HAAS

Public Relations
YVONNE MIELATZ-POHL,
JENNIFER NOTHNAGEL

Engagement
HANNA BELZ

Art Handling
SABINE GWOSDEK

Conservation
FRIEDERIKE
ZIMMERN-WESSEL,
MONIKA
LIDLE-FÜRST

Education
LUTZ FICHTNER
AND TEAM

Technical Management
ANNETTE SCHRÖDER
AND TEAM

Realization
WOLFGANG KOCH,
BERND SCHUR
AND EXHIBITION
CONSTRUCTION TEAM

The exhibition is
sponsored by
FREUNDE DES
LANDESMUSEUMS
DARMSTADT

**Fondazione
Donnaregina per le
arti contemporanee /
Madre · Museo
d'Arte Contemporanea
Donnaregina, Naples**
March to May 2021

President
LAURA VALENTE

Vice-President
MARIA LETIZIA MAGALDI

Counselor
FERDINANDO PINTO

Administrative
Coordinator
GIANNI LIMONE

Project Coordinator
SANA LAVROFF

Exhibition and
Collection
Coordination
SILVIA SALVATI

Exhibition Assistant
LAURA MARIANO

Exhibition Design
DOLORES LETTIERI

Conservation and
Restoration
GABRIELLA RUSSO

Editorial and
External Projects
ANNA CUOMO,
EDUARDO MILONE

Protocol and
Public Relations
BEATRICE BUTI

Presidence and
Direction Office
FEDERICA DE CARO

Administrative Office
LUIGI D'ANGELO

General Coordinator,
Research Department
VINCENZO TRIONE

COMMUNICATION
SCABEC SPA

The project has
been organized
entirely using
POC Funding
(Programma Operativo
Complementare)
2014-2020 provided
by the Campania
Region.

Imprint

**EACH AND EVERY TASCHEN BOOK
PLANTS A SEED!**
TASCHEN is a carbon neutral
publisher. Each year, we
offset our annual carbon
emissions with carbon credits
at the Instituto Terra, a
reforestation program in Minas
Gerais, Brazil, founded by
Lélia and Sebastião Salgado.
To find out more about this
ecological partnership,
please check:
www.taschen.com/zerocarbon
Inspiration: unlimited.
Carbon footprint: zero.

Want to see more? Visit
taschen.com to view our
current publications,
browse our latest magazine,
and subscribe to our
newsletter.

© 2024 TASCHEN GmbH
Hohenzollernring 53,
D-50672 Köln
www.taschen.com

Photographs by
Peter Lindbergh
© 2020 PETER
LINDBERGH FOUNDATION

Texts
FELIX KRÄMER
PETER LINDBERGH
WIM WENDERS

Design
STUDIO PETER LINDBERGH

English Translation
MONICA BLOXAM, FOR GRAPEVINE
PUBLISHING SERVICES
KAREN WILLIAMS

Printed in Italy
ISBN 978-3-8365-9700-5

Front Cover:
Linda Evangelista,
Michaela Bercu &
Kirsten Owen
Pont-à-Mousson, 1988

Back Cover:
Eiffel Tower
Paris, 1989

Front Endpapers:
Nevada, 1997

Back Endpapers:
Paramount Studios,
Hollywood, 1999

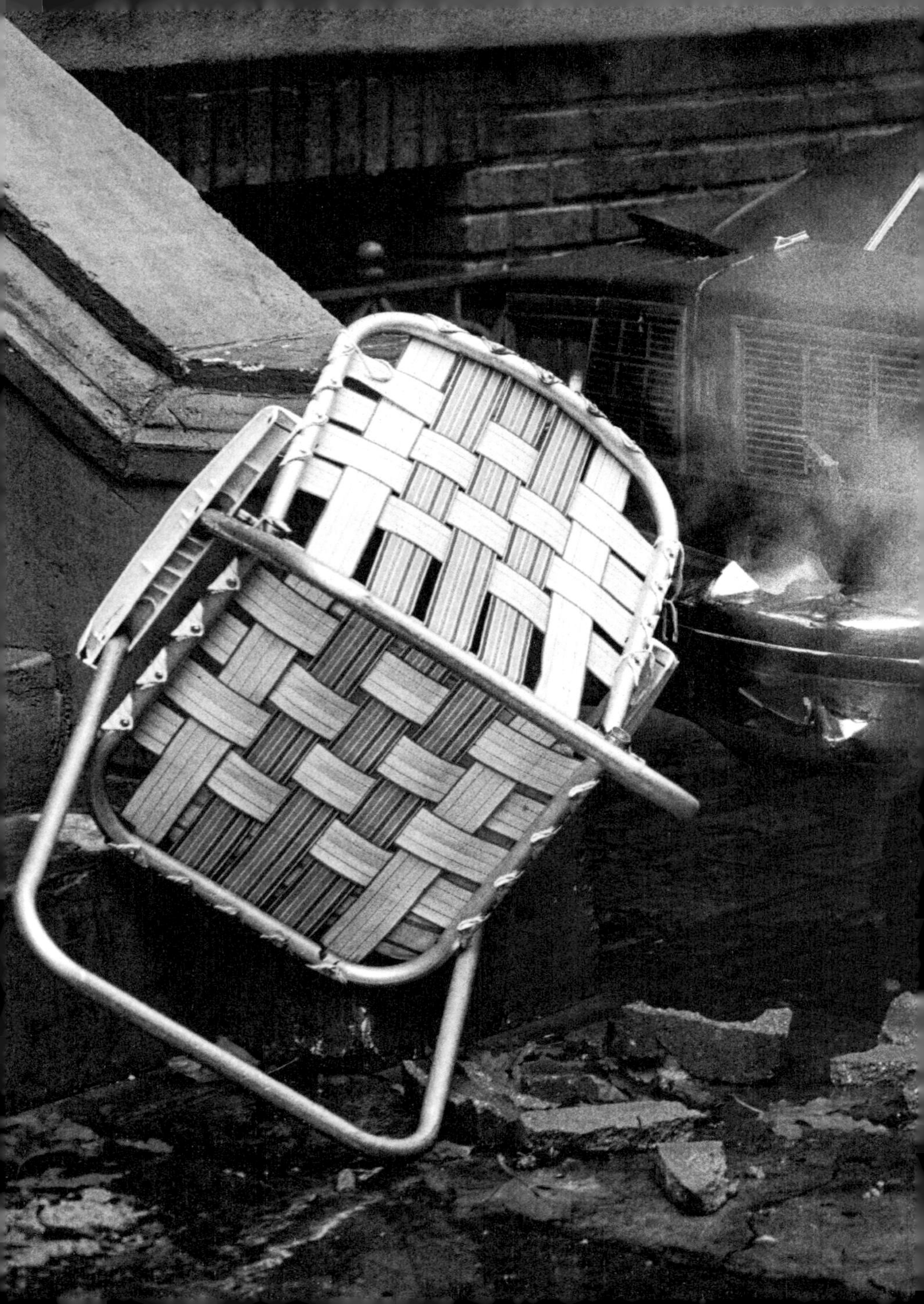